中国 B2B2C 在线教育平台用户课程购买意愿的影响因素研究

（中英双语）

Determinants of Purchasing Online Courses through Education Platform in China

王绍峰　著

ZHEJIANG UNIVERSITY PRESS
浙江大学出版社

图书在版编目（CIP）数据

中国 B2B2C 在线教育平台用户课程购买意愿的影响因素研究 / 王绍峰著. —杭州：浙江大学出版社，2021.12
ISBN 978-7-308-21767-5

Ⅰ．①中… Ⅱ．①王… Ⅲ．①网络教育－购买行为－影响因素－研究－中国 Ⅳ．①G434

中国版本图书馆 CIP 数据核字（2021）第 191779 号

中国 B2B2C 在线教育平台用户课程购买意愿的影响因素研究

王绍峰　著

责任编辑	杜希武
责任校对	夏湘娣
封面设计	刘依群
出版发行	浙江大学出版社
	（杭州市天目山路 148 号　邮政编码 310007）
	（网址：http://www.zjupress.com）
排　　版	杭州好友排版工作室
印　　刷	广东虎彩云印刷有限公司绍兴分公司
开　　本	710mm×1000mm　1/16
印　　张	18.25
字　　数	354 千
版 印 次	2021 年 12 月第 1 版　2021 年 12 月第 1 次印刷
书　　号	ISBN 978-7-308-21767-5
定　　价	59.00 元

浙江大学出版社市场运营中心联系方式：(0571) 88925591；http://zjdxcbs.tmall.com

作者简介

王绍峰,1990年1月生。浙江万里学院物流与电子商务学院教师,北京师范大学智慧学习研究院博士后。电子科技大学(UESTC)—葡萄牙里斯本大学学院(ISCTE-IUL)联合培养博士、高级工程师(计算机技术与软件)、经济师(工商管理)、国家二级技师(创业咨询师)、房地产经纪人、信息系统项目管理师、电子商务设计师、系统集成项目管理工程师。澳大利亚堪培拉大学工商管理硕士。电子科技大学经济与管理学院业界导师、宁波大学国际学生创新创业导师、宁波工程学院大学生创业导师、深圳市人工智能产业协会专家。研究和擅长领域:电子商务、在线教育。主持浙江省教育科学规划课题等7项,参与国际合作(联合国教科文组织)、国家级、省部级等科研项目4项,发表论文6篇,出版和参编专著2本、电子文献1本,实用新型专利1项,软件著作权3项。*Smart Learning Environments* 期刊审稿人。曾服务于PHPWIND(阿里巴巴旗下)、中关村在线、电脑之家(PCHOME)、建玛特购APP。

Author Introduction

Shaofeng Wang is a senior computer technology and software engineer and an economist specializing in business administration. In addition, he teaches at Zhejiang Wanli University's School of Logistics and e-Commerce, as well as being a postdoctoral fellow at Beijing Normal University's Smart Learning Institute. He has got a doctor's degree of Management from the Instituto Superior de Ciências do Trabalho e da Empresa (ISCTE)-Lisbon University Institute (IUL), Portugal, and a master's degree of Business Administration from the University of Canberra, Australia. His current research interests are e-commerce and smart education. Previous to his academic career, he founded www. NB. com. cn, a digital marketing and Internet software company. In recent years, he has presided over seven research projects, participated in four international cooperation and other empirical research projects, published six papers, co-authored two monographs, acquired a utility model patent and three software copyrights, and served as a journal reviewer for *Smart Learning Environments*.

前　言

　　在国家大力推进信息产业和数字经济发展的背景下，立足于国内外在线教育和知识付费行业快速发展的现状，本书先梳理了中国在线教育平台的发展脉络和商业模式，发现在线课程成为在线教育平台的主要收入来源，开展在线教育平台用户课程购买意愿影响因素的探讨有着重要的意义。针对在线课程购买意愿低的问题，通过调研大量相关文献提炼了影响在线课程购买意愿的相关因素，基于感知价值理论、技术接受模型并结合当前的研究情境引入了中介变量、调节变量（网络口碑）和多群组变量（复购历史），提出了中国 B2B2C 在线教育平台课程购买意愿影响因素模型，剖析了影响在线课程购买意愿的相关因素和各因素之间的作用关系，并对是否复购的异质性进行分组建模，得出不同购买历史的用户存在影响机理的差异。本书在数据分析的基础上还进行了相应的讨论并给出了对应的建议，如保证课程质量，提供口碑，根据用户的购买经验进行分组，使用人工智能为用户推荐在线课程；优化时间和空间自治功能，提高 5G、虚拟现实和增强现实的用户体验；使用云服务和大数据技术降低课程价格，提供更多免费试用，以减少用户的感知风险。

　　本书为深入剖析中国在线教育平台课程消费情景下在线课程购买意愿提供了系统的研究，融合多理论的预测模型和 MGA 多群组技术，为开展相关理论研究提供参考，丰富了本领域的理论研究和研究方法。为了同步国内外研究动态和文献语境，本书采用中英双语进行写作，也便于读者同步了解本领域的中英文表述。

Introduction

In the context of China's vigorous promotion of the information industry and digital economy, it is based on the background of the rapid development of online education and knowledge payment industries at home and abroad. This book first sorts out the development context and business model of online education platforms in China, and finds it is of great value to explore the factors affecting users' intention to buy online courses. Aiming at the problem of low online course purchase intention based on the current status quo, this book researched a large number of relevant documents, it refined the relevant factors that affect online course purchase intention, based on the perceived value theory, technology acceptance model and combined with the current research situation, introduced mediation variables, moderation variables (Internet word-of-mouth) and multi-group variables (repurchase history), and proposed a model of influencing factors of China's B2B2C online education platform course purchase intention, and identified the influence factors of online education platform course purchase intentions, analyzed the relevant factors that affect online course purchase intentions and the relationship between the factors, and the heterogeneity of whether to repurchase is grouped and modeled to find that users with different purchase histories have differences in the influence mechanism. Based on the data analysis, this study also discussed the corresponding recommendations, such as guaranteeing course quality, providing word-of-mouth, grouping users according to their purchasing experience, using artificial intelligence to recommend online courses for users; optimizing functions of time and space autonomy, improving user experience with 5G, virtual reality, and augmented reality; reducing course price with cloud services and big data technologies, and providing more course free trial in an attempt to reduce users' perceived risk.

This book provides a systematic research for the in-depth analysis of online course purchase intention under the course consumption scenario of China's online education platform. It integrates multi theoretical prediction model and MGA multi group technology to provide reference for relevant theoretical research, and also enriches the theoretical research and research methods in this field. For researchers and practitioners to keep abreast of domestic and foreign research trends and literature context, this book is written in both Chinese and English, which is also convenient for readers to understand the Chinese and English expressions in this field.

目　　录

第1章 绪 论

1.1 研究背景

中国互联网络信息中心(CNNIC)数据显示,截至 2020 年 12 月,中国的网民数量已达 9.89 亿;其中在线教育用户规模达 3.42 亿,依然保持着高速的增长态势;通过手机使用在线教育的用户规模达 3.41 亿。中国手机在线教育用户占比再创新高,在线教育用户进一步向手机等移动终端集中[1]。

据中国人民银行《2020 年支付体系运行总体情况》,2020 年移动支付业务共 1232.20 亿笔,金额合计 432.16 万亿元,同比分别增长 21.48% 和 24.50%。在线支付的增长依旧强势,反映中国在线交易环境已趋成熟[2]。

工业和信息化部等发布了《扩大和升级信息消费三年行动计划(2018—2020 年)》,经过估算,到 2020 年中国的信息方面消费产业规模将达 6 万亿元人民币,每年的平均增长超过 11%[3]。互联网技术的迅速发展,智能终端的大量使用,加之移动互联网的应用覆盖面越来越广,使得目前在线教育平台成为我国公民获取知识的重要途径。这样的形式突破了线下教育在空间和时间上的束缚,通过计算机和手机等移动终端提供随时随地的在线教育服务,成为一种新型的商业模式。

近年来国家开始着眼于在线教育并加大扶持力度,公众也开始越来越多地接触到网络学习,开始尝试并接受这种在线教育模式。腾讯研究院发现 96% 的用户选择拥有规模和品牌的 B2B2C 在线教育平台进行学习,B2B2C 在线教育平台用户数量呈现激增态势[4]。艾瑞咨询在《中国 B2B2C 在线教育平台行业研究报告》中提及:中国在线教育行业的整体市场规模已于 2017 年超过 1941 亿元人民币,相较上期增长 22.9%[5]。网经社在

《2018 年度中国在线教育市场发展报告》中称：在 2018 年，该行业的市场总规模已超 3000 亿元人民币，较 2017 年增长 45％[6]。面对这块新的市场空间，幼儿教育、成人高等教育、青少年 K12 教育、求职职业教育等各种细分的需求呈现快速增长的态势，在线教育课程内容形式也愈发丰富。当前，在线教育市场分为：综合平台、外言学习、幼儿教育形式、境外留学形式、K12 教育形式、职业教育形式、技能提升形式、网络学习工具形式、考试考证培训形式、影音知识形式等[5,7]。用户对于知识种类的不同需求，产生了各种线上教育的市场，随着需求的不断增长，市场也不断扩张，而在某些特定的细分领域，线上教育显得尤为适合，其发展的前景更为广阔。

然而，随着更多企业开始加入在线教育产业中，行业竞争也越发激烈。随着百度、阿里巴巴、腾讯等网络行业中的龙头企业进入，市场的竞争更加激烈。综上所述，借着新一代网络技术的普及热潮，以此为基础发展起来的在线教育产业也更容易被用户接受，更加便捷的学习方式使得在线教育逐步成为未来教育的一大重要模式。目前，B2B2C 模式在线教育平台的用户急速增加，但依旧停留在潜在客户阶段，并未真正发生购买并产生收入，此现状还带来了包括服务器和人员开支在内的成本增加。《2019 年中国在线教育行业市场前瞻分析报告》中提及中国在线教育平台企业用户课程购买比例不高，导致本身已经入不敷出的平台经营状况更加严峻[8]。如何认清影响用户网络课程购买意愿的相关因素，把握用户需求，提高用户购买意愿和购买率，成为当前 B2B2C 在线教育平台迫切需要研究解决的问题。

购买意愿是用户购买相关产品或服务的可能性，已被多次验证可以进行预测[9]。综合以上研究，在本研究中购买意愿是指 B2B2C 在线教育平台用户购买网络课程的主观意愿。基于上述背景，本书将中国 B2B2C 模式在线教育平台用户作为研究对象，使用理论分析结合实证检验的方法，将从感知价值视角来探讨用户在线教育课程购买意愿，研究产生 B2B2C 模式在线教育平台用户的在线教育课程购买意愿影响因素，分析不同因素对用户购买意愿影响程度的高低，以此来探索可以提高在线教育水平和在线教育平台盈利能力的运营策略。

1.2 研究问题描述

伴随着互联网使用者对在线学习模式的接受程度的逐步提高,这些在线教育平台的用户数量迅速增长,在线教育的市场容量不可小觑,这也让更多资本和创业者投身这个行业。但是多数平台依旧处在成本投入而没有产出的局面,盈利模式的不清晰是大多数平台无法良性运转的核心问题。当前在线教育平台的收入来源为内容费用、软件收费、服务费用、成交佣金以及付费广告。然而,在线课程的收费是 B2B2C 模式在线教育平台将来具有很大潜力的盈利方向。当前成立时间较长的行业企业,正在不断尝试寻找课程销售和在线服务售卖的盈利方式来获得更多的用户和更大的市场规模。

李雅筝(2016)认为在中国互联网发展的情景下,使用"免费"的互联网服务已经成为中国网民的普遍共识[10],在这一背景下,如何提高在线教育平台用户的购买意愿获得更多收入成为在线教育平台迫切需要破解的困境。目前的研究成果中,把在线课程作为电子商务的虚拟商品,并以此为出发视角来研究单个用户的消费购买行为还为数不多。国内学者许亚楠等(2018)认为在互联网信息爆炸的时代,找到用户课程购买意愿的影响因素,可以帮助在线课程提供方获得更多用户[11]。陈昊等(2019)发现知识付费作为一种全新的商业模式正在被逐渐接受,这说明用户为知识课程付费已成为一种切实可行的商业模式[12]。由此可见,在线教育平台用户购买意愿的培养已成为在线教育平台盈利和沉淀商业模式的关键所在。

在线教育平台行业急需更多的研究来填补研究领域的空白,使企业对用户购买意愿有更深入的了解,以帮助相关企业针对性调整经营策略,同时提升在线教育类企业的市场竞争力,争夺更多在线教育行业的市场占有率。本文涉及以下研究问题:

(1)甄别在线教育平台用户网络课程购买意愿的相关因素;

(2)分析在线课程的购买意愿相关因素及其影响程度;

(3)当感知价值设置为模型的中介变量时,对在线教育平台用户购买意愿的影响研究;

(4)当课程口碑设置为模型的调节变量时,对感知价值和购买意愿两者之间的作用研究；

（5）探讨买过和未曾买过在线课程的两个用户组在购买意愿影响因素方面的差异。

1.3　研究目标

本研究的研究目标如下：

（1）揭示影响用户购买网络课程意向的相关因素；

（2）在揭示影响在线教育平台用户的购买影响因素后，确定影响用户购买网络课程意向的关键因素和影响程度；

（3）为在线教育行业企业提供制定企业经营战略、产品研发策略、市场营销方案等有价值的参考建议，同时为提升潜在用户的在线教育产品购买转化率提供有效的决策依据，使在线教育平台企业能够熟知潜在用户的购买行为和其特征，在洞察顾客需求后实施正确的解决办法，从而推动企业的可持续发展并形成新的企业竞争优势。

1.4　研究方法

（一）文献回顾法和内容分析方法

通过对相关文献和数据的整理，确定影响用户在线教育平台购买意愿的各种因素，先分析再总结研究模型所包含的结构变量，之后再建立对用户在线课程购买意愿的作用因素研究模型，而后确认本研究对应的目的和研究假设，最后再提出本研究模型包含的结构变量和相关测量的指标。

（二）问卷调查法

在总结中国 B2B2C 模式在线教育平台的特征和研究假设后，参考国内和国外已经成熟的量表，吸纳专家的意见完善问卷相关题项，最后设计出调查问卷。为了保证本研究问卷中内容的效度，本研究的潜在变量与测量的题项都来自或参考已有的出版文献。

本研究将通过问卷调研来获取用于实证分析的样本数据。初步完成问卷设计之后，将采用互联网问卷发布工具"问卷星"（https://www.

sojump. com)发布问卷(问卷星,2018)[13]。

研究过程中将会开展预测试,用来检验研究题项的信度与效度,获得结论之后对相应题项做精确修订。为保证正式调查的时候被调查者能正确地了解测量题项的内涵并同时回答,第一次预测会通过微信平台邀请一些在在线教育平台上有购买使用经验的用户进行调查,根据反馈对有歧义的测量题项进行完善。之后再开始全面的正式调研,具有在线课程购买或使用经验的被调查者才可参与详细调查。由于调查问卷会面向所有的用户开放,相应用户可自行参与问卷调查;另外我们以 QQ 群、E-mail 和微信群为载体随机选出受访者并邀约用户参与问卷调查。最后获得用于本研究分析的数据。

(三)描述性统计分析

获得本研究所需的调查数据后,开展相关的描述性统计分析,以此掌握本次研究数据的整体情况。

(四)信度和效度分析

信度和效度可以用于分析本次问卷调查的质量状况。

(五)实证分析(PLS-SEM)

本研究分别使用 SPSS、SmartPLS 来对数据进行实证分析,并对本研究的研究假设进行验证。

1.5 研究框架

1.5.1 研究路径

本研究先回顾了大量文献,并对中国在线教育发展这一研究背景进行了分析,在线教育的市场规模、服务提供者、潜在用户都呈现明显上升趋势,然而众多在线教育平台却出现亏损且用户课程购买意愿不高的情况。因此很有必要开展识别在线教育平台用户课程购买意愿相关影响因素及其影响程度的研究,以此寻找提高用户购买意愿的解决之道。基于该研究背景,作者提出了在线教育平台用户课程购买意愿的影响因素研究问题。在梳理现有文献、回顾相关理论的基础之上,基于用户感知价值、在线口碑、用户感知风险等基础理论,建立本研究理论模型的同时提出有关联的研究假设,采用网络问卷调研回收数据,再开展实证分析来检验假设。最后,揭示了在线教育平台用户课程购买意愿的影响因素,之后进行了相应的讨论并给出了对应的建议,阐述了研究的贡献和局限性,并提出了今后的研究方向。所采取的研究路径如图 1-1 所示。

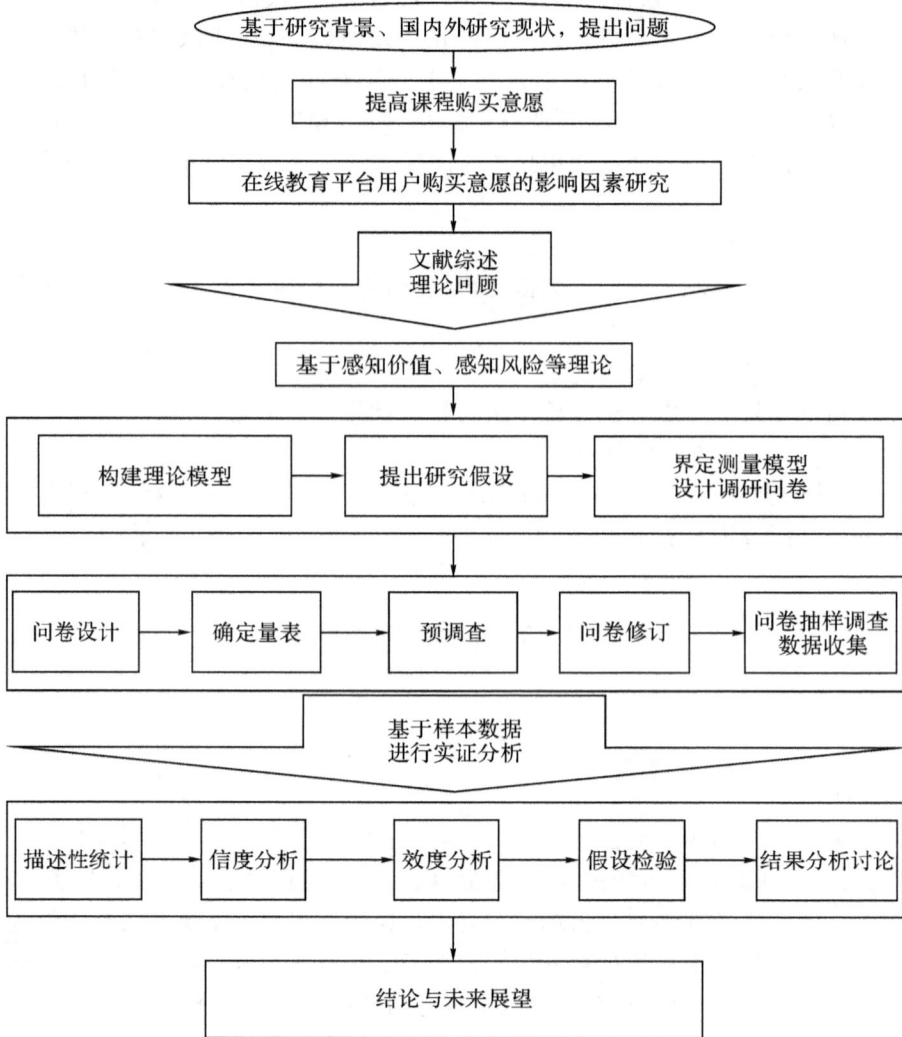

图 1-1 研究路径

1.5.2 研究章节安排

本研究以 B2B2C 在线教育平台用户的购买意愿为研究对象,从感知价值理论视角开展研究。在 B2B2C 在线教育平台的研究背景下,以感知价值的因素为基础,将 B2B2C 在线教育平台的网络课程视为网络虚拟商品,结合电子商务虚拟商品在线销售的场景分析情景变量,如课程口碑、感知易用性等影响用户购买行为的因素。本书共有六章,主要内容如下。

第一章绪论。第一章作为本研究的发起做了详细说明。首先介绍在中国互联网高速发展和在线教育市场规模持续增长的背景下,大部分在线教育平台出现亏损的突出问题,通过背景的研究,提出问题,在本章中重点研究、描述本研究的研究目的。描述了本研究所使用的研究方法、研究框架,并从整体上对本研究如何实现进行阐释。最后阐述了本研究的理论价值和现实价值,提炼出本研究的创新与贡献。

第二章文献综述与理论基础。本章内容是整个研究的理论支撑部分,梳理了国内外有关在线教育和用户购买意愿的研究成果,同时阐述了现有研究成果的不足之处和新事物等待研究的内容,更加突出本研究问题的重要性和急迫性。同时在国内外有关在线教育平台、在线学习、网络购买意愿、在线口碑、用户感知价值等方面研究成果的基础上,分别对涉及的变量特点、维度和测量方法进行了归纳与总结。本研究所采用的基础理论都是在购买意愿、顾客感知价值、电子商务等领域的成熟理论和成熟模型,而后提出本研究模型的相关因素。因此本章内容尤为关键,是本研究的理论依据。检索和翻阅有关资料,开展进一步探究,结合本研究主题的研究背景与研究目标,详细描述用户感知价值理论、在线感知风险理论和信息系统中技术接受模型理论的含义。此后将对相关理论在本研究过程中的影响进行分析。

第三章 B2B2C 在线教育平台概述。本研究属于在线购买意愿的影响因素研究,而 B2B2C 在线教育平台作为专业性电子商务网站,也应具备电子商务平台所具备的特性。因此本章先对我国在线教育的商业模式进行概念界定,对在线教育平台重新进行分类,并对 B2B2C 在线教育平台进行定义,整理归纳其所具备的特点,描述了其发展来源与未来发展趋势。

第四章研究设计与数据收集。对有联系的文章和参考书目进行研究,结合已得出的研究结论和有关结果提出本研究的假设,并建立了以用户感知价值作为中介变量的研究理论模型。为确保问卷和潜变量的信效度,问卷会采用已被多次验证的成熟量表,首先针对模型中的变量进行量表设计,再开展调查问卷的设计。本书采取预先测试来对调研问卷回收的数据开展测验和题项优化。最后,在屏蔽违反逻辑的题项后,确定问卷并开始面向目标发放,收集问卷数据,并对数据进行有效整理。

第五章数据统计与分析。本章主要是对本研究所提出的研究假设展开检验,对调查的问卷进行回收后开展描述性分析,对所包含的测量问项开展信效度的测验。在做完模型的信效度分析后,先对本研究提出的模型展开路径的分析,再开展调节效应的分析。最后,揭示影响消费者行为的关键因素以及作用大小。

第六章结论与展望。该部分内容主要是在整合理论研究成果和对样本数据开展了实证分析的基础之上,梳理出本研究的成果和发现,并提出对在线教育平台有一定指导意义的相关建议,同时说明本研究依旧存在未覆盖的领域,不足以适用所有情景下的模式,从而给出后续研究的参考方向,为在线教育方面的进一步研究提供一定程度的帮助。

1.6　研究价值和贡献

1.6.1　现实价值

(1)对在线教育行业而言:深度解析在线教育的主要收入来源,让投资方、创业者、参与企业等了解商业模式以产生兴趣,号召更多社会力量参与到在线教育行业的发展中来,推动中国在线教育行业的发展。

(2)对企业而言:揭示在线教育平台用户课程购买意愿的实现过程,为在线教育行业企业提供制定企业经营战略、产品研发策略、市场营销方案等有价值的参考建议,同时为提升潜在用户的在线教育产品购买转化率提供有效的决策依据。使在线教育平台企业能够熟知潜在用户的购买行为和其特征,在洞察顾客需求的基础上实施正确的解决办法,从而推动企业的可持续发展并形成新的企业竞争优势。

(3)对产品营销而言:为参与企业实施营销策略提供参考。研究影响在线教育课程购买意愿的因素,有助于企业针对客户制定合适的营销策略,降低盲目营销支出,促进我国网络教育产业的发展。

1.6.2　理论价值

(1)研究对象聚焦商业化在线教育平台。本文调研的样本数据全部来自真实商业环境的用户反馈。主要数据来自数据城堡(DataCastle)、腾讯课堂、淘宝教育等真实在线教育平台的用户,而不是采用学生问卷的方式来获得样本数据,因此本研究较大程度还原了真实商业场景中的消费行为。相比较采用学生问卷的方式,本研究更加具有说服性和商业的参考价值,能够给在线教育平台企业和从业者一些参考。

(2)研究方法上的创新。本研究采用了 PLS-SEM 研究方法对在线教育平台用户课程购买意愿影响因素构建模型并且进行相关检验。然后对拥有在线教育平台课程购买经验和不曾拥有购买经验的用户进行分组讨论。采用 PLS-MGA(PLS Multi-Group Analysis)进行多群组比较分析,进一步讨论不同购买经验的用户购买意愿影响模型中各潜在变量之间的相互关系与强度,以探讨不同用户分组购买意愿所包含的因素与对应因素的影响强度。

(3)研究模型的整合创新,具有一定的理论创新,构建了在线教育平台用户课程购买影响因素的研究模型。根据在线教育平台的消费情境,引入了课程免费试听和时空自主性两个情境变量,加入了口碑调节变量和控制变量,扩大了模型的解释范围,完善了感知价值理论。

(4)调研使用的数据来自一手真实用户,研究所得出的结论具有参考价值。由于以往在线教育平台用户的数据获取较难,更多采用在校学生作为样本群体,样本的代表性不足,其普适性也存在不足。

1.7　本章小结

中国互联网高速发展,为中国的众多产业创造了新的机遇。在线教育享受着中国网络用户数量加速扩张的红利,其市场规模快速扩张,然而大部分在线教育平台出现了亏损的问题。本章从背景出发,说明了本研究的明确方向和详细问题,描述了研究目的,阐述了本研究所使用的研究方法、研究框架。本研究开展了对 B2B2C 商业模式在线教育平台用户对在线课程的购买意愿作用因素研究,希望能为在线教育平台提供在企业营运、产品研发、市场营销等方面富含意义的考量建议。最后阐述了本研究的理论价值和现实价值,提炼出了本研究的创新与贡献。

    在下一章中,作者将对本书所涉及的文献进一步深入分析与梳理。同时阐述本研究的重要性和急迫性,也为之后各章奠定研究理论基础。

Chapter 1　Introduction

1.1　Research Background

China Internet Network Information Center (CINIC) conducted a survey which illustrated that the number of Internet users in China reached 989 million by the end of December 2020, of which users of online education reached 342 million. The number of users using online education through mobile phones was 341 million. Users of mobile online education in China set a record high, and online education users further concentrated on using mobile phones and mobile terminals.

The People's Bank of China argued that the number of mobile payment services reached 123.220 billion, at a total amount of 432.16 trillion yuan, an increase of 21.48% and 24.5% respectively. The scale and growth of online payment is still of great momentum, reflecting that China's online payment has been widely popularized and accepted by users.

China's Ministry of Industry and Information Technology and the National Development and Reform Commission jointly pointed out that the scale of China's information consumption shows a clear growing trend. By 2020, China's information consumption is expected to reach 6 trillion yuan, with an average annual growth rate of at least 11%. The promotion of information technology is obvious. The rapid development of Internet technology, the large-scale popularization of smart terminals, and the comprehensive penetration of mobile application services are revolutionizing people's habits of shopping, entertainment, travel, and knowledge acquisition. The traditional industry can also harness advantages of the advantages of the Internet to be better integrated with the Internet industries. At present, the online education platform (OEP) is an important communication channel for Chinese people to obtain information and knowledge. These platforms aim at using application technologies of the Internet and mobile Internet to provide online and mobile learning services to the public, breaking the limits brought by traditional education models and becoming a new type of business model.

In recent years, with the growing support of the state for online education and the increasing acceptance of online learning methods, Tencent Research Institute (TRI, 2019) found that 96% of users choose B2B2C OEP with relative decent scale and branding. The scale of B2B2C OEP users has grown rapidly. According to iResearch (2018), the online education market in China reached 194.12 billion yuan in 2017, an increase of 22.9% on the previous year. E-commerce Research Center of Internet Economy Institute (ERCIEI, 2019) reported that the market size of China's online education industry (OEI) has exceeded 300 billion in 2018, which is 45% larger than that in 2017. The vast market is attracting many traditional educational institutions and Internet companies to accelerate their process of online education deployment. With the increasing demand for online education courses in the fields of education for children, K12, higher education, vocational education, etc., the online education curriculum market is continuously segmented, and the curriculum service model of online education presents a diversified trend. At present, from the perspective of business, the domestic online education market can be divided into: comprehensive platform (e.g. Tencent Classroom, Taobao Education, Baidu Teaching), language learning (e.g. 91 foreign teachers, 51 talk), early childhood education (e.g. 61 Time Network, Beva Network), K12 education (e.g. Xueersi Network School), consultation of studying abroad (e.g. Huatuo Network School), vocational education and skills enhancement (e.g. Dube. com,

Baidu Chuanxun), exam and training (e. g. Highso, Huanqiu Network School), e-learning tools (e. g. YY voice, dictionary), audio and video knowledge (e. g. Himalaya FM, Litchi FM). The diversification of new demands of Internet knowledge users has driven the online education market to be more segmented, the industry scale has continued to grow, and the prospects in many sub-sectors are promising.

However, while the OEI is welcoming the prosperity, it also indicates that the competition among OEP companies is becoming increasingly fierce. With the intervention of Internet giants such as Baidu, Tencent, and Alibaba, the online education market has ushered in a battle for intensified competition. The homogenization of products and services in the OEI and the low purchase rate are becoming more prominent.

Ni (2018) published an article, mentioning that VIPKID, an online English education platform for children, which was founded nearly four years ago, received 500 million dollar at its round of financing on June 21st, 2018, the largest one in the global OEI to date. In July 21st, Hyphen Education announced the completion of its third round of financing, and Zuoye Bang completed its fourth funding round at 350 million dollars. New Oriental Education, Hujiang Net School and many other pace setters of the OEP were submitting their IPO prospectus. In addition, it is said that one of the Internet unicorns, Today's Headlines, intended to touch the water of OEI through the acquisition of an OEP called "Xue Ba 100". The investment and financing situation seems a hot streak. However, most online education companies are facing losses. Through the IPO prospectus of Hujiang Net School, and financial statements of Suntech and 51talk in 2018, it is known that all the companies above had a net loss. According to the survey conducted by Internet Education Research Institute (2016) on business operation of 400 OEPs, results showed that 70.58% were making losses, with 13.24% in break-even and only 16.18% making a profit. The overall profitability of start-up projects of online education is expected to be less than 5%, with a failure rate of about 15% and a loss rate of 70%. It can be seen that most

OEP companies do not have a clear profit model, and the phenomenon of burning money is serious. Therefore, it is urgent to explore effective profit methods in this industry. For some online education service providers who started earlier and have a larger scale, it is also an urgent need to explore new business models and how to achieve user realization after the accumulation of original users. At present, the profit model of China's B2B2C OEPs mainly rely on course fees, online learning service fees, software fees, platform commissions and advertising revenue. Among them, providing high-quality learning content and cultivating more paid users is the key to the profit model of the majority of large-scale OEPs. The Institute of Journalism and Communication of the Chinese Academy of Social Sciences (IJCCAS, 2018) pointed out that the number of users in the knowledge-paid market continued to expand from 93 million in 2016 to 188 million in 2017, with an annual growth rate of 102.2%, reflecting the willingness of users to pay for high-quality knowledge content and it is feasible to cultivate knowledge-paid model for profitability on the OEP. However, how to persuade users to pay for content or services needs innovative strategies.

In summary, thanks to the mature development of Internet technology and its application services, online education has become a universally accepted method of learning and a trend in the development of digitized education. Nowadays, the user scale and industry scale of the B2B2C OEP are still growing rapidly. The OEI has promising market prospects and became an emerging industry, which is widely acknowledged. However, the rapid growth of the B2B2C OEP has not brought more revenue to the platforms. Instead, it has increased the burden on the platforms, at higher expenses on servers, development and personnel maintenance. Foresight Industry Research Institute (FIRI, 2019) reported that the course purchase ratio on OEP is not high, resulting in many platforms unable to make ends meet. How to recognize the relevant factors that impact purchase intention (PI) of online courses, grasp the user's needs, and improve the user's PI and purchase rate become urgent problems that B2B2C OEP needs to solve.

Purchase intention (PI) is the possibility that a user purchases a particular product or brand and is proven to be an important indicator to predict consumer behavior (Feng, Mu, & Fu, 2006). Many e-commerce researches show that users' PI is an important indicator for participating in e-commerce transactions. Based on the previous studies, PI in this study refers to the subjective willingness of users to purchase online courses on B2B2C OEPs. In this context, this study deemed users on commercial B2B2C OEP as the research object, explore the intention to purchase online education courses from the perspective of perceived value (PV), identify factors that impact users' PI on B2B2C OEP, and analyze the extend of impacts of the above-mentioned factors through theoretical analysis and empirical study, in order to deliver strategic benefits for the commercial operation of B2B2C OEPs, and improve their profitability.

1.2   Research Problems

Nowadays, with the increasing acceptance of the online learning method and the rapid growth of online education users, OEI has a huge market potential, attracting many investors and entrepreneurs to join in the search of wealth. However, most OEPs are still in the stage of burning money, and the unclear business model is a key issue holding many platforms from sustainable development. Currently, the main probability models for OEPs are charging through paid content, online learning service fees, software fees, platform commissions and advertising revenue. Among them, the paid online course is a profit model with great market potential for B2B2C OEP in the future, which is also the key to achieve user realization and sustainable development. While competing for user resources and occupying market share, some of the relatively mature commercial OEPs, such as Tencent Classroom, Taobao Education, Baidu Lectures, etc. are also gradually exploring and improving the business model of paid courses and paid services.

Li (2016) argued that the use of "free" Internet services has become a common consensus among Chinese netizens in the context of China's Internet advancement. However, for OEPs, how to improve their users' intention to purchase so as to generate more income has become an urgent issue for these platforms. The online course on OEP is regarded as a commodity according to the existing researches, but rare researches adopt the perspective of commodity and individual consumption behavior to study users' intention to purchase courses on OEP. Xu, Zhang, and Dong (2018) considered that finding factors that exerts impacts on users' intention to purchase courses can help online course providers access to a greater number of users in the era of information explosion. Chen, Jiao, and Li (2019) found that paid knowledge is gradually being accepted as a new business model, indicating that it is a practical business model that users pay for knowledge and courses. Therefore, the cultivation and fostering of users' PI has become the key to the profitability and business model of OEPs.

The industry of OEP urgently needs more research to fill these gaps, so that enterprises can have a deeper understanding of their users' PI, helping the business enterprises to adjust their business strategies in a targeted manner, and at the same time enhance their own competitiveness and strive for larger market share. Therefore, the following research questions have been covered in this study:

(1) Identifying the leading factors of users' intention to purchase online courses.

(2) Researching on the role of PV in mediating the impacts of PI on OEP.

(3) Analyzing the impacts of the factors related to users' intention to purchase online courses on B2B2C OEPs.

1.3　Research Objectives

The research objectives of this study are as follows:

1. Under the background of the OEP in China, revealing the relevant factors that affect users' intention to purchase online courses.

2. After revealing the factors affecting the purchase of OEP users, determining the key factors and impacts of the factors that affect users' intention to purchase online courses.

3. Provide valuable reference and suggestions for enterprises in OEI in terms of formulating business strategy, product development strategy, marketing plan, etc., and providing effective decision-making reference for improving the conversion rate of potential users' purchasing online education products, so that OEPs can master purchasing behaviors of their consumers in China's e-commerce environment, thus better responding to complex and volatile market conditions, promoting sustainable development and forming new competitive advantages for corporate by implementing accurate solutions to customer needs.

1.4　Research Methods

Based on the basic research of management, economics, psychology and sociology, comprehensive and in-depth research was carried out, combining qualitative research and quantitative research. The research objectives are achieved through the effective combination of normative research and empirical research. The main research methods of this study are as follows:

（1）Literature investigation and content analysis

Through the collation of relevant literature and data, determining various factors that impose impacts on users' intention to purchase on OEP, analyzing and summarizing the structural variables in the model and then constructing a theoretical model of factors impacting online PI of consumers, and determining the research objectives and hypotheses, to further determine specific measurement indicators of structural variables in the theoretical model.

（2）Questionnaire survey

Based on mature scales at home and abroad, items in the questionnaire were selected through advice from experts, and the questionnaire was designed based on the characteristics and research hypotheses of B2B2C OEPs in China. In order to ensure the validity of the questionnaire, potential variables and measurement items in this study were derived from or referenced by existing literature. In addition to that, the structure and content of the initial questionnaire were further adjusted through the pre-investigation.

Samples for empirical analysis were obtained through questionnaire survey. After the preliminary design, the questionnaire was released via an online tool to issue questionnaire, Questionnaire Star. The number of questionnaires issued to its users exceeded 26. 8 million in 2018 and the number of questionnaires collected on this platform exceeded 1. 77 billion since it was launched online in 2006 (Questionnaire Star, 2018).

This study includes a pre-investigation to test the reliability and validity of the items, and then make further analysis of the items after drawing the conclusion. The first pre-investigation invited users with experience in the OEP to conduct surveys through the WeChat platform, in order to ensure that the respondents can understand the meaning of the measurement items and accurately fill in the formal investigation. Then, the study provided carefully modified items with ambiguous meanings and wordings according to the feedback of these respondents. The first pre-investigation was the premises of a large-scale formal investigation later where only users with relevant experience in using online courses are eligible to participate in the survey. The questionnaire respondents were consisted of two parts. On the one hand, the questionnaire was available to all users on the Questionnaire Star. Users can participate in the survey without any invitation. On the other hand, the study was based on randomly selected respondents via sending invitations through QQ groups, WeChat groups, and emails.

Finally, the revised questionnaire was distributed and collected through multiple channels of OEP in an electronic format. Users of B2B2C OEP were invited to fill out the questionnaire and raw data were collated and analyzed.

(3) Descriptive statistical analysis

After obtaining the sample data needed for sending the questionnaire, statistical software was used to perform descriptive statistical analysis to understand the structure and distribution of the samples, so as to grasp the basic statistical characteristics of the data.

(4) Reliability and validity analysis

Reliability and validity analysis were conducted to evaluate the quality of the questionnaire. The stability and consistency of the questionnaire to test related variables were measured by reliability analysis, and the validity of the questionnaire was tested by factor analysis.

(5) Empirical analysis (PLS-SEM)

This study adopted statistical analysis software, SPSS and SmartPLS, for comprehensive analysis. Descriptive statistical analysis could be performed using SPSS, while SmartPLS could not only analyze the reliability and validity of structural equation modeling (SEM) model, but also test hypotheses.

1.5 Research Framework

1.5.1 Research Path

This study starts with an extensive review of the literature, including the research background of online education development in China. The market size, service providers and potential users of online education all show a clear upward trend. However, many OEPs suffer losses and a decreasing number of users. The intention to purchase the course is not high. Therefore, it is necessary to carry out research on identifying factors impacting the intention to purchase online courses of users on OEP and the degree of impacts of these factors, in order to find ways to improve users' PI. This is also the commercialization goal for OEPs to increase their income. These act as the foundation for him to study factors imposing impacts on users' intention to purchase courses on OEP. Based on the existing literature and reviewing relevant theories, theories about PV and perceived risk (PR), a theoretical model was constructed, and relevant research hypotheses are proposed. The hypotheses are tested through questionnaire survey and empirical analysis. Finally, the results reveal factors imposing impacts on users' intention to purchase courses on OEP. The author explains contributions and limitations of the research and proposes direction for future research. The research path taken is shown in Figure 1-1.

1.5.2 Chapter Arrangement

This study takes users' intention to purchase courses on OEP as the research object, focusing on the perspective of PV. Against the background of B2B2C OEP, and based on the PV, online courses on B2B2C OEP are regarded as network virtual goods. Situational variables

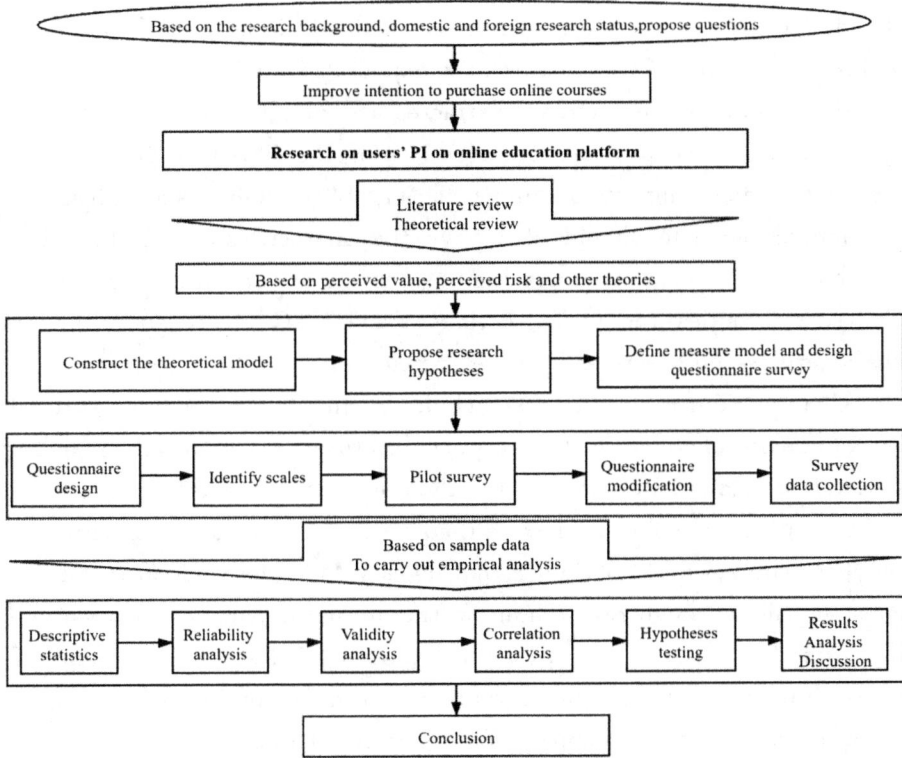

Based on the research background, domestic and foreign research status,propose questions

Improve intention to purchase online courses

Research on users' PI on online education platform

Literature review
Theoretical review

Based on perceived value, perceived risk and other theories

| Construct the theoretical model | Propose research hypotheses | Define measure model and desigh questionnaire survey |

| Questionnaire design | Identify scales | Pilot survey | Questionnaire modification | Survey data collection |

Based on sample data
To carry out empirical analysis

| Descriptive statistics | Reliability analysis | Validity analysis | Correlation analysis | Hypotheses testing | Results Analysis Discussion |

Conclusion

Figure 1-1　Research path

including word-of-mouth (WM), perceived ease of use (PEU) that impact users' purchase behavior is selected in combination with the scene of selling virtual goods in e-commerce. A total of six chapters are arranged for thesis writing. The main research contents are as follows:

　　The introduction includes a detailed description of the launch of this study. Firstly, under the background of the rapid development of Internet in China and the continuous growth of the online education market, most OEPs have a common outstanding problem, operating loss. Then from the research background, the main research questions of this thesis are proposed, and the research purposes of this research are described. The research methods and the frameworks used in this study are depicted, and the implementation of this research is explained. Finally, the theoretical and practical value of this research are expounded, and the innovation and contribution of this research are extracted accordingly.

Chapter Three provides an overview of the B2B2C OEI, to study factors that exert impacts on online PI. The B2B2C OEP as a professional e-commerce website should also have the characteristics of the OEP. Therefore, this chapter defines the business model of online education in China, reclassifies the OEP, defines the B2B2C OEP, sorts out its characteristic and describes its development source and future trends.

Chapter Four covers the research design and data collection. Through the summary of relevant theoretical literature, based on the existing research as a foundation and related theories, combined with the research objectives and his point of view, a theoretical model of users' intention to purchase courses on B2B2C OEP that takes WM as the moderator of PV is constructed. Through researching on the mutual impacts of each variable in the model, research hypotheses are put forward accordingly, and the research model with perceptual value as the mediator is constructed. In order to ensure the reliability and validity of the questionnaires and variables used in this study, the questionnaire used in the study adopts mature scales that have been verified for multiple times. Firstly, the scales are designed targeted for the variables involved in the model, and then the questionnaire is designed. The author also utilized pre-investigation to test the reliability and validity of the questionnaire and optimize the items. Finally, after deleting the unreasonable items, the final version of questionnaire is ready to distribute, and after collecting answers to the questionnaire, the collected data are effectively organized and arranged.

Chapter Five focuses on data processing and analysis, testing the research hypotheses proposed in this study. After the questionnaire was collected, descriptive statistical analysis was carried out, and the reliability and validity of the items to measure the construct variables are tested, after which the path analysis and moderating effect analysis of the research model are performed. Finally, the results can reveal the key factors affecting consumer behavior and their impacts degree.

Chapter Six summarizes the conclusions and paths for further research. This chapter is based on the results of theoretical research and empirical analysis, sorting out the results and findings of this research, proposing recommendations for the OEP, explaining the inadequacy and limitation of the study and providing direction and a certain degree of assistance for further research in the direction of online education.

1.6   Research Value and Contribution

1.6.1   Realistic Value

(1) For the OEI: deeply analyzing the main sources of income for online education, allowing investors, entrepreneurs, companies and other institutions to understand the business model, triggering their interest to participate, and calling for more social forces to participate in the development of the OEI so as to promote the development of China's OEI.

(2) For enterprises: revealing the realization process of users' PI on OEP, providing valuable reference and suggestions for enterprises in the OEI to formulate business strategies, product development strategies, marketing plans, etc. , offering an effective basis for decision making to enhance the purchase conversion rates of their potential users, enabling OEP companies to grasp the characteristics of consumers' purchasing behavior in China's e-commerce environment to cope with complex and volatile market conditions, and promoting sustainable development and forming new competition advantage by understanding customers' real needs and implementing correct solutions.

(3) For product marketing: providing reference for companies in this industry to better implement marketing strategies. Studying the factors

that imposing impacts on PI on online education courses helps enterprises to develop appropriate marketing strategies for customers, reduce blind marketing expenditures, and promote the development of China's OEI.

1.6.2 Theoretical Value

(1) The research object focuses on the commercial OEP. Previous scholars paid more attention to the analysis of factors impacting user behavior in the context of MOOC and self-built online learning systems, but less on the usage scenarios of the commercial OEP. Nowadays, the development trend of online education has shown a good momentum and has become a hot spot for the business and education sectors. The OEP for commercial operation is more dynamic and sustainable. Therefore, this thesis analyzes factors that impact users' purchasing behavior through empirical analysis, which has a positive effect on breaking through the limitations of previous research, enriching the research situation of user behavior on online education, and promoting the sustainable development of online education industrialization.

(2) Innovation in research methods. In this study, the PLS-SEM method was used to construct and test the model of factors that impose impacts on users' PI on OEP. Then users are classified into two groups based on whether they have experience in purchasing courses on OEP. PLS multi-group analysis (PLS-MGA) was used for comparison analysis to further discuss the relationship and strength between potential variables that have impacts on the PI of users with different purchase experiences in the model, to explore the factors that have impacts on PI users with different purchase experiences and the impact strength of the corresponding factors.

(3) The innovation of integrating the research model, which is a theoretical innovation, to some extent since a model of factors that have impacts on users' intention to purchase courses on OEP was constructed. Based on the previous research, PV is studied as a mediator. According to the current advancement of new technologies, such as mobile Internet, the

contextualized variables are added to conduct in-depth research, and the variable of "WM" was introduced a new moderator, which enriches the research on the impacts of each dimension on the dimensions on PV.

(4) The sample data come from real users, so the research results are more reliable. Because the data acquisition of online education users was difficult in the past, normally students are used as sample groups, whose representativeness and universality are insufficient. The sample data of this study are all first-hand data from genuine users on OEP.

1.7   Chapter summary

The rapid development of the Chinese Internet has created new opportunities for many industries in China. Online education enjoys the rapid development of the Internet with continuously growing market scale but most OEPs are suffering losses, an acute challenge facing this industry. This chapter takes the background as the starting point, puts forward main research questions and describes the research purpose of this research. The research methods and framework used in this study are also elaborated in this chapter. Analyzing the factors that impact the users' intention to purchase courses on B2B2C OEP, this study intends to provide valuable reference and suggestions for enterprise management, product development, marketing and other OEPs. Finally, the chapter sets forth the theoretical and practical value of this research and extracts the key innovation and contribution.

In the next chapter, he conducted an in-depth review of the relevant literature involved in this study, and expounded the importance and urgency of the research questions, laying the theoretical foundation for the later chapters.

第 2 章　文献综述与理论基础

2.1　购买意愿相关研究综述

2.1.1　购买意愿相关研究综述

Eagly 和 Chaiken(1968)指出,意愿是有计划和有意识地实施某一行为的个人动机[14]。而在后期,有相关学者将意愿这个概念引入营销学科,Fishbein 和 Ajzen(1975)将购买意愿判定为消费者购买某种商品或者服务的主观概率,认为客户的购买意愿是一种主观的可能性,即客户可能进行某种特定的购买[15]。Bagozzi 和 Burnkrant(1979)指出,购买意愿被视为消费者决定购买货物的倾向[16]。Burke 等(1985)认为顾客对商品或服务的主观态度形成了顾客的购买意愿[17]。Dodds 等(1991)则将买受人消费的意愿视为潜在用户购买所选标的的可能性[18]。Ajzen 和 Driver(1992)认为意愿是购买行为产生之前的关键因素,也是产生下一步行为的必经过程[19]。Spears 和 Singh(2004)研究发现,潜在用户购买货物或服务的概率是购买意愿[20]。当购物者对某种商品或服务的态度和印象达到满意时,就会产生购买意愿。

中国的研究人员也对购买意愿相关内容开展过一系列的定义。韩睿和田志龙(2005)认为用户的购买意愿指主观判断消费概率,这个结论与国外的学者是一样的[21]。冯建英等(2006)指出消费行为的一个先决条件是产生用户的购买意愿[9]。张金鑫(2017)认为购买意愿决定着是否采取购买行为[22]。庞玉玮(2018)认为个体拥有了购买意愿之后才会做出购买决策,当个体的购买意愿越强烈则购买行为实施的可能性越大[23]。刘遗志等

(2019)研究后认为拥有购买意愿是购买行为的前提[24]。

众多学者针对购买意愿开展研究,随着这个概念的明晰和深入,大家开始用这一概念来预估消费者的购物走向。用户网络环境中的购买意愿同线下环境无太大差异,因此众多学者也发现了用户购买意愿是触发潜在用户产生购买行为的先前因素。

2.1.2　感知价值与购买意愿相关研究综述

Monroe(1973)指出,用户往往在做出购买决定之前比较所付出的成本和从产品中获得的利得,如果所收到的利得超过所付出的成本,顾客对产品有积极的看法[25]。当顾客感知的利得超过感知的成本时则形成购买意愿,感知价值越高,其购买可能性越大。Dodds 等(1991)研究发现,预期获得的价值对购买意愿有积极影响[18]。Teas 和 Agarwal(2000)得出消费者所接受的主观价值左右了他们的购买意愿,消费者感知价值是行动与否的先行条件[26]。Tam(2004)发现用户主观价值产生的购买行为可能性比用户的满意程度所产生的可能性更高[27]。Wu 和 Hsing(2006)为评估消费者感知的牺牲与感知的利得同时对用户购买意愿的作用,开发了相应的研究模型[28]。结果表明,主观感受获得的价值观对用户的购买倾向产生了明显的积极影响。

宋亦平(2006)表示,消费者感知价值经常会影响消费者的购买决定,用户对获得利益的评估会对用户的购买倾向产生作用[29]。钟凯(2013)通过调研发现了潜在用户的主观感知的价值会对其是否做出消费行为产生作用[30]。此外,刘遗志和汤定娜(2015)认为强化推广可以提升用户的购买倾向[31]。王赟芝(2017)在进行实证研究后发现用户的感知价值越大,其对商品或服务的购买意愿越强烈[32]。许亚楠等(2018)通过对大学生在线课程付费意愿的研究发现,感知价值显著影响大学生的购买意愿[11]。林婷婷和曲洪建(2019)通过对感知价值与购买意愿之间的关系进行研究,验证了用户的主观感知的价值与用户是否做出消费行为存在关联[33]。

根据前人的研究成果分析,多种因素对是否做出消费行为产生作用。然而,以上因素是否对在线教育的用户课程付费意愿也有明显的影响,各因素之间的作用如何,需要联系在线教育课程购买场景,通过实证分析加以验证。

2.1.3 在线口碑与购买意愿相关研究综述

在传统的市场营销及消费者购买行为的研究领域,口碑被认为是影响消费者购买行为和市场推广的重要部分,在关于传统销售和用户消费行为的专业领域,都认同口碑是会作用于消费者行为的一个重要部分(黄英、朱顺德,2003)[34]。鉴于网络消费的快速崛起,网络产品上的评论和说明对潜在用户的选购非常重要。在线购物平台用留言征求用户对商品的反馈意见,以供之后的用户考察。这些评价构成了特定的商品或服务的网络点评和在线口碑,对消费者网络购买的意愿和行为产生关键影响。

Park 等(2007)认为,网上评论的质量更高数量更多,对用户购买商品的意愿产生更积极的作用[35]。Lee 和 Youn(2009)发现积极的评价可能会刺激消费者购买商品的意愿,而不是消极的影响[36]。Gui 等(2012)在对亚马逊购物平台上的数据做研究时发现,评论在销售初期对产品的影响更加明显[37]。

Hennig-Thurau 等(2003)研究了消费者在网络平台上查找商品口碑的动机,发现消费者认为查看评价可以更快地了解产品,节约时间,更快地做出购买决策[38]。

中国学者在有关研究中也发现,在网络购物的情境下,网络口碑对消费者购买行为有明显的影响和作用,商品或服务的积极网络口碑能正面影响顾客的购买意愿,良好的在线点评能对用户的消费意愿产生积极影响(毕继东,2009;李佳,2015;黄文彦,2013;卢长宝等,2017;许亚楠等,2018)[11,39,40,41,42],在线的负面点评对消费意愿有负面作用(毕继东,2010;郭菲,2015;张景,2015)[43,44,45]。叶阳和王涵(2018)在对有声阅读平台的付费影响因素研究中发现,网络口碑和用户感知的质量都会左右用户付费意愿[46]。王建军等(2019)发现,熟人之间的口碑会正向地调节感知的价值对用户的购买意愿的影响[47]。王君萍等(2019)对点评的来源和发表人的可信度进行了深入探讨,发现以上这些都对用户的消费意愿产生了积极作用[48]。

综合以上研究成果来看,在众多研究中已多次验证过相关因素,以及这些因素对购买意愿的影响程度和关系。

2.1.4　在线购买意愿相关研究综述

消费者对购买商品和服务的意愿实际上并不会因为线上线下而产生不同,都是指购买商品或服务的可能性或概率。线上消费的购物方式和环境与线下消费不同,在虚拟渠道产生交易是其自身的特质。

Sharma(2002)的研究表明,网点的服务质量对消费者的购物意愿也有着较大的影响,例如优秀的客服人员、较短的回应时间、完善的售后服务以及其他相关配套服务对网络消费者的购物意愿有着较为积极的影响[49]。所以网站应该在维系客户关系及相关服务上增加客户黏性,提高客户的购买意愿。Belanger 等(2002)则发现一个购物网站的界面也对消费者的购物意愿有影响,更加简洁方便的页面有助于客户了解产品和服务,继而提高消费者购买意愿[50]。

Pavlou(2003)认为,与线下购物模式相比,在线购物时消费者可以更快地浏览种类更多的商品,并进行比较,可以以较少的时间和精力来获得更优的产品和更多的服务,但是网络消费也会带来一定的风险[51],例如无法触摸实物,无法感受实物质地,售后服务难以保障,同时也存在个人信息被泄漏等问题,这些潜在的风险会对消费者的购物意愿产生一定的影响。如果这些问题得不到解决,线上购物将难以得到长远的发展。

周劲松(2006)对假设的模型进行路径分析,结果表明 B2C 模式电子商务网站的信任度受到上述关联因素影响,网站可在以上内容上采取有效措施来赢得消费者的信任[52]。

孙娇娇和孙永波(2017)基于感知价值的理论探讨了用户对生鲜产品的在线购买意愿影响因素,得出了娱乐性和感知成本等因素对用户的购买倾向有明显作用[53]。孙小丽(2018)发现用户的性别对在线购买意愿的作用并无显著性差异,但在线购物年限、在线购物频率对用户购买意愿的作用则存在较大差异[54]。崔剑峰(2019)探讨了感知风险与网络冲动性购买的关系,将感知的风险来源划分为产品、在线平台、在线提供的服务、用户自身所处环境四类,并发现感知风险会显著影响用户的购买意愿[55]。李梦吟和王成慧(2019)基于技术接受模型在社会化媒体环境中对用户的网络购买意愿进行了研究,认为信任是影响网络购买意愿非常重要的因素之一[56]。

综上所述,每个研究在设定研究对象上均有所不同,在定义购买意愿和对其概念的分析上也存在一定的差异。本研究对用户购买意愿的操作性定义为:在中国 B2B2C 模式在线教育平台的购物环境下,消费者产生在线课程的服务价格感知后,愿意达成交易的概率。

2.2 顾客感知价值相关研究综述

2.2.1 顾客感知价值相关研究综述

顾客购买的不仅仅是商品本身,还有商品或服务所提供的价值。顾客感知的最高值并不是产品和服务,而是消费者的真实需求。企业所做的任何一个决定都应该以获取客户这一稀缺资源为出发点。范秀成和罗海成(2003)觉得顾客真正所在意的价值才是顾客感知价值[57]。Peter 和Tarpey(1975)提出购物者在消费时会产生两个感知:需要的部分为正面的价值,不想要的部分便为负面的价值[58]。Zeithaml(1988)结合众多前人已经发布的结果,采用用户访谈的研究方式,综合概括出潜在用户对自己感知价值的四种观点,并在总结消费者思想行径的前提上,把用户的感知价值定义为客户对商品使用效果的总体评价[59]。Zeithaml(1988)提出,公司应该从客户的角度出发进行创造、设计等服务,应该将消费者的感知价值判定为关键因素。他把潜在客户的感知价值概括为四项内容:(1)价值表示较低的消费,一部分客户把价值看作较低的消费,如果有促销或者让利的商品,他们就认为这些商品具有较高的价值,这表示在他们的认知中,消费的金额是价值感受中关键的部分。(2)价值表示期待从商品中得到的利益,和那些认为消费额重要的人不同,有另一部分人认为从商品或服务中可以获得的利益才是价值的重要因素。(3)价值表示有性价比,部分客户认为只有在消费额和获得的品质对等,或是可以用便宜的价格获得质量更高的商品时才是有价值的。(4)价值表示所有的成本换得的所有的回报。他们将自己购买商品时产生的时间和精力也当作成本的一部分,当然他们也将品质以外的利益当作回报。Zeithaml(1988)把消费者对价值的四种观点总结归纳为:消费者的感知价值是消费者在对付出和回报进行比较后,能够感知到的商品和服务的整体效果的反馈。此定义包括了两个内容:第一,每个人对价值的感受均不相同;第二,价值是付出与回报两者之间的衡量,消费者会综合考虑多种因素后做出消费行为,而不是片面的思考。

Butz 和 Goodstein(1996)提出,用户主观感知到的价值的形成是因为客户对这家企业的信任,从而产生对商品和服务的信任,这种信任会让客户感受到收获大于付出[60]。Gardial 等(1994)提出,顾客在选购商品时所感知到的价值与后期使用中感知到的价值是不一样的[61]。Woodruff(1997)表示,消费者的感知价值为用户在产品质量、体验等方面的主观判断,最后这些特性能让消费者实现自己的期望[62]。Grewal 等(1998),Parasuraman 和 Grewal(2000)表示,客户的感知价值是客户在不断比较感知的利益和感知成本的非静态的概念,可以总结为四个类型:①获得的价值,即支付相应金额可以获得的回报;②相互交换价值,表示客户通过消费行为得到的心理愉悦的感受;③使用价值,表示在使用商品或者体验服务的过程中得到的效果反馈;④赎回价值,表示将旧的商品出售后获得的收入[63-64]。目前中国学术界对顾客感知价值的研究开始大幅增加,并把顾客的感知价值和用户的购买意愿、消费者购买行为以及顾客的忠诚度等关联在一起。江林和袁宏福(2009)的研究较为新颖,他们将消费者的个性因素作为影响顾客的感知价值因素,通过研究不同个性的消费者,来探究不同个性对感知价值的影响方式和影响程度[65]。郝俊峰(2011)对企业的创新行为和品牌的形象、品牌的管理能力、顾客的感知价值与顾客的购买行为之间的相互作用进行研究,用缜密的研究架构进一步探讨了潜在消费者的感知价值等因素对消费者的消费行为的作用结果[66]。钟凯(2013)把感知价值的理论作为前提条件,发现网络点评在用户感知价值和用户消费意愿之间起到一些调节的作用[30]。赵岩(2013)表示,顾客的感知价值由整体顾客利益与整体顾客成本两部分组成[67]。陈超等(2017)基于感知价值的视角研究用户对转基因食品的购买意愿,发现用户的负面点评会对买方的购买意愿产生负面作用[68]。方爱华等(2018)针对虚拟社区用户知识付费意愿的研究发现,感知有用性、感知信任正向影响感知价值,从而影响虚拟社区用户的付费意愿[69]。陈凯等(2019)对感知风险和感知价值两个理论进行了整合,将感知风险和感知价值都进行了进一步的因素细分,探讨其对用户新能源汽车购买意愿的影响,结果发现主观感知的风险和价值对用户的购买意愿有明显影响[70]。

通过以上的研究和调查可以发现,顾客的感知价值不单纯是顾客的购买意愿和顾客的购买行为发生的基础,同时也是企业在营销活动中较为在意的关键因素。对顾客的感知价值的探索基本是通过三方面开展的:首先,把顾客的感知价值定为关键变量,采用实证研究的方法或是参考梳理先前的研究结论,探索顾客的感知价值和企业有关影响因素的关联;其次,引入感知价值作为模型的中间变量进行探讨;最后,结合在线教育行业特点,帮助企业在激烈的市场竞争中参考经营策略以获得具有优势的地位。

2.2.2 网络顾客感知价值相关研究综述

Keener(1999)提出网络顾客的感知价值通过基础目标和手段目标两个目标展开[71]。基础目标是指网购站点应该确保提供的商品的质量、降低购买的成本,便利消费者,不泄露顾客隐私,让消费者产生愉悦的感受。手段目标是指网站必须做到诚信,保证各方面的信息安全,上新及时以便消费者可以经常得到新的商品和服务,降低网上购物的风险。Bourdeau 等(2002)指出使用 E-mail 的人更看重社会价值,使用网络可以让他们建立并维系好人际关系,他们使用网络并不是追求知识,而是比较注重便捷的交流方式[72]。在对网络顾客的感知价值研究中,钟小娜(2005)提出了可以使网络购物的顾客提高感知价值的建议,以有效地降低用户主观感知到的风险[73]。许统邦等(2006)表示购买的情境对网络顾客感知价值也存在影响,同时在理论上对感知到的利得与利失和感知风险进行了深入的研究,得出新的网络消费的感知价值研究模型[74]。孙强和司有和(2007)认为满意度主要可以从购买商品是否便捷、商品是否低廉、客户的个性、客户的知识层面和售后方面进行探讨,信任感可以从网站提供的安全服务、网站在专业领域的知识等方面进行体现,以上两方面共同组成了用户的感知价值[75]。张明立(2007)提出客户的心理状态、收入高低和消费模式等也会对感知价值产生影响[76]。除以上之外,还有包括家庭、工作、周遭环境在内的各种购物环境也会对感知价值产生影响。钟凯(2013)表示好的感知价值会增加网络客户的购买意愿,在注重价格合理给客户带来感知价值的同时也要更加注重在线口碑的积累[30]。叶阳和王涵(2018)以有声阅读平台作为研究空间,对其用户进行了和内容付费有关的影响原因研究,得出每个人的付费倾向、感知价格等多方面的因素对用户的购买意愿有直接影响,而间接影响用户购买意愿的影响因素中则有感知质量和网络口碑[46]。高翔(2019)以感知价值作为中介变量研究用户行为,主观感知的价值会直接作用于顾客的购买倾向,再间接地影响感知品质[77]。

2.2.3　感知风险与顾客感知价值的相关研究综述

Bauer(1960)是第一个提出感知风险这个概念的人,他认为感知风险是每个人对不同的风险和风险的严重程度的感受,就是消费者认为在做出一个错误的决策或是不确定的决策后会产生的负面的后果[78]。比如,消费者购买了某一项在线课程,在购买课程之前会做很多功课,但购买课程之后课程质量是否和预期的一样高,个人吸收和理解能力是否与课程匹配的风险都可能存在,如果答案是否定的,那么消费者在前期金钱、时间和精力上的付出都是浪费的,从而产生风险。随着研究领域的不断扩展和深入,越来越多会产生感知风险的因素也逐渐扩充。Stone 和 Grønhaug(1993)在研究中证实了感知风险的六个重要组成[79]。Jacoby 等(1972)分别提出了财务、社会、业绩、身体和心理共计五个种类的风险[80]。Peter 和 Tarpey(1975)首次提出了新的类型:时间风险[58]。

王晰巍等(2017)为探讨用户在汽车新媒体环境下交互意愿的影响因素,基于感知价值理论构建了相应模型,用户感知到的风险会对使用者的交互意愿产生负面作用[81]。此外,赵士雯等(2018)在研究用户对智慧型房产商品的购买意愿时,基于感知价值和感知风险理论构建了结构方程模型,验证用户主观感受到的风险是经用户主观感知的价值来间接地作用于用户的消费倾向[82]。其他学者如刘遗志等(2019)从感知风险与感知成本的视角出发,使用问卷调研的方法回收数据,并采用结构方程模型进行数据分析,得出在网络环境中的感知成本与感知风险都会影响用户的线下购买意愿,并最后影响到用户的线下购买行为[24]。陈凯等(2019)把感知风险与感知价值引入研究中,共同研究用户对新能源汽车的购买意愿,最终发现感知风险显著负向影响用户的购买意愿,其中财务风险是主要的影响因素之一[70]。

2.2.4　感知成本与顾客感知价值的相关研究综述

Klemperer(1987)提出感知成本包含了交易成本(Transaction costs)、学习成本(Learning cost)、契约成本(Contractual costs)[83]。Zeithaml(1988)表示感知利失是包含感知成本的,用户所感知到的成本是消费者在选购和运用商品时感知到的费用[59]。

Dick 和 Basu(1994)提出消费者在进行支付的过程中产生认知的成本主要包括：时间成本，即消费所需要消耗的时间；金钱成本，即消费需要消耗的资金；认知成本，即消费所需要消耗的认知[84]。而认知成本的产生多数是因为不熟练掌握网络支付技术和在消费过程中感受到了风险。Venkatesh 等(2003)采用感知成本作为变量来研究客户的使用意愿[85]。在时间和资金成本之外，还提出了学习成本，表示学习成本是消费过程中因为学习使用所消耗的精力。

本研究以感知价值理论为基本理论，结合之前的研究结论，对用户购买 B2B2C 模式在线教育课程进行研究，也加入了感知成本理论。Jones 等(2002)针对在银行业和理发行业的研究中指出，感知成本包含沉没成本等六种类型[86]。Lam 等(2004)开展对于旅游代理业的研究，提出感知成本包含了资金成本(Money)、不确定性成本(Uncertainty)等[87]。王英迪(2016)提出，进行产品创新有助于用户减少感知成本，提高购买意愿[88]。孙娇娇和孙永波(2017)提出消费者在互联网消费模式中的价格认知、犹豫行为、品牌信任感和感知成本会对用户的购买意愿产生影响[53]。万静(2018)在研究多种渠道用户购买意愿之间的关系中，得出线下的感知成本也会显著影响用户在线下的购买意愿[89]。卢恒等(2019)在对使用语音进行问答的虚拟社区用户付费意愿的研究中，从感知收益和感知成本两个方面研究用户的购买意愿，得出沉没成本和信息获取习惯都负向影响感知收益，转移成本与个人免费观念均正向影响感知成本，最后得出感知收益正向影响购买意愿、感知成本负向影响购买意愿[90]。

2.2.5　在线口碑与顾客感知价值的相关研究综述

Arndt(1967)在研究中提出了口碑一词[91]。他着重指出口碑是消费者在接触了解产品、品牌或者服务后等形成的一种非官方的、个性化的传递信息和沟通的方式。提出消费者在使用产品和获得服务后，可以给出满意的反馈(Brown and Reingen，1987)[92]，也可以给出不满意的反馈，这些反馈都会给潜在消费者的购买决策带来影响(File 等，1992)[93]。

在线口碑随着互联网的普及而逐步产生。已有研究对在线口碑的描述不一，但其本质基本相同，本文统一采用在线口碑(Online Word-of-Mouth)这一提法。Gelb 和 Johnson(1995)[94]、Chatterjee(2001)[95]提出大量的消费者可以在网络消费后进行在线口碑的发表和相互联系。Bhatnagar 和 Ghose(2004)[96]、Sun 等(2006)[97] 表示随着互联网的普及,在线口碑可以被文字记录,这种形式的口碑的传播范围、传播速度不受限制,传播效率高于传统口碑。

在线口碑和传统口碑的本质是一样的,只是存在的形式和载体不同。传统口碑较多的是口口相传,扩散面不广,利用率不高。在线口碑也是通过个人描述传递信息,但其通过互联网传播可以被文字化,传播面广,传播速度快,便于查找和分享。陈超等(2017)的研究发现,口碑因素会调节感知价值对购买意愿的影响[68]。叶阳和王涵(2018)在对声音阅读的在线平台用户开展购买意愿的研究中,发现网络口碑会显著影响用户的感知价值[46]。王建军等(2019)在探讨网络口碑、感知价值、购买意愿三者之间关系的研究中,将口碑按照熟人口碑和陌生口碑进行细分,最终发现陌生口碑会影响用户的购买意愿与感知价值,熟人口碑会产生较为积极的调节作用[47]。

在线口碑产生的平台较为丰富,如电子消费平台、在线购物 app、微信、邮件、第三方口碑平台等。但无论在线口碑是以何种形式体现的,其本质都是消费者使用互联网平台对产品或者服务进行评价后分享。互联网的发展让口碑分享更加简便,也让在线口碑的数量快速增加,使在线口碑成为当前研究的热点之一。

2.3　理论基础

2.3.1　顾客的感知价值

在市场营销学与消费者行为的研究领域,研究者均认可顾客的感知价值是消费者产生消费决策时的重要考量因素,顾客购买的可能性会随着所感知的价值增高而提高。

Porter(1985)首次发表了买方价值理论,是指购买商品获得和服务获得的净收益[98]。他指出企业给到的总价值只有在高于用户的期待价值时,才可以让产品或服务获得青睐。站在企业的位置,若期望提升买方价值有两种方法,第一种为提升整体收益,第二种为减少用户所支付的成本,其中成本除了金钱以外,也要考虑时间、精力等其他成本。

　　Annika 和 Christian(1996)根据损益权衡,制定了客户的价值过程相关理论[99]。但事实上,顾客价值的产生是一个漫长的过程,其期间顾客需要对企业进行不断了解,顾客和企业之间也需要不断地接触,并不是消费者单纯考量的结果,所以 Annika 和 Christian 其实并没有很好地对消费者和企业的关系进行全面的研究。Woodruff(1997)发现消费者的感知价值和购买之间的关系是动态的,是不断变化的[62]。科特勒(1998)认为用户在购物前会将预期与期望价值做比较来做出消费决策[100]。

　　在用户的感知价值方面,先前研究多以增加前置变量来开展实证分析,其中有的研究是划分为感知利得与感知利失两类前置变量来进行研究(Dodds 等,1991)[18];也有研究者以产品质量等因素来作为影响消费者感知价值的前因变量(Wood and Scheer,1996;钟凯,2013)[30,101]。孙娇娇和孙永波(2017)引入消费者决策的风格和感知价值理论来展开移动互联网的生鲜产品购买意愿研究[53]。叶阳和王涵(2018)对声音阅读平台用户展开购买意愿研究时采用了感知价值的视角构建用户付费意愿模型[46]。陈昊等(2019)基于感知价值理论和期望确认模型来进行用户的知识付费意愿研究[12]。

　　综上,先前研究者从不同维度对顾客的价值理论进行了多方面的研究,对其本质意义理解基本一致,都认为价值感知是购买意愿的决定因素,同时也决定了购买行为。在网上进行消费时,和线下消费类似,顾客的感知价值和购买意愿呈正比。本研究以顾客感知价值理论为基础理论,提出了如图 2-1所示的在线课程购买意愿的作用模型。

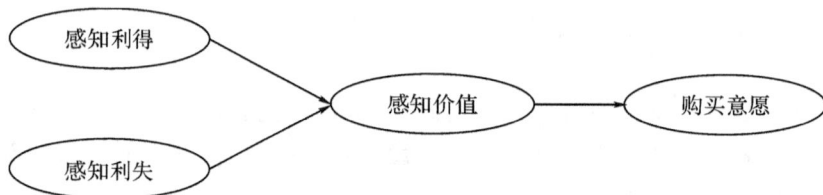

图 2-1　在线课程购买意愿的作用模型

2.3.2　感知风险理论(PR)

感知风险已多次被证实是消费者购买意愿的其中一个重要影响因素。感知风险有关研究得出,消费者在购物时,会出现难以预判的个人感受,从而影响到用户潜在的消费倾向。

Stone 和 Grønhaug(1993)[79]、Shim 等(2001)[102]提出了感知风险所构成的具体内容,本次研究来判定用户的感知风险主要是通过研究消费者在网络上购买付费课程所花费的时间和金钱是否换取了等价的学习效果。以往的研究还表明,消费者网络消费的风险被认为对消费意愿产生了影响(McKnight 等,2002;黄英、朱顺德,2003;黄文彦、劳陈峰,2013)[34,41,103]。感知风险也被多次引入用户的购买意愿研究(赵士雯等,2018;万静,2018;陈凯等,2019;孟陆等,2019)[70,82,89,104]。

在线课程消费的主要内容是在线课程及其相关服务,相对于传统的购买来说风险较小。研究了已有的文献后,接下去本研究会对感知风险进行相关探讨,用实证分析来检验感知风险在网络消费的环境下是否也会影响在线教育平台用户的付费课程的购买意愿。

2.3.3　技术接受模型(TAM)

Davis(1986)提出的技术接受模型[105],用于解释与预测使用者采纳信息系统的接受度,详见图 2-2。

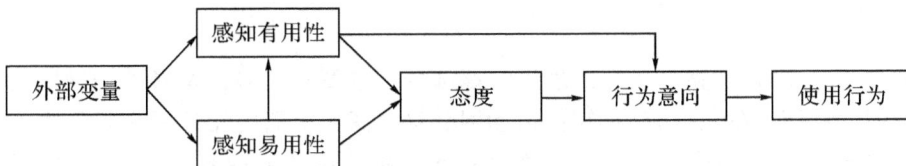

图 2-2　技术接受模型

此模型以理性行为理论为基础,提炼出用户的感知易用性和感知有用性两类变量。感知易用性是用户在使用系统中能够感知到系统简单易用的状态。感知有用性则是用户感受到系统是真实有效的。

Davis(1986)表示用户需要消耗时间来感知系统是否有效,因此感知易用性也会直接影响感知有用性[105]。用户会因为系统操作不方便而放弃使用,导致他们无法感知到系统的有用性。

Venkatesh 和 Davis(1996)修订了技术接受模型[106],删除了"态度"因素,使现有的模型更为简洁明了,如图 2-3 所示。

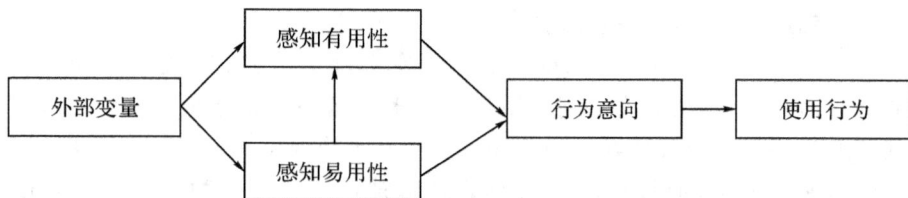

图 2-3　改进后的 TAM 模型

目前,多种信息技术已经被大规模地应用,包括但不局限于各种在线教育平台、购物网站、商务办公等,各国学者以此为基础,开展了数量庞大的研究和实证,进一步确定了该模型的适用性。

根据大量的文献检索和内容分析,笔者发现技术接受模型也在大量的实证研究中被使用,以探讨用户的购买意愿(李同强,2016;黄彬,2017;马健,2018;李梦吟、王成慧,2019)[56,107,108,109]。因此,本研究也会使用技术接受模型对在线教育平台用户课程购买意愿影响因素进行探讨。

2.4　本章小结

本章内容是整个研究的理论支撑部分。本章是对各国学者关于网络购物影响因素、在线口碑、感知价值和网购消费意愿等研究结论的概括。本章也描述了现有研究成果的不足之处和新事物的待研究内容,更加突出本研究问题的重要性和急迫性。同时在前人研究成果的基础上,依次对涉及的相关变量、概念与衡量方式做了总结。本研究将采用的基础理论都是在购买意愿、顾客感知价值、电子商务领域方面的成熟理论和成熟模型,因此本章内容尤为关键,是本研究的理论依据。

Chapter 2 Literature Review and Theoretical Foundation

2.1 Literature on PI

2.1.1 Literature of PI

Intention is the premise of behavioral activities. Only when individuals have the intention, can they take certain behavioral activities. Therefore, the individual's intention can be considered as determination of the individual's behavioral activities. The term "intention" is initially a concept of psychology, which refers to the willingness of consumers to act and a change in the state of mind of the consumer. It is the possibility that the consumer engages in a certain behavior in the case of receiving certain information or stimuli. In consumer behaviorism, the intention to purchase is considered as a decision-making process, meaning that the consumer has the possibility to purchase or attempt to purchase a product or service.

Eagly and Chaiken (1993) considered that intention is a psychological state different from attitude, and it is an individual motivation to implement a certain behavior with consciousness and plan. Since then, some scholars have introduced the concept of "intention" into the discipline of marketing. Fishbein and Ajzen (1975) identified PI as the subjective probability of consumers purchasing a certain product or service, and they believed that the customer's PI refers to the subjective probability that the customer engages in a particular purchase. Bagozzi and Burnkrant (1979) defined PI as the consumer's tendency to buy commodity. They believed that the purchase behavior can be predicted by the PI that is a key indicator to understand the buyer's subjective tendency. Burke, Hatfield, and Kein (1985) proposed that consumers' attitudes towards a certain product or brand, as well as certain environmental factors, ultimately constitute consumers' PI that is the subjective tendency of consumers to choose a certain commodity. He also confirmed that the PI can be used as an important indicator to predict consumer buying behavior. Dodds, Monroe, and Grewal (1991) defined consumers' PI as the probability and likelihood that a consumer will buy a particular product or service. Ajzen and Driver (1992) defined PI as a determining factor before behavioral performance and a necessary process for doing the next step. Spears and Singh (2004) concluded that PI is the subjective probability that a customer buys a certain good or service after research. When the attitude and impression of consumers reaches the level of satisfaction with a product or service, they will form an intention to purchase.

Chinese scholars have also defined PI in series of wording and phrasing. Han and Tian (2005) believed that PI is the possibility of consumers purchasing certain goods, which coincides with foreign scholars. Feng, Mu, and Fu (2006) considered PI as the basis for consumers' buying behavior. Zhang (2017) proposed that PI determines whether consumers will buy or not. Pang (2018) argued that an individual has a PI before making a purchase decision, and when the individual's PI is stronger, the individual is more likely to implement the purchase behavior. Liu, Hu, and Tang (2019) argued that having PI is a prerequisite for conducting purchasing behavior.

The research of the majority of scholars on the PI is also deepened with the clarity of this concept. Everyone is more willing to use this concept to predict the shopping trends of consumers in the future. Compared with the traditional PI, consumers' online PI is not much different. Most scholars also believe that online PI refers that consumers are likely to purchase a certain product or service in a virtual environment. Although there is no shopping environment of actual offline consumption in the online environment, consumers are driven by the PI to buy when making shopping behaviors.

2. 1. 2   Literature of PV and PI

Monroe (1973) pointed out that customers usually compare the perceived benefit and perceived cost (PC) of purchasing products when making purchasing decisions. When the perceived benefit is greater than PC, the customer has a positive PV for the product. Positive PV will increase consumers' willingness to buy. Similarly, when the perceived benefit of the consumer is greater than PC, the customer will have a PI, and higher PV always causes higher PI. Dodds, Monroe, and Grewal (1991) pointed out that PV has a positive impact on PI in empirical research. Assael, Dymond, and Papadaki (1992) pointed out that higher PV for goods or services during the shopping process brings stronger PI. From the perspective of consumer psychology, Zeithaml (1988) conducted a large number of empirical studies to prove that the higher the consumer's perceived benefit to the product or service is, the higher their feeling of value will be, and higher PV of the product or service will increase the consumer's willingness to purchase the product or service. Teas and Agarwal (2000) argued that the subjective PV of consumers determines their willingness to purchase, and that PV is an important factor in consumers' decision-making. Eggert and Ulaga (2002) also pinpointed that consumer satisfaction is a necessary driver for purchase, but PV is the most important driver for consumers to purchase. Tam (2004) showed that consumers' PV is more likely to trigger consumer buying behavior than consumer satisfaction. Wu and Hsing (2006) constructed a model that how perceived sacrifice affects PV and then PI. The conclusions showed that PV has a significant positive impact on consumers' PI.

Song, Wang, and Xu (2006) pointed out that the PV of consumers usually affects their decision whether to purchase or not. The evaluation result of PV determines the willingness to purchase. Wang, Li, and Ye (2007) suggested that consumers' perceptions of purchasing interests and purchasing risks affect consumers' PV and their purchasing decisions. In the study of online consumers' willingness to purchase, Zhong (2013) took the purchase cost, perceived product quality, PR, perceived website service quality as antecedent variables of consumer's PR online, and concluded that consumers' perceived product quality and perceived website service quality have a significant positive impact on their PV and PI, while PC and PR have a significant negative impact on their PV and PI. Ji (2013) also found that perceived benefits, purchase costs, and PR has direct impacts on users' willingness to consume in the context of online shopping. In the study of the factors affecting the willingness of free customers to pay for value-added services, Li, Li, and Shi (2014) used the network externalities, virtual social capital and network viscosity as explanatory variables of customer PV, and concluded that network externalities and virtual social capital can directly affect customers' PV, which indirectly affects customers' intention to pay, while PV has a direct positive impact on customers' intention to pay. In a study of PV and willingness to channel change, Zhao (2015) found that the improvement of PV promotes higher PI and likelihood of purchase behavior of online consumers. Liu and Tang (2015) believed that it is possible to enhance the PV of consumers by strengthening publicity, thereby stimulating online consumers' PI and shopping behavior online. After conducting an empirical research, Wang (2017) found that the greater the PV of the user, the stronger the willingness to purchase the goods or services. Xu, Zhang, and Dong (2018) found that the PV significantly affects college students' intention to purchase through their research on college students' willingness to pay for online courses. Lin and Qu (2019) conducted a study on the relationship between PV and PI, finding that users' PV has a positive impact on their PI.

From the above researches, it can be concluded that factors such as PV, perceived benefit, PR, and PC are the key factors affecting PI in the empirical analysis of consumer PI. Then, whether these factors have a significant impact on the intention of purchasing online courses, and how the various potential factors affect each other needs to be verified through empirical analysis in combination with the situation of purchasing courses on online educational platforms.

2.1.3   Literature of online WM and PI

In the field of traditional marketing and consumer buying behavior research, WM is considered to be an important factor affecting marketing and consumer buying behavior (Huang & Zhu, 2003), since it is able to deliver information about the product or service that helps other consumers make purchasing decisions to the audience. With the rapid development of e-commerce, comments and WM on online products also have an important impact on consumers purchasing a certain product. In the online shopping situation, the e-commerce platform collects consumers' relevant evaluations of a certain product or service based on the comment function to help other consumers make judgments at the time of purchase. These evaluations constitute online consumer reviews or electronic WM for specific goods or services, which can have a significant impact on consumer online PI and behavior.

Park, Lee, and Han (2007) believed that the online comment is an important factor affecting consumer decision-making after empirical research. The quality and quantity of online reviews can positively impact consumers' PI. Lee and Youn (2009) argued that positive online reviews have a positive impact on consumers' willingness to recommend and purchase a product, while negative reviews can have a negative impact. Cui, Lui, and Guo (2012) collected users' consumption data and online comment data for electronic products and video games on Amazon. com when studying the impacts of online consumer reviews on new product sales. The analysis found that the number of online reviews at the beginning of the sale has a significant impact on selling new product.

Hennig-Thurau and Walsh (2003) conducted a research on consumers search for online WM and reading motivation on the online consumer opinion platform, finding that consumers read other consumers' comments of related products when they shop online so as to save time in making their decision on which good to buy and help them make better purchasing decisions.

Chinese scholars have also confirmed in relevant research that in the context of online shopping, online WM has a significant impact on consumers' purchasing behavior, and positive online WM of goods or services can positively affect customers' PI (Bi, 2009; Huang & Lao, 2013; Li, 2015; Lu, Huang, & Li, 2017; Xu, Zhang, & Dong, 2018), negative online WM has a negative impact on PI (Bi, 2010; Guo, 2015; Zhang, 2015; Chen, Wu, & Zhang 2017). Wang (2018) found that both Internet WM and users' perceived quality affect the intention of users to pay in the study of the factors affecting the payment on the audio book platform. Wang, Wang, and Yang (2019) found that WM between acquaintances positively moderates the impacts of PV on PI. Wang, Wang, and Yang (2019) deeply explored the source of WM and the reliability of commentator, all of which demonstrated that both have a positive impact on the user's PI.

It can be seen that Internet WM is an important factor affecting consumers' purchasing behavior in the context of online consumption. OEP users may also pay attention to other users' online comments about a course when purchasing the paid courses. When comments of a course show a good reputation and meets the user's learning needs, the user's PI may be higher. Therefore, in the study of factors influencing user's intention in paying for online courses, he believed that the comment WM may be an important factor affecting the users' intention for buying the course, introducing relevant models for analysis.

Based on the above research results, factors such as PV, PR, PC, and online WM (online comments) have been confirmed to impose impacts on users' PI (the willingness to pay) in buying a product or service in the Internet context in many studies. Therefore, in constructing the model of factors influencing users' intention in purchasing courses on OEP, he learns from the previous research and involves factors that have been confirmed to impose impacts on consumers' PI in other consumption scenarios, and he adds some contextual variables that may affect the user's PI in buying paid courses based on the specific situation of online education. In this way, this study can batter verify which factors affect the user's intention to purchase a paid course and how different factors affect each other.

2.1.4   Literature of online PI

Whether in a physical or an online shopping environment, consumers' intention to purchase goods or services is essentially the same, and it refers to the probability or likelihood of purchasing goods or services. Due to a different way of shopping and environment, the activities of online consumers reflect their own characteristics, which is that the virtual channel, Internet, has been taken as the medium to purchase. The consumer's online PI refers to the probability or possibility that the consumer buys certain product or service after being informed of related information provided by the online store when browsing the online store.

Baker, Grewal, and Parasuraman (1994) believed that the "soft environment" of online shopping is the internal psychological reaction of marketing strategies of e-commerce enterprise. When customers shop online, the shopping environment and atmosphere provided by the website exerts a significant impact on the psychology of customers, and its impacts outweigh the impacts of the product itself on the customer to some extent. Dowling and Staelin (1994) argued that although online shopping provides consumers with a convenient and fast way to shop, it still contains more new risks compared with traditional offline shopping, such as personal privacy leakage, stolen credit card number and password, lack of product quality assurance, lack of satisfactory service, no delivery after payment, etc. These risks seriously restrict consumers' PI. Shelanski and Klein (1995) proposed that transaction cost is an important factor in affecting consumers' PI, whether it is online or offline. Chiles and McMackin (1996) pointed out that in the online shopping environment, transaction costs refer to the sum of time and risk involved in order to complete online transactions, including purchasing equipment, searching information, learning knowledge, currency, and time. The transaction cost of online shopping is lower than traditional offline shopping.

Sharma (2002) studied the factors affecting consumers' online PI, and he found that among these factors, in addition to the product quality and product price that have an impact on consumers' PI, the website's service to consumers also has a significant impact on their PI. The website's services include its information quality, response time, reliability, and product delivery and after-sales maintenance. He believed that high-quality and fast service can not only reduce the time and effort spent on purchasing products, transaction costs, but also relieve consumers' worries. He pointed out that websites should maintain and develop close relationships with customers through good service, creating value for them. Belanger, Hiller, and Smith (2002) pointed out that aesthetically pleasing, reasonably designed and easy-to-use web design helps to stimulate consumers' desire to purchase, otherwise it has a negative impact on consumers' PI.

Pavlou (2003) argued that compared with the traditional shopping model, it is fair to say that online shopping brings convenience to consumers, so that consumers can get the goods and services they need at a lower price and enjoy the fun. However, it also causes certain risks to consumers, such as difficulty in guaranteeing product quality, poor after-sales service quality, personal privacy leakage, unavailable easy to be leaked, non-delivery after payment, and stolen credit card information etc. All the above-mentioned factors exert negative impacts on consumers' PI and hinder the development of online shopping at the same time. Based on previous studies, Lim (2003) summarized the PR of online shopping for consumers into seven categories (quality risk, economic risk, personal risk, social risk, psychological risk, health risk, time risk), and researched the root causes of these risks, which can be summarized as the following four aspects: products, network technology, vendors and consumers. Lim (2003) believed that the risks caused by insufficient technology are the main reason that hinder consumers' online shopping. Lim (2003) surveyed 1,000 Internet users through requiring each of them for their opinions on each of the following questions and found that 88% of the respondents believe that losses caused by technical issues are relatively more serious for consumers; 82% of respondents believe that losses caused by sellers are more serious for consumers; 78% of the respondents believe that the losses caused by product quality are more serious for consumers; and 92% of the respondents believe that the losses caused by consumers' own are more serious. Liu and Wei (2003) argued that when online consumers choose different categories of goods, the degree of their PI is also different.

Gupta, Su, and Walter (2004) classified consumers into risk-neutral and risk-averse types based on attitudes toward risk, and constructed a purchase decision model including factors such as commodity prices, search costs, time required for purchase, and PR. The quantitative methodology was also used to analyze the different characteristics of decision-making in the context of online shopping and offline shopping for these two types of consumers. The results of the study showed that risk-neutral consumers tend to shop online, while risk-averse consumers tend to shop offline. Among the factors affecting consumers' online shopping, the variety of goods and the time required for purchase are important factors affecting their PI, while the price of goods is not the main factor determining the purchase. Consumers are more willing to visit a retail website with great varieties and easy-to-order operation. Gefen and Straub (2004) believed that trust is generated in the long-term and frequent communication between the two parties. Consumers in the context of online shopping cannot communicate with seller face to face, so it is difficult to establish a trust relationship with the shopping site in the context. Teo and Yu (2004) argued that trust is built gradually through frequent contacts and exchanges between people or organizations, but in e-commerce shopping environment, there exist difficulties in establishing trust between the buyer and the seller because the consumer cannot have face-to-face contact with people. Dailey (2004) proposed that that under the conditions of e-commerce, consumers buy goods online based on their recognition of the design of online stores, so the quality of the interface design of the virtual store directly affects customers' PI. If the interface design of the virtual store conforms to the customer's aesthetic psychology and facilitates the customer to search for information, it helps to create trust between the customer and the company, thus enhancing customer's PI. Dailey (2004) also proposed that e-commerce enterprises should optimize the design of web interface in the four aspects: structure, content, illustration and interaction, so as to convey the information that the enterprise enjoys integrity when operating business to viewers. In this regard, the trust between the viewer and the enterprise can be enhanced, and the viewer can be converted into the customer of the enterprise.

Liu, Huang, and Liu (2004) constructed a model that how service quality affects consumers' online PI. The criteria used to judge the quality of the website include the rationality of web design, interaction and communication, convenience to place an order and delivery speed. Through questionnaire survey and multivariate regression, impacts from these four aspects on the online consumers' PI were studied, and the empirical results show that the rationality of web design and delivery speed affect the consumers' online PI significantly and positively. Wang and Emurian (2005) believed that the quality of service exerts a greater impact on consumers' PI in the process of purchasing goods online comparing with traditional shopping. The service includes not only online services, such as whether the product information provided online is comprehensive and detailed, whether the questions raised by customers can be answered in time, whether the interface design of the web page is reasonable, etc., but also includes product distribution and after-sales service, and all of these factors have a significant impact on consumers. Zhou (2005) conducted an empirical study on the factors affecting consumers' trust on website, and proposed the following hypotheses: (1) the more familiar consumers are to the website, the more likely they trust it; (2) the higher the security of the website is, the easier it is for consumers to form trust with the website; (3) the quality of website information contributes to the cultivation of website brand trust; (4) the shopping experience helps the establishment of website trust; (5) the establishment of WM trust in website brand and development is crucial. He used the online bookstore *Dangdang* as the website to research on consumers' trust. Through the path analysis of the hypothesis model, the results showed that the trust degree of B2C e-commerce website is affected by the abovementioned factors, and the website can effectively establish and maintain the trust between consumers and websites by taking corresponding measures.

Xue (2005) summarized the cost factors in online transactions into the following categories: search cost, learning cost, time cost, currency cost, asset-specific cost, risk cost, and proposed that transaction cost factors influencing online transactions in China include computer and network equipment costs, website design convenience and interface friendliness, network information, time factor, distribution and after-sales service, transaction uncertainty. He believed that in the growth of e-commerce in China, it is necessary to fully consider the transaction cost factors affecting consumers' online purchases and design an e-commerce model that conforms to China's national conditions, thereby reducing transaction costs and increasing consumers' online PI. Liu (2017) argued that the degree of willingness to make purchases via the Internet varies with the purchase of different goods. He divided goods into two categories: tangible goods and intangible goods. Through the research, it is found that consumers purchase both tangible and intangible goods online, and the three factors of perceived effectiveness, perceived convenience and PR exert impacts on consumers' online PI. Therefore, he constructed a hypothesis model about how online PI is affected and conducted empirical research accordingly. The empirical results show that PR has the greatest impacts on consumers' online PI. Zhong and Zhang (2013) constructed an empirical model of how consumers' PV affect their online PI and proposed that consumers' PV can be considered in three dimensions: functional value, emotional value and social value. Wu, Chang, and Pan (2014) considered that the online PV consists of three dimensions: online result value, online emotion value, online procedural value that impose positive impacts on online PI. Based on the theory of PV, Sun and Sun (2017) explored the impacts on users' intention when buying fresh products online, and found that PC, entertainment and functionality significantly affect users' online PI, which validates the mediating role of PV. Sun (2018) found that the gender of the user has no significant difference in their online PI, but the online shopping period and online shopping frequency have great differences in the user's PI. Exploring the relationship between PR and online impulse purchase, Cui (2019) divided causes of PR into products, online platforms, online services, and users' own environments, and found that PR affects users; PI significantly. Based on the technology acceptance model (TAM), Li and Wang (2019) studied the user's online PI in the social media environment and proposed that trust is one of the most important factors affecting online PI.

In summary, the definitions and conceptual analysis of each researcher about users' PI are different according to various research objects. The operational definition of PI in this study is in the shopping environment on Chinese B2B2C OEP, the probability of being willing to close a deal after perceiving the price and service of the online course.

2.2　Literature of CPV

2.2.1　Literature of CPV

Drucker (1954) pointed out that consumers buy and consume not only the product, or in a more accurate way, it is not the product and the service that is purchased or consumed, but the value that is conveyed to consumers. In other words, the real needs of customers are the key to determining the maximum customer value, rather than the product or service that the company now offers to customers. It is precisely because customers are the rarest resources for an enterprise, therefore any decision made by the company should be based on obtaining this resource. Fan and Luo (2003) believed that customer value is the value that customers care about in their heart, also known as customer PV, which means that customers consider what they want from their own point of view, and they believe that they can obtain the value via purchasing and using the product. Slywotzky (1996) also pointed out that creating and providing good customer value to customers increases the overall value of the company. Peter and Tarpey (1975) argued that two perceptions exist when purchasing products: characteristics they would like to obtain known as positive value while characteristics they would not like to obtain known as negative value. The margin between these two is the net perceived reward. Positive value is perceived rewards, while negative value is PR. Integrating the research results of various scholars, Zeithaml (1988) summarized the four views about consumers' own PV through conducting interviews, and defined customer's PV as the overall evaluation of the product's utility for the customer, that is, the difference between the customer's perceived benefit and the perceived pay based on the perspective of consumer psychological behavior. According to Zeithaml (1988), when companies design, create, and provide value for consumers, they should start being consumer-oriented and use customer perceived value (CPV) as a determining factor. CPV is divided into four meanings: (1) value is a low price. Some consumers equate value with low prices. As long as they are discounted or ultra-low-priced products, they have high value, indicating that the currency they pay in their value perception is the most important. (2) Value is what you want to get from the product. Unlike the money paid for, some consumers see the benefits they receive from services or products as the most important value factor. This is the same as the definition of utility in economics and is a subjective measure of satisfaction with consumer products. (3) Value is the quality of the price paid. Some consumers conceptualize value as a trade-off between "doing money" and "quality". It is valuable to get quality products at the lowest price. (4) Value is all that you can get with all your efforts. Some consumers consider the factors they pay (time, money, effort) and the benefits they receive. Zeithaml (1988) summarized the consumer's expression of these four values into an all-round definition: CPV is the overall evaluation of service utility that consumers perceive the trade-off between the perceived benefits and cost of acquiring a product or service. This concept contains two layers of meaning: firstly, value is personalized, different from person to person. Different consumers have different PV for a same product or service; secondly, value represents a trade-off between utility (revenue) and cost (price), and consumers make purchase decisions based on the value they feel that is not affected just by a single factor.

Sheth, Newman, and Gross (1992) analyzed the composition of PV and concluded that products provide customers with five values, namely functional value, social value, emotional value, epistemic value and situational value. Anderson, Jain, and Chintagunta (1992) and others believed that value is the customer perceived utility comparing the price, which can be reflected in economic, technical, service and social benefits. Gale and Wood (1994) refined this concept as customer value is the market perceived quality comparing to the price of the product. From the perspective of corporate strategy, Butz and Goodstein (1996) analyzed CPV and concluded that when customers believe in a product or service provided by a company or enterprise, this belief enables company to bring more net value to the consumer comparing with its competitors, in which context the benefit is greater than the cost. By developing this differentiation from competitors, CPV is formed. Gardial, Clemons, and Woodruff (1994) also pointed out the value that consumers feel when they buy goods is different from the value that consumers feel when they use the goods. When consumers buy and use a certain product, they measure the value of the product according to the different feelings formed in each stage. Woodruff (1997) pointed out that CPV is the customer's preference and evaluation of product attributes, results after using it, etc. , and these attributes and results can help customers achieve their intended goals when using products. Grewal, Monroe, and Krishnan (1998) mentioned that whether consumers buy or not depends on the comparison of the benefits he receives from the products and the price he pays for the product, which is the CPV of a product is derived from the benefits of the product and the cost of obtaining the product. When the perceived benefit is higher than PC, CPV is greater. The magnitude of PV depends on the relative relationship between perceived benefits and the cost that needs to be paid. From the perspective of customer relationship management system, Keeney (1999) pointed out that the total net value of the benefits and costs paid by consumers through the customer relationship management system is CPV. Parasuraman and Grewal (2000) argued that CPV is to weigh customer perceived profit and PC, therefore it is a dynamic concept. It includes four values: firstly, acquisition value, which refers to benefits obtained after paying a certain currency; secondly, transaction value, which refers to the joy obtained by the customer from the transaction process; thirdly, use value, which refers to the utility obtained due to the use of the product or service; fourthly, redemption value, which refers to the residual value obtained after the product is trade-in or the service is terminated.

Sweeney and Soutar (2001) proposed four dimensions of CPV through empirical research: firstly, emotional value which refers to the utility obtained by customers from the sensation and emotion of consuming this product; secondly, social value which refers to utility brought to the society due to the improvement of society self-concept concept; thirdly, quality value which refers to the utility obtained by the customer from the comparison between the perceived quality of the product and the expected performance; fourthly, price value which refers to the utility of the short-term and long-term PC of the customer. Sanchez, Callarisa, and Rodriguez (2006) perfected the definition of CPV from the perspective of travel culture, pointing out that CPV is a series of dynamic variables of consumers at the time of purchase, use and after use. The subjective measurement of CPV also varies over time and culture.

The research on CPV in Chinese academic sector has begun to increase substantially, and these researches link CPV with PI, purchase behavior, customer loyalty and many other elements. Li and An (2008) explored the interrelationship between CPV and perceived quality, brand image and customer experience through literature reviews. Based on CPV, Wang and Xue (2010) carried out an empirical research of a bicycle rider association in Shanghai, researching on the social capital dimension, characteristics and impacts of the brand community, and revealing the mechanism by which the brand community exerts impacts on brand loyalty through the measurement of CPV. Liao and Lin (2009) explored the PV of luxury goods by taking luxury goods as the object of his empirical research. Jiang and Yuan (2009) innovatively introduced consumer personality factors into the measurement of CPV and perfected the research system of CPV theory from the perspective of driving factors. The starting point of his research is that the difference in individual psychology has a significant impact on their PV. Five dimensions of personality were included in this research, which are of openness, extroversion, pleasantness, rigorousness and neuroticism. The impacts of these five dimensions on CPV and the five customer perception models were evaluated comprehensively to study how to improve CPV. Hao (2011) studied the relationship and interaction between corporate innovation behaviors and its brand image, brand management capabilities, CPV, and customer buying behavior, and used an integrated research framework to explore how corporate innovation behaviors, brand image, brand management capabilities, CPV affect consumers' purchasing behavior. Based on the theory of PV, Zhong (2005) found that perceived product quality and perceived website service quality have a significant positive impact on PV and PI of online consumers, while PR imposes a negative impact on PV and PI; purchase cost has a positive impact on CPV but has no significant impacts on PI; PV (functional value, emotional value and social value) has a significant and positive impact on PI; online WM moderates the impacts of PV on PI. Zhao (2013) found that CPV is composed of the overall customer benefits and the overall customer costs in his study. The overall customer benefit is the total amount of money consisting of a set of economic, functional, and psychological benefits expected from its particular supply of the product; total customer cost refers to the estimated total expenditure of assessment, acquisition, use, and abandonment of its particular supply of the product. From the perspective of PV, Chen, Wu, and Zhang (2017) studied the user's intention to purchase genetically modified food through the questionnaire survey, and they researched on the impacts of social value, functional value, economic value and emotional value on the user's PI. It is found that WM plays a role in regulating the four dimensions of PV, and PV also positively affects the user's PI. It is also concluded that negative WM negatively affects the user's PI. Fang, Lu, and Liu (2018) found that perceived usefulness (PU) and perceived trust positively affect PV, thus affecting the consumers' intention to pay in virtual community. Chen, Gu, and Hu (2019) integrated two theories, PV and PR, and further broke down PV and PR to explore how the intention to purchase new energy vehicles is affected. It is found that both PV and PR have a significant impact on the user's PI.

Related literature illustrates that CPV is not only the premise of their PI and behavior, but also the most important indicator of marketing activities. The research on CPV is mostly carried out from the following three perspectives: firstly, taking CPV as the core variable, through empirical research or summarizing previous literature to explore the relationship between CPV and enterprise-related variables in order to develop and improve the corporate strategic framework centered on CPV. Secondly, CPV is used as a mediator variable to modify the existing classic models. Thirdly, combining CPV and Chinese practice so that the core concept, CPV in marketing, can be applied to various industries, and guide the development strategy of the enterprise, and finally providing strategies for business operation through the introduction of concepts. Helping companies to gain a dominant position in the fierce competition.

2.2.2　Literature of online CPV

Keeney (1999) argued that PV of online customers should combine the underlying goals and the means objectives. The basic goal is that the shopping website should ensure product quality to minimize the cost of online customer purchases, provide convenience to consumers, protect their privacy, and make consumers feel entertaining during the shopping process. Meanwhile shopping websites that cannot take fraudulent behavior, ensure system security, provide comprehensive information and make it easier for consumers to compare goods, often update the variety of products to meet consumers' motivations for new purchases, minimize online trading risks, etc. Bourdeau, Chebat, and Couturier (2002) conducted a comparative study of website visitors and email users in college students, from which it showed that the network provides five values to college students, including utilitarian value, social value, and hedonic value, purchasing value and learning value. Bourdeau, Chebat, and Couturier (2002) concluded that most website visitors are looking for a learning experience, enjoying the fun that the network brings to them and thinking that the network brings them new knowledge that does not make them feel painful. They are happy to learn this new knowledge and think that browsing websites can help them to buy the goods they need online. E-mail users pay more attention to social values. They can establish good interpersonal relationships with others through online channels. They use e-mail not to learn as website visitors, but to focus on the communication function of e-mail. Chen and Dubinsky (2003) suggested key factors influencing CPV in the B2C e-commerce environment by establishing a theoretical framework, including perceived product quality, PR, product price and experience value. Perceived product quality includes sub-factors such as shopping website credibility, product price, and experience; PR includes sub-factors such as shopping website credibility, product price, and perceived product quality; experience value includes sub-factors such as website information, consumer service, and ease of use. Mathwick, Malhotra, and Rigdon (2001) conducted an in-depth study on the experience value of online shopping behaviors through the experiential value scale.

In the research on PV of online customers, Zhong (2005) constructed a model of the generation process of online CPV, and argued that online customer perceived profit and loss, characteristics of online customers, and PR impose significant impacts on their PV. According to the research results, Zhong (2005) summarized some suggestions for improving PV of online customers, such as improving product quality, reducing transaction costs, and reducing PR of online customers. Based on the model constructed by Zhong (2005), Xu, Liang, and Xia (2006) added the purchase situation factor to the model and believed that the purchase situation can also exert certain impacts on the PV of online customers. They also conducted an in-depth theoretical research on perceived profit and loss and PR, so as to construct a perceptual value model of online customers. Sun and Si (2007) studied the PV of online customers and constructed a theoretical model for the PV formation of online customers. Through empirical research, it is considered that PV of online customers includes two aspects, satisfaction and sense of trust. The PV of satisfaction is reflected in convenience, commodity price, personalized experience, online customer expertise and service remedy. The PV of trust is reflected in the security of the shopping website, the protection of the privacy of online customers, and the expertise of shopping websites. Zhang (2007) thought that there are many factors affecting PV of online customers. For example, the personal factors of online customers, including their physical and psychological factors, economic status and lifestyle. All these factors have an impact on their PV. Environmental factors also have an impact on PV of online customers, including social environment, natural environment, shopping environment, family, related groups, and their roles and status. Zhang (2007) also thought that social and cultural factors have a certain impact on the PV of online customers, including cultural and subculture, consumer prevalence and social class. Therefore, these factors should be emphasized in research. Through empirical research, Zhong (2013) found that PV (functional value, emotional value and social value) has a positive impact on the PI of online customers, and their PI is not depending solely on the price. At the same time, more attention should be paid to the accumulation of online WM. Liu (2017) found that the exclusive price on platform has the greatest impacts by studying the factors affecting the PI of online customers, followed by entertainment, self-efficacy, convenience and ease of use. Wang (2017) introduced online WM, PV, PU, and PEU into his empirical study to research on the intention of users to purchase agricultural products online. The results showed that PV moderates the impacts of WM on PI, and PV significantly and positively affects PI. Ye and Wang (2018) conducted a research on factors influencing users' intention for content payment on audio-reading platforms. The results showed that personal awareness of payment, PV and perceived price directly affect PI, and perceived quality and online WM indirectly affect PI. Gao (2019) used perceptual value as a mediator to study factors influencing users' intention to purchase fresh products online, and perceived service quality as a moderating variable of the impacts of perceived product quality on PV. The results also demonstrated that PV has positive impacts on PI and mediates the impacts of service quality on PI.

2. 2. 3　Literature of PR and CPV

Bauer (1960) first proposed the concept of PR, which often refers to the subjective judgment of the characteristics and the severity of the risk, that is, the uncertainty of the decision-making result and the seriousness of making wrong decisions. For example, when an OEP user purchases a course, even if he has a comprehensive understanding of its content and related information, whether he can successfully complete the course after the purchase, whether the course can be as useful as his initial expectation, and whether service provided by the platform can meet his needs still remain uncertain. However, when making incorrect purchase decisions, users may suffer from serious consequences such as delays in learning plans, wasted time and money.

In different situations, researchers have conducted in-depth research on PR and continuously enriched its content. Jacoby and Kaplan (1972) divided PR into financial risk, performance risk, social risk, physical and psychological risk in the study. Peter and Tarpey (1975) considered time risk as an important factor in related research. In order to explore factors influencing users' intention to interact in the new media environment of automobiles, Wang, Li, and Wang (2017) constructed a structural equation model based on the theory of PV, and concluded that information usefulness, PV, and PEU impose positive impacts on user interaction intention while PR negatively affects user interaction intention. Zhao, Chen, and Du (2018) constructed a structural equation model based on PV and PR theory when researching users' intention to purchase smart real estate. Through empirical analysis, it was found that PR negatively affects PV and perceived quality, while PR positively affects the user's PI. Her research also indicated that PR indirectly affects PI through PV. Based on the perspectives of PR and PC, Liu, Hu, and Tang (2019) used questionnaire survey to collect data, and structural equation model for data analysis. They concluded that in the online environment, both PC and PR affect users' PI, and ultimately affect users' offline purchase behavior. Chen, Gu, and Hu (2019) introduced PR and PV into the research to jointly study users' intention to purchase new energy vehicles, and divided PR into event risk, financial risk, functional risk and physical risk. In the end, it is found that PR negatively affects users' PI, and financial risk is one of the main factors.

2.2.4   Literature of PC and CPV

Perceived transaction costs originated in the field of economics, emphasizing that the transaction subject is rational, and the trader makes decides on transactions in the principle of maximization of interests. Online transaction is full of uncertainty and complexity. Klemperer (1987) studied the banking industry and found that PC includes transaction cost, learning cost, and contractual cost. Zeithaml (1988) proposed perceived sacrifice contains PC in the study of PV, and PC is the cost perceived by the user when using a product.

Dick and Basu (1994) divided PC into time cost, money cost, and cognitive cost perceived by consumers in the payment process. The time cost refers to the amount of time the consumer perceives to spend on the payment. The monetary cost refers to the amount of money the consumer needs to pay. The cognitive cost refers to the cognitive resources that the consumer perceives to pay. The cognitive cost is mainly due to the unskilled mobile payment operation (new technology acceptance) or the risk in the payment process. PC mainly includes property cost, time cost and learning cost. Property cost refers to the money paid for the purchase of the product and its supporting products or services. The time cost refers to the time wasted when using the product, and learning cost refers to effort devoted to learn to use the product.

In this research, when studying the intentions to purchase paid courses on B2B2BC OEP, he based on the results from previous researches on PV and also added theories of PC. Jones, Mothersbaugh, and Beatty (2002) pointed out that PC includes opportunity costs, risk costs, search and evaluation costs before switching, action and cognition costs after switching, set up cost, and sunk costs in the banking industry and hairdressing industry. Lam, Shankar, and Erramilli (2004) conducted research on the tourism agency, suggesting that PC includes money, energy, time, new technology, and uncertainty. Bunduchi (2005) pointed out that e-commerce reduces the time cost in the process of information exchange and decision-making. Rabinovich, Knemeyer, and Mayer (2007) argued that PC depends on the effort spent in the transaction and all transaction-related activities. Wang (2016) found that when studying factors influencing users' intention to pay on WeChat, improved product technology is beneficial to reducing users' PC and increase their PI. When researching on consumers' decision-making styles, Sun and Sun (2017) found that the awareness of price, the awareness of choice confusion and brand loyalty affect users' PI in the mobile Internet environment, and that PC significantly affects users' PI. Wan (2018) concluded that offline PC significantly affects users' online PI in the study of the relationship between users' PI in multiple channels. Lu, Zhang, and Zhang (2019) researched on users' PI from the two aspects, perceived benefit and PC in the study on intention to pay of users who use voice to answer questions in virtual community, and concluded that sunk cost and information acquisition habits affect perceived benefit negatively; switching cost and the individual free concept positively affect PC; perceived benefit positively affects PI; and PC negatively affects PI.

2.2.5 Literature of online WM and CPV

Arndt (1967) coined the terminology WM in the study. He emphasized that WM is an informal, non-commercial way to communicate information about products, brands or services. The real development of WM is mainly due to the research on the impacts of WM on consumer purchasing decisions. Brown and Reingen (1987) believed that WM is feedback generated by consumers after purchasing goods that can positively express consumers' satisfaction with goods or services. File and Prince (1992) pointed out that WM can also negatively express consumers' complaints about goods or services, and they directly impact the expectations and purchase decisions of subsequent consumers.

With the development of the Internet, online WM came into being. At present, there are different forms of online WM, such as virtual WM, online forum review, online WM, and electronic WM. Although the definition of online WM is different, the basic connotation is the same, therefore this thesis uses the wording of online WM. Research conducted by Staus (1997) showed that online WM is a way for consumers to consult, feedback, express their satisfaction or dissatisfaction about products, and this way of existence can even be the on the message board and information release column on the company website. Gelb and Joson (1995) and Chatterjee (2001) pointed out that online WM is the communication of information on goods and services by consumers through the Internet platform and experience discussion on the Internet after a large number of consumers using the goods or services. Bhatnagar and Ghose (2004) and Sun, You, and Wu (2006) proposed that the widespread use of Internet platforms has caused the spread of WM without boundary restrictions, greatly enhancing the speed and scope of WM communication and making WM easier to store.

Online WM and traditional WM have the same connotation. The only difference is that the form of existence and support is different. Traditional WM is spreading and passing from mouth to mouth, and this form of communication is not easy to record. Online WM continues the form of traditional WM communication, while with the help of the Internet, the original mouth-to-mouth mode can be recorded on the Internet, which is more conducive for consumers to review and storage and for the communication of WM. Chen, Jiao and Li (2017) carried out a research on users' intention to purchase genetically modified foods and found that the factor of WM moderates the impacts of PV to PI. Ye and

Wang (2018) found that online WM significantly affects users' PV in the study of users on an audio platform. Wang, Wang, and Wang (2019) divided WM into WM from acquaintances and WM from strangers in the study of the relationship between Internet WM, PV, and PI, and discovered that WM from strangers affects users' PI and PV while WM from acquaintances positively moderates the affect from PV to PI.

Online WM exists in a variety of ways, such as online shopping mall, blog, microblog, email, instant messaging (such as QQ, Wechat), discussion group, user comments sites (such as dianping, Maoyan) and other cyberspace.

In summary, different communication platforms and different interactions make online WM have four different forms. However, regardless of the form of online WM, its essence refers to the dissemination of relevant comments on products or services by consumers through the Internet platform. The development of Internet technology has made WM communication more convenient, and the number of online WM has soared, making online WM one of the hot topics of current research.

2.3 Theoretical Foundation for PI

2.3.1 CPV

In the field of marketing and consumer behavior research, scholars generally believe that CPV is an important reference for consumers to make purchasing decisions. Higher value perceived by customers when purchasing goods indicates higher possibility of purchasing actions take place.

Porter (1985) proposed the buyer value theory which refers to the cost of the purchase of products or services minus the cost. He believed that companies can only gain a dominant position in the competition by providing consumers with more than expected value. There are two ways to increase the value of the buyer. One is to increase the consumer's income, and the other is to reduce the cost of the consumer. In addition to the monetary cost, the cost of the consumer includes time cost, opportunity cost, etc., and the shopping conditions are convenient. Whether it is or not is also an important part of consumer costs. Porter elaborates the theory of buyer value from the perspective of enterprises. He believes that in order to obtain competitive advantage, enterprises must pay attention to and take certain measures to improve the buyer's value of consumers.

Zeithhaml (1988), a well-known American marketing guru, studied CPV on a product or service after weighing the benefits of perceived benefits and costs. The overall utility evaluation, that is, the PV of the consumer is the result of the consumer's evaluation of the trade-off between benefit and cost. This view was widely recognized in subsequent research and further developed. For example, Dodds, Monroe, and Grewal (1991) considered PV as "perceived benefit" and "perceived sacrifice" when consumers purchase goods or services. He also defined the boundary of perceived benefit (including product entity characteristics, service characteristics, etc.) and perceived sacrifice (including acquisition costs, transportation, maintenance, and potential failure risks). Kotler (1994) considered CPV as the difference between the value of all products (cognitive monetary value) and the cost (estimated cost) from the perspective of the value of the transfer. In the relevant research, Sirdeshmukh, Singh, and Sabol (2002) proposed that PV refers to the time, money, energy and other costs that the consumer pays when acquiring the product or service. It is worthwhile to purchase the product or service. Many scholars in China also conduct relevant researches. PV is generally considered to be based on the overall utility evaluation of income and trade-offs (Bai, 2001; Fan & Luo, 2003). According to the above connotation of PV, it is believed that CPV is not inherent in the product or service, nor is the company's desire or imagination, but determined by the customer's perception (Ji, 2013).

Ravald and Gronroos (1996) proposed the theory of customer value process based on the relationship between customer profit and loss and believed that PV is the overall evaluation of utility by consumers based on the perception of profit and loss. In fact, this view does not consider the relationship between consumers and businesses. Because the customer value is based on the premise that the company and the customer are constantly understanding and interacting with each other, this is a long process. Therefore, customer value is the result of a period of accumulation, which is the process of value generation. Woodruff (1997) pointed out in the study of the change in value perception during the consumer purchase process that the customer would evaluate the value that the product or service brought to itself before deciding to purchase, and then proceed to purchase on this basis. After receiving the goods or services, the customer also makes a final evaluation of the personal experience of the goods or services. This final evaluation is the starting point for the next purchase and decide whether to make another purchase. At different stages of the purchase process, the PV of the customer is different. When the prior value is evaluated as positive, the consumer will purchase and vice versa. Woodruff (1997) built a hierarchy of customer values that explains the value attributes, evaluation results, and final goals. Through this constant process of PV, it is pointed out that CPV alternates between comment and purchase. Kotler (1994) explained the customer value from the perspective of customer transfer value and customer satisfaction and proposed the customer transfer value theory. He believed that the customer transfer value refers to the difference between the total value obtained and the total cost paid. Among them, the total value includes personnel, products, services and image, etc. The total cost includes physical strength, time, currency and so on. At the same time, it is pointed out that before purchasing a product or service, the customer compares the value of the desired product or service with the expected value. If the value of the desired product or service is greater than the expected value, the consumer is satisfied with the product or service and it is possible for him/her to make a purchase again, but if the value of the desired product or service is less than the expected value, the consumer will be dissatisfied and give up the purchase.

In addition, domestic and foreign scholars also defined PV from the perspective of PV components. The consumer value model proposed by Sheth, Newman, and Gross (1992) divided CPV into epistemic value, functional value, social value, and emotional value, contingent value. The value component model proposed by Kaufman (1998) divided CPV into reputation value, exchange value and utility value. Sweeney and Soutar (2001) thought that CPV can be measured in terms of quality, price, emotional and social factors.

As for factors affecting CPV, previous studies have increased the antecedent variables of PV for empirical analysis. Among them, there are direct causes of perceived benefits (e. g. perceived profit) and perceived sacrifices (e. g. perceived loss) as the antecedent variables of PV (Dodds, Monroe, & Grewal, 1991). Some scholars used PR, purchase cost, service quality, and product quality as an antecedent variable that affects CPV (Wood & Scheer, 1996; Zhong, 2013). Sun and Sun (2017) introduced the style of consumer decision-making and the theory of PV to research on consumers' intention in buying fresh products on the internet. Ye and Wang (2018) used the PV perspective to construct a model of users' PI on audio reading platform. Chen, Gu, and Hu (2019) conducted a research on the use's intention to pay for knowledge based on the PV theory and ECT.

Therefore, CPV is the user's perception of the product and service's perceived profit and the balance of profit and loss. The overall utility evaluation of the production is generally recognized and confirmed by previous scholars. The author analyzes the effect of PV on the user's willingness to purchase the course. PV was used to measure the user's perceived benefits for the purchase of paid courses; PC was used to measure the user's perception of the price of the paid course, the cost of purchase, etc. As a factor of perceived loss and loss, construct the basic model of the impacts of PV on users' intention to purchase courses.

Although scholars in the past have comprehensively explained the theory of customer value based on different angles, they had a relatively consistent understanding and understanding of the essence of customer value. Scholars believed that consumers' perception of value determines their PI and behavior. When purchasing goods or services in an online store, greater consumer value brings greater likelihood of a willingness to purchase, and vice versa. Therefore, under the guidance of the CPV theory, it is necessary for this study to conduct an in-depth study of the relationship between PV and PI. Finally, based on the PV theory, this study puts forward the impacts model of PV on the intention to purchase the course, as shown in Figure 2-1.

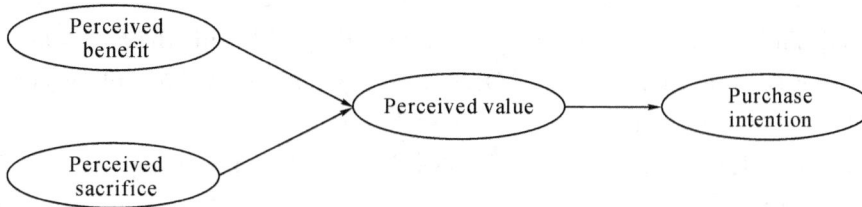

Figure 2-1   Theoretical framework of CPV

2.3.2   PR

The concept of PR originated in the field of social psychology and was later introduced into the field of information technology acceptance and consumer shopping behavior research. It has been verified by many scholars as one of the important factors influencing consumers' PI. PR-related theories hold that consumers have a subjective feeling that cannot be accurately predicted when making a shopping decision. The uncertainty of the outcome of the purchase decision causes consumers to have negative consuming sentiment, which in turn affects their ultimate PI.

Based on the research conducted by Stone and Grønhaug (1993) and others, this study has drawn the composition of PR proposed by Shim, Eastlick, and Lotz (2000), and this study mainly focuses on the time (time risk) that users spend on choosing to purchase paid courses, money (cost risk) that is whether the cost spent is worthwhile, whether the learning expectation and the purpose can be achieved (performance risk) to measure PR. According to the research related to online consumer behavior in the context of Internet, the impacts of PR on consumer PI has also been confirmed in previous studies (McKnight, Choudhury, & Kacmar, 2002; Huang & Zhu, 2003; Park, Lee, & Han, 2007; Huang, 2017). PR has also been introduced to study users' PI for many times (Liu & Tang, 2015; Zhao, Chen, & Du, 2018; Wan, 2018; Chen, Gu, & Hu, 2019; Meng, Jiao, & Liu, 2019).

It can be seen that PR is a key factor affecting consumers' PI. Higher risk perceived by consumer imposes greater negative impacts on their purchasing decisions, therefore reducing their PI. In the context of Internet consumption, users of OEPs also have different levels of decision-making risk when purchasing a course. Based on previous researches, this study introduces PR as a variable negatively influencing users' course PI when constructing the model of factors that impact users' intention to purchase courses, and the study also verifies whether PR is also applicable in the context of Internet consumption scenarios for paid courses through empirical analysis.

2.3.3 TAM

Davis (1986) proposed a TAM which consists of six variables: external variables, PU, PEU, attitude, behavioral intentions, and usage behavior. It is mainly used to explain and predict the acceptance of users' continuous use of information systems.

The model is based on the theory of rational behavior, and two concepts, PEU and PU were proposed. Among them, PEU mainly refers to the user's subjective ease of use of the information system and PU mainly refers to the subjective performance improvement of users using the information system. Davis (1986) also argued that PU and PEU can replace "subjective norms", so the model excludes "subjective norms" and their corresponding influencing factors "normative beliefs" and "compliance motivation".

Davis (1986) found that the usage behavior is mainly affected by the user's behavior intention that is determined by the user's attitude and PU. At the same time, the user's PU and PEU have a direct impact on the user's attitude to some extent. In addition, PU is directly affected by PEU because the user's perception of the usefulness of the system takes time. If the system is not easy to use, it may stop user from continuous use of the system, therefore the user will not be aware of the usefulness of the system. External variables in the model generally refer to system characteristics, user intervention design, and the nature of the setup process.

Venkatesh and Davis' TAM (1996) continued to improve the "attitude" in the original model, and the reconstructed model was more intuitive and clearer, as shown in Figure 2-2.

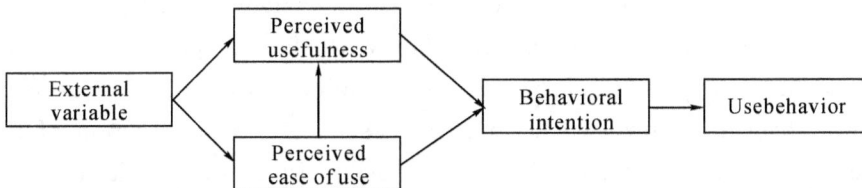

Figure 2-2　Improved TAM according to Venkatesh and Davis (1996)

Zhou (2014) believed that the explanation of the TAM and the validity of the scale are continuously verified in different user groups, different technologies, and different organizational environments, and the model itself is continuously improved. Foreign researchers have launched a large and extensive range of empirical research in the context of different technology applications, such as office automation software, various educational websites, telemedicine, search engines, electronic bulletin systems, e-commerce websites, electronic supermarkets, virtual stores, etc. The research results confirm the explanation and effectiveness of the model to a considerable extent.

According to a large number of literature and content analysis, it is found that the TAM is also used in a large number of empirical studies to explore the user's PI (Li, 2016; Huang, 2017; Ma, 2018; Li & Wang, 2019). Therefore, this study also used the TAM to explore the factors affecting PI of users on OEP.

2.4　Chapter summary

This chapter is the theoretical support for the entire study. This chapter summarizes the research results of domestic and foreign scholars on the factors affecting consumer online shopping, CPV, online WM and online consumers' PI. The focus is the arrangement of relevant research on CPV, including its connotation dimensions, and online consumers' PI. At the same time, it is found that the use of PV theory to study the consumers' intention to purchase online is not systematic enough, because this perspective ignores the role of online WM. This chapter also sorts out the research progress and achievements of online education and PI at home and abroad and provides a theoretical basis for the construction of the theoretical model of factors influencing users' PI on online platform. In this chapter, theresearches pointed out inadequacies of existing research results and the content of new things that need to be studied, which highlights the importance and urgency of the research questions in this study. Based on the research results of online education, PV, PI, online WM, etc., the characteristics, dimensions and measurement methods involved are summarized. The basic theories adopted in this study have been verified and proved for many times in the field of PI, CPV, and e-commerce. Some mature models with good measurement criteria for users' PI are included here in this chapter, and on this basis, the suitable model is extracted. Therefore, the research content of this part is especially important, which lays a theoretical foundation for this research.

第3章 B2B2C 在线教育平台概述

3.1 在线教育概述

Williams 和 Peters(1997)将在线学习(E-learning)定义为使用互联网和电脑学习模式[110]。Miltiadou(2001)介绍网络学习作为丰富、全面和动态的教学形式,提供了一个吸引人的学习项目,它依赖于互联网和计算机,为许多不能上大学的人提供终身学习的机会[111]。Piccoli 等(2001)认为在线学习是一种开放的系统,强调技术、交互性和自我控制在整个在线学习过程中的重要作用[112]。Harasun 等(1995)指出在线学习是一种利用互联网提供突破时间和地点限制的学习方式[113]。

何克抗(2005)回顾教育技术的发展历史:在 20 世纪 90 年代初,美国教育界曾兴起对"无界的虚拟学校是否会最终替代有校舍的经典"的可能性进行探讨[114]。赞同未来会取代和不会取代观点的辩论双方各执一词,无法得出统一的结论。这场关于未来教育方式的辩论逐渐从美国本土传播至全世界,引起了美国和全世界众多学者、教育学家的参与,然而讨论观点仍然分成两派未能达成一致意见。但是,美国的教育界人士和国际教育界人士通过近 10 年的在线教育探索与经验积累以后,深入总结了在线教育形式的优势和缺点,对于在线教育未来是否会取代有围墙的传统学校也有了更深入的认识,持有不同观点的两派都意识到没有绝对意义上的取代,在线教育与传统学校教育能优势互补,如同电子书籍和纸质书籍一样会继续共存互补。

2000 年 12 月,美国教育部(2000)草拟了《美国教育技术白皮书》[115],提出线上学习可以辅助传统学习,使其具有更佳的效果;E-Learning 不会取代传统的学校教育模式,但是会极大地改善并提升教学的体验和教学方式。报告中对"在线学习"进行了较为全面的界定:首先,该方式需要以互联网为媒介教学和配套服务;其次,可以给到一种新鲜的学习模式,提供了不受时间和地点限制的学习载体;最后,信息计划和各种工具的搭配使用能很好地实现部分教育目标,帮助提升教学效果,但并不能代替传统的课堂教学,也不会取代传统的学校教育。这为在线教育(在线学习)这个新名词在美国甚至今后在全世界的流行奠定了基础。

在 2003 年时,毛向辉分享了《教育与学习》期刊选出的 10 项"2003 年度美国教学技术最佳应用项目"[116]。从中看到了许多借助信息技术发展开展在线教育行为的教学项目,也充分显示了信息技术的发展、互联网的普及推动了在线教育内容生产的热潮,进一步完善了在线教育上下游产业的发展。

Moallem(2003)提出在线交流工具不能单独促进学习,但通过精心设计,它们可以成为一种有效的在线学习工具[117]。Carson(2004)对麻省理工学院的在线教育进行了调查,得出的结论是大多数用户来自北美,但国际化趋势更加明显,大部分学习人员都是学士及以上学历[118]。

2008 年,加拿大教授唐斯和乔治首先提出了 MOOC 成体系的公开课程概念[119]。MOOC 课程主要就是人与计算机的互动学习,借助 BOLG 和 BBS 等社交平台,提供网络课程资料、教学流程和学习讨论。这种新的教学模式和教学组织完全不同于传统的大学课堂教学。它有两个显著的特点:第一,学习人群的开放。课程不仅允许校内学生注册,还允许校外学生注册。第二,没有时间空间的限制。MOOC 突破了传统大学课堂教学的时间和空间限制,使教学和学习更加灵活,扩大了课堂教学,可以容纳更多的参与者。

董晓迪(2015)通过对中国网络教育商业模式的分析,发现网络教育的内容可以从以下四个方面来描述:第一,网络教育是一种存在于互联网环境中的行为,打破了时空限制,允许用户在任何时间和地点进行教育和学习,为最终的学习创造了良好的学习环境;第二,借助移动终端的普及和技术升级,在线教育已经不再局限于传统的个人电脑,可使用智能手机、Pad 等终端开展教育与学习,使教学具备可移动性、碎片利用时间、智能化成为其特色;第三,在线教育不只是单纯的教育信息化或者教育设备更新,更多的是对教育内涵、教育模式、教育目的等全流程的变化,只要有一技之长的用户都可以成为在线教育平台入驻开课的老师,刷新了以往对老师的传统定义;第四,得益于互联网传播的便捷性,在线教育平台可以把分散在全球各地的个性化学习需求汇总到在线教育平台上,通过大数据的匹配实现个性化与定制化的教育,这样的学习方式不但可以提升教育效果,还可以进行教育阶段的细分,从而可以对不同的学生量身定制课程,在进行针对性学习的同时进一步提升学习体验[120]。

Allen 和 Seaman(2016)通过调查,在 *Online Report Card-Tracking Online Education in the United States* 报告中对传统面对面教育、在线教育、混合教育进行了界定,认为至少有 80% 的课程内容在线学习才能明确认为属于在线教育[121]。

艾瑞咨询(2018)认为计算机与因特网的普及应用,加上数字化多媒体技术开始大量应用于教育培训的过程中,为获取教育资源提供了新的途径,也正式推动了在线教育的发展[5]。在线教育正式诞生之前,教育信息化推进了教育的现代化发展,幻灯片、投影仪、广播、电视、录音、录像带等教学形式加快了信息传递的过程,提高了教育的效率,为在线教育的诞生奠定了基础。

网经社(2019)则将在线教育的发展阶段划分为 20 世纪末—2009 年、2010—2014 年、2015 年至今,依次定义为初始阶段、成长阶段和稳定阶段[6]。还指出 2013 年为在线教育的元年。指出未来借助 AI、Big Data、AR 等科技的应用,在线教育将走向更加完善的人机交互。

自从在线教育提出以后,中国的学者近年来也从多个角度对在线教育发表了诸多的观点。余胜泉和林君芬(2003)从中国教育信息化的应用案例分析,指出中国在线教育的发展存在概念定义上的模糊,在线课程内容宽泛,学习环境的搭建缺少良好的设计,教学的表现形式单一,并且缺少互动和课程评价反馈机制[122]。丁兴富(2004)从加快远程教育学科建设从而推动在线教育长远发展提出了意见,鼓励学科内容创新、教学形式的创新推进其创新发展[123]。方柏林和刘常庆(2006)通过针对马歇尔的研究认为应从教师、课程开发、课程评估、组织高效、外部关系等五个方面对在线教育平台进行全面的推进[124]。彭立宏和周丽涛(2006)以基础设施划分了基于互联网的在线教育和基于校园网的在线教育,并且提出了应开发更多优质网上课程、加大技术平台的研究、提供更好的交互性、建设评价反馈机制、提供个性化学习服务,从而提升在线教育平台的服务水平[125]。高峻(2008)通过研究国外网络教育平台,提出了引领式的在线学习模式,倡导通过在线平台的人际交互进行学习从而解决用户自主学习模式下的一些问题[126]。姜卉等(2008)以在线课程《e-Learning 导论》为案例进行研究,结果发现辅导老师的积极参与和有效组织与课程作业的完成有显著的关系;辅导老师的组织教学和讨论与小组协同知识构建的水平有显著的关系;辅导老师的情感支持与小组协作知识建构水平、良好沟通氛围的构建有显著的关系[127]。

胡晶等(2010)通过对数学文化课程的研究认为,在线课程教学设计要注重课程的性质与特色,在线教学也要营造愉悦的学习环境,教师的积极参与可以增加学习中的信心,课程的交互设计可以提高课程的趣味性[128]。张玲燕(2008)对我国目前快速发展的网络大学进行研究后提出了其优点和缺点,并认为网络大学的便利性、经济性、共享性为教育资源的普及提供了新的渠道和方式,但由于教学活动完全通过网络进行,对于学生的人际交往能力、集体主义观念、团队合作能力、价值观教育存在不足,而且在线教育无法对学生进行监督和提醒[129]。陈巍(2010)以成人高等教育开展在线教育为研究视角,对中国成人高等教育目前所面临的问题,结合在线教育时空限制小、学习资源丰富、学习形式灵活的特点开展了实证研究,肯定了在线教育对于中国成人高等教育的作用,并对其存在的不足提出继续加大创新改革力度的建议[130]。齐振国(2012)从在线教育适合的学习对象、在线培养人数、在线教学成本、教育质量、学习环境、适合课程内容、学习自觉性、学员计算机操作能力等方面阐述了在线教育的一些常见误区,提出应客观认识在线教育的优势和不足之处以真正达到在线教育的教学目标[131]。韩勇(2012)对 web2.0 时代的在线教育新模式做出了新的阐述,重点强调了web2.0 在线教育平台构建的网络学习环境可以实现社会化的学习并以人性化为导向,最终提升在线学习的效果和体验[132]。王立慧和徐文清(2012)指出继续教育、在线教育、自学考试教育是中国成人教育的主要组成部分[133]。2010 年,中国成人教育在校生人数达 536 万人,网络教育在校生人数为 453 万人,自考助学班在校人数为 59.5 万人。三种成人学历模式呈现出互补、融合发展的态势,建议从转变教育观念、完善课程系统、改进教学形式、提升教师队伍等方面推动成人高等学历教育的发展。中商产业研究院(2019)在《2018 年度中国在线教育市场发展报告》中指出在线教育就是利用信息技术和互联网科技进行知识传播和课程学习的方式[134]。中国互联网络信息中心(2019)发现直播、Big Data 等科技的普及,为在线教育的学习课堂营造了良好的学习氛围,因材施教的教学形式可以增强教学效果,打破时间、空间的限制,为方便教学和学习提供了非常大的便捷[154]。苏幕遮

(2019)认为在线教育汇聚更多优质资源、课程内容透明、突破时空限制、节省花销、满足用户碎片化学习需求,因而得到了快速的发展[135]。

中国学者从 2012 年开始对 MOOC 进行相关研究并发表观点。李晓明(2013)指出 MOOC 理念将为传统的教学办法提供创新的思想来源,MOOC 与以往的公开课也存在许多不同点,MOOC 更加关注谁来参与、评价如何、有何问题与想法。MOOC 对于改变延续了几百年的传统课堂教学模式有着重要的启迪,MOOC 模式也会给教育带来更多创新空间[136]。袁莉等(2014)以破坏式创新理论、维持性创新理论为基础,充分认可了 MOOC 模式为高等教育做出的贡献,促进高等院校对新的教学方法、商业模式和灵活学习的思考[137]。李明华(2013)提出 MOOCs 的兴起挑战了以传统大学打包出售学历的市场,发现 MOOCs 对于提高中国高等教育课程质量并淘汰劣质课程有着帮助[138]。MOOCs 模式不光把世界上的优秀课程带来中国,同样把中国的优秀课程以 MOOCs 方式推向世界带来了机遇。顾小清等(2013)通过分析 MOOC 的发展历史与其国际化的发展背景,比较中国本土 MOOC 的发展环境与可能性[139]。汪琼(2013)发现世界众多知名高等院校开始拥抱 MOOCs,认为应该对 MOOCs 持有开放性的学习观,但是 MOOCs 未来是否会与高等教育结合也需要进一步看 MOOCs 技术的发展趋势[140]。如果未来的 MOOC 技术发展能够帮助用户分析并找到想要学习的内容,让学习变得有趣且高效,也许未来的 MOOC 会取代现行的高等教育系统成为学习的主要阵地。焦建利和贾义敏(2011)研究得出世界范围内开放教育资源的运动可以令中国的高等教育获得参考,例如从提供创新机会、共同创建资源与开源、优秀课程再分配等方面着手[141]。

通过文献检索和研究总结,发现在线教育的定义存在多个版本,界定不清。中商产业研究院(2019)指出在线教育、网络学习、网络培训、online education、e-learning 等名词从说法上有些差别,但经过新技术、新模式近三十年的发展,验证了几者的内涵和本质并无实质性区别[134]。因此本研究将在线教育定义为一种基于互联网获取知识的学习行为,是以互联网为传播媒介的教学方式,是学生与教师通过互联网媒介展开的教育学习活动。得益于网络课件、网络视频、网络音频、在线问答等在线工具的帮助,学生也可以在任何时间、任何地点开展学习行为,有别于传统学校教育,打破了时间和空间的限制。在线教育的优势在于:超越时空和人力物力的限制,最大限度地利用资源;在任何时间和任何地点自主选择学习行为;师生互动交流;学生自主学习、自主掌握进度并能即时得到反馈;个性化教学形式的创新,使用新的教育工具,使网络教学管理自动化等等。

3.2 在线教育商业模式

3.2.1 在线教育平台分类和商业模式

中商产业研究院(2019)在《2019 年中国在线教育市场前景研究报告》中对在线教育的类型进行了划分,主要分为十大类:学前教育、母婴类、成人外语、职业技能、少儿英语、兴趣爱好、留学生、高校学生、中小学和职业资格考试[134]。互联网教育智能技术及应用国家工程实验室和北师大智慧学习研究院(2017)指出外语培训和课后培训的市场需求旺盛,公务员考试、研究生考试和英语也是在线教育的热门领域[142]。但是,在线教育的学习内容远不止于此,每个在线教育平台都推出了各种有偿在线学习服务,覆盖范围十分广泛。

艾瑞咨询(2018)在《2017 年中国 B2B2C 在线教育平台行业研究报告》中对在线教育平台的各种类型进行了整理划分,具体可以划分为综合平台、垂直平台、慕课平台[5]。

在当前以市场为导向的在线教育行业中,在线教育服务涵盖了广泛的形式,并且有许多类型的公司参与在线教育行业,比如有从事线下教育的,刚涉足培训的以及成熟的互联网公司。在线教育行业有两种主要方式向消费者收费:一个是收取学习课程费和材料费,主要是一些由供应商提供的高质量数字原创课程内容;另一个是为用户提供相关的考证咨询、线上模拟、教育咨询,感兴趣的用户可以购买相关的专业性服务。

艾瑞咨询(2018)认为目前的在线教育商业模式主要依靠销售课程赚取利润,企业是在网络上教学的教师和学习者的桥梁,今后可以探索各种盈利模式[5]。学生通过平台向网络教师支付课程费用,对课程收费是主要收入来源,这是该行业参与者的主要盈利模式。在教学的过程中,平台可以通过类似直播的方式运营,学生可以在线奖励网络教师,平台也可以从中抽取分成佣金。网络教师和入驻平台的供应商进入平台后,仍需进行宣传和推广工作,平台提供的招生、教学、管理和服务工具也可以提高教学工作的效率。

因此,未来的平台可以在广告资源和网络工具资源上收取一些额外的费用。尽管增加收入的方式多样,但目前在线教育平台的收入来源依旧以在线课程的销售为主。

3.2.2　商业模式比较

极光大数据(2017)发现受到众人追捧的知识付费主要是指软性知识,即消费者用付费的方式获取知识认知者的实践总结等信息[143]。艾瑞咨询(2018)发现 B2B2C 商业模式的在线教育企业发挥着多种多样垂直课程领域聚合发布的作用;而 B2C 在线网校则是教育主体自我管理的网络载体,一般以比较垂直的教育领域为主要课程产品[5]。庞东梅(2018)指出 B2B2C 这类商业模式在线教育平台提供了渠道、信息系统功能和其他相关服务支持,在这个实施过程中同时实现内容变现[144]。B2B2C 在线教育、B2C 网校、知识付费的比较分析如表 3-1 所示。

表 3-1　**B2B2C 在线教育、B2C 网校、知识付费分析**

	B2C 网校	B2B2C 在线教育	知识付费
定义	相关机构聚焦于直营的网络平台。	集合多个领域的公开化平台	以碎片化轻知识分享传递为主
共性	以开展技能培训与在线教育为目标,将传统的教学场景搬到线上实施		
	公开化平台,集合多类内容为生产者和购买者提供桥梁		
	同属于信息消费领域,包含了对信息产品和服务的购买、使用的过程		
教育主体	平台的教学教研团队	独立教师、教育机构、大 V	知识大 V
知识领域	相对专注几个类目	涉及多种类型科目	各类经验等轻知识
课程消费	平台定价,课程费用为直接收益,课程单价较高	平台协助定价,佣金收益,课程单价较高	课程单价相对较低
传播模式	重平台价值,直/录播为主	重平台价值,直/录播为主	图文音频等。
课程体系	成熟且结构化的课程	成熟且结构化的课程	碎片化的知识传递

续表

	B2C 网校	B2B2C 在线教育	知识付费
学习目的	目标明确的教育投资,以达到教育效果为目标的刚需用户为主	目标明确的教育投资,以达到教育效果为目标的刚需用户为主,也含轻知识的需求用户	需求多样的求知消费,也含轻知识的需求用户

3.2.3　B2B2C 在线教育平台相关介绍

庞东梅(2018)将 B2B2C 在线教育平台界定为知识课程生产者和消费者的在线服务载体[144]。艾瑞咨询(2018)认为 B2B2C 这类商业模式在线教育平台更多承担的是教育的互联网载体平台角色,为教学过程中的各个环节提供多方面支持和互联网技术服务[5]。

腾讯研究院(2019)认为 B2B2C 商业模式在线教育平台是指在线教育的培训机构、个人通过入驻在线教育平台为个人用户提供大量的教育课程服务,B2B2C 在线教育平台的内容综合性更强,借助平台庞大的数据优势为课程提供方和课程需求方提供精准匹配的服务[4]。

在本研究中,将 B2B2C 这类商业模式的在线教育平台界定为知识课程生产者和消费者的在线服务载体。同时将课程消费方定为"用户",将 B2B2C 在线教育企业和平台定为"平台",其历史轨迹见表 3-2。

表 3-2　在线教育发展历史

时间	阶段	代表事物	特征
20 世纪 90 年代前	传统教育	函授、收音机、电视转播	一些新的技术手段的初步探索和应用
1990—2000	数字化教育	电子计算机、互联网、远程教育	网络的普及,数字化技术应用到教育教学的过程中
2000—2010	互联网＋教育	网络学校、学习社区、视频课件	BBS、视频等形式开始繁荣
2010—2013	移动＋教育	录/直播、MOOC、移动化、大数据应用	录播付费形式、MOOC 兴起,直播形式出现
2013 年至今	智能＋教育	知识付费平台、B2B2C 平台、AI	知识付费崛起,综合类的 B2B2C 的规模持续扩大

3.3　全球在线教育发展概述

3.3.1　美国、英国等国的在线教育行业概况

Docebo(2016)指出截至 2016 年底,美国在线学习市场价值超过 270 亿美元。在线学习的观念开始被用户接受,越来越多人采纳在线学习对市场规模产生积极影响,促进在线教育需求的增长,推动未来几年的行业增长[145]。

Allen 和 Seaman(2017)在报告 *Distance Education Enrollment Report* 2017 报告中指出,就在 2015 年的秋季,超过 600 万名美国学生参加了至少一个远程学习课程,该数据比上一年增加了 3.9%。这一增长率高于之前两年中的任何一年[146]。

BestColleges(2018)在报告 *Online Education Trends Report* 2018 中指出,40% 的受访者计划在接下去的时间增加在线教育的预算,79% 的在线教育学生和 76% 的校友认为在线教育是"优于"或"等于"传统的学校教育,而 57% 的学校表示雇主也有类似的感受,在线教育继续在美国呈现上升的趋势[147]。

美国的在线教育形式以 MOOC(Massive open online course)、远程教育(Distance education)、开放大学(Open university)这三种形式为主。而美国的 MOOC 市场更加接近于中国的在线教育平台。而在名词使用上,在线教育(online education)、在线学习(e-leaning)则是从不同角度讲述了在线教育,本研究以在线教育平台为研究对象,则以上名词的含义没有本质区别,因此同时进行检索研究。

诞生于美国的在线教育形式,MOOC 在线教育平台在 2011 年已拥有 190 多国累计 16 万的学习用户[148]。相信这将对高等教育的发展产生巨大影响,甚至改变高等教育的格局。过去,只有少部分人获得顶尖大学优秀课程的学习机会,不仅是因为高昂的学费,其招收的学生人数也往往很有限。现在,随着 MOOC 在线教育平台的出现,只要互联网连通,任何人,任何时间地点都可以获得学习机会,这也让新的在线教育模式受到了极大的

追捧[149]。

美国教育部 2014 年 11 月发布的报告 *The Future Ready District Professional Learning Through Online Communities of Practice and Social Networks to Drive Continuous Improvement* 中指出,将会进行更多的在线学习社区的有益探索,从而推进专业学习的持续改进。并且列举了三个关于使用在线社区提升教育效果的故事,如 *Sherri's Story* 中提及 Sherri 作为一个中学教师开展日复一日的教学工作,当她遇到教学中的一些问题时感觉非常苦恼和无助,她庆幸加入了一些在线教学论坛并发现了一些对她有价值的教学方法,最后也帮助她解决了教学上所遇到的问题。报告中同样描述了未来将会开展更多的关于如何利用信息化工具和在线教育平台来提升教学效果的探索[150]。

Dhawal(2018)在文章 *A Review of MOOC Stats and Trends in* 2017 中提及美国 MOOC 的规模已经发展到超过 9400 个课程,拥有超过 500 个基于 MOOC 课程的证书,以及十多个研究生学位。根据 Class Central 收集的数据,2017 年约有 2300 万新学员报名参加了他们的第一次 MOOC 课程[151]。这与 2016 年注册 MOOC 的 2300 万新学员相似,据统计,目前 MOOC 学员总数约为 8100 万。

英国开放大学于 1969 年 4 月 23 日建立,是一家灵活、创新和世界性的领先大学。英国开放大学独特的体系更加了解兼职学生的需求,以方便学员更好地平衡工作和学习。超过 200 万人次在该学校进行学习,研究生部分的人数就超过了 30 万,属于英国最大规模的大学(250000 名学生)[152]。

Docebo(2016)发布的 *ELEARNING MARKET TRENDS AND FORECAST* 2017—2021 认为目前印度一半的人口实际上不到 25 岁,预计到 2022 年面临 2.5 亿技术工人的短缺,因此认为印度的教育将会很大程度上依赖于在线教育[145]。截至 2015 年,印度已经是仅次于美国的第二大在线教育市场。KPMG 和 Google(2017)认为印度的在线教育市场将从 2016 年约 160 万用户增长到 2021 年的 960 万用户[153]。拉丁美洲预计将在 2016 年至 2020 年间实现可观的增长,2016 年拉丁美洲在线教育市场份额估值约为 21 亿美元,并且可能在之后的几年内以超过 14% 的复合年增长率持续增长 5 年。根据 Ambient Insight 的数据,2014 年巴西移动学习产品和服务的收入达到了 3.333 亿美元,增长率高达 25.7%,到 2019 年收入将激增至 10 亿美元以上,巴西也是拉丁美洲中移动学习增幅最大的国家。

近年来,拉丁美洲的一些国家已经更大规模地采用了 MOOC。墨西哥和巴西是 MOOCs 使用率最高的 10 个国家中的两个。Veduca 是一个巴西 MOOC 平台,在 21 个知识领域提供 300 多个免费在线课程。根据 Ambient Insight 的数据,截至 2016 年底,美国的电子学习市场规模超过 270 亿美元,美国也是在线教育市场的最大消费国,其次是日本、韩国、中国和印度。根据 Ambient Insight 的数据,2016 年欧洲西部在线教育市场规模约为 80 亿美元,而欧洲东部市场约为 10 亿美元,东欧最大的消费国是俄罗斯联邦,英国则是西欧最大的消费国。世界部分国家在线教育发展情况如表 3-3 所示。

表 3-3　世界部分国家在线教育发展情况汇总

国家	发展概况
美国	在 2016 年末,市场总规模超过 270 亿美金。学员超过 600 万,MOOC 学员总数约为 8100 万。40％的受访者计划在明年增加在线教育的预算
英国	2016 年欧洲西部在线教育市场规模约为 80 亿美元,英国是西欧最大的消费国。超过 200 万人次在英国开放大学进行学习,研究生部分的人数就超过了 30 万,属于英国最大规模的大学(250000 名学生)
印度	截至 2015 年,印度已经是仅次于美国的第二大在线教育市场。并测算到 2018 年印度的在线教育市场将达到 12.9 亿美元,年复合增长率为 17％。印度 5 亿互联网用户将推动在线教育的发展,用户数量将从 2016 年约 160 万增长到 2021 年的 960 万
巴西	2014 年巴西移动学习产品和服务的收入达到了 3.333 亿美元,增长率高达 25.7％,到 2019 年收入将激增至 10 亿美元以上,巴西也是拉丁美洲移动学习增幅最大的国家

3.3.2　中国在线教育行业概况

自 1998 年开始,中国在线远程教育开始进入快速发展时期,中国高校的在线教育也开始起步,这也推进了中国在线教育行业发展。2000 年以后,舒宁(2016)认为中国在线远程教育开始迎来高速发展时期;借助多媒体技术、在线视频课件、在线问答网站系统等技术在在线教育行业的应用,加上多种在线教育的内容提供者类型开始出现[149]。

中国互联网络信息中心(2019)数据统计,截至 2018 年 12 月,中国的网民数量已达 8.29 亿;其中在线教育用户规模达 2.01 亿,比 2017 年增加 4605 万用户,年增长率高达 29.7%;通过手机使用在线教育的用户规模达 1.94 亿[154]。网经社(2019)在《2018 年度中国在线教育市场发展报告》中报道,2018 年中国在线教育行业的市场规模已超 3000 亿元,较 2017 年增速为 45%。随着在线教育行业的逐步成熟,以及风险投资机构的回归理性,传统线下教育机构寻求开展在线教育转型的难度更大[6]。

2018 年以来,中国在线教育市场的投融资局面十分火爆。倪明(2018)发表的《在线教育普遍严重亏损》中提及,在线教育平台融资局面火爆的同时,也有大量的在线平台处于亏损状态[155]。苏幕遮(2019)在《2019 中国 K12 在线教育行业研究报告》中指出,在 2019 年上市的新东方网校依然面临着获客成本高等急需解决的问题,中国在线教育发展局面不容乐观[135]。

尽管中国在线教育行业的众多企业依旧亏损,但是网络普及和网民数量持续增长、用户电子支付习惯的养成、政策面的利好、风险投资机构的看好、用户需求的持续增长,这五大因素仍推动中国在线教育市场进入高速发展的快车道。网经社(2019)指出,中国在线教育的人均消费金额远比欧美发达国家的人均投入更少[6]。因此,中国的在线教育目前仍然处于发展阶段。随着中国家庭收入的提高,加上中国庞大的人口基数以及政府鼓励生育的政策引导,相信未来中国在线教育的发展机会巨大。

3.3.3　中国在线教育平台典型企业分析

中国科技部火炬中心和长城战略咨询(2018)公布的信息中提及了"独角兽"这类企业。自从"独角兽"的定义被提出后,迅速获得了华尔街日报、财富、TechCrunch、CB Insights 等全球科技界和投资界众多机构的认可[156]。科技部认定独角兽企业的标准为:

(1)中国境内注册并有法人资格;

(2)成立少于 10 年;

(3)获得过私募投资,且尚未 IPO 上市;

(4)符合(1)(2)(3),且估值超 10 亿美元称为独角兽;

(5)符合(1)(2)(3),且估值超 100 亿美元称为超级独角兽。

网经社(2019)[6]在线教育"独角兽"统计数据显示,中国在线教育行业共诞生了 11 只"独角兽",表 3-4 是其名单。

表 3-4 在线教育行业"独角兽"名单

企业	估值(亿美元)	建立时间	注册地	排名
VIPKID	35	2013	北京	1
猿辅导	30	2012	北京	2
ItutorGroup	20	2009	上海	3
一起作业	12.5	2013	上海	4
网易有道	11	2007	北京	5
沪江网校 （含 CCtalk）	11	2015	上海	5
慧科在线教育	10	2010	北京	7
学霸君	10	2013	上海	7
哒哒英语	10	2013	北京	7
作业帮	10	2015	北京	7
直播优选	10	2017	武汉	7

　　CCtalk(2019)为沪江旗下 B2B2C 商业模式在线教育平台,CC 的含义是 Content(内容)和 Community(社区)两个单词的结合,属于横跨知识分享和在线教育两大领域的 B2B2C 在线教育平台[157]。教育内容方面有语言类、职业教育、中小幼、兴趣爱好 4 个分类,已拥有超过 50 多个子类目。学习性社区让学生们不再是孤独的自己学习。沪江(2018)宣称 3 万多人次的网师、几千家企业都已加入了平台,网络课程的存量数超过 85 万,服务学生超过 1000 万名[158]。2017 年,CCtalk 平台业务量实现了"阶梯式"增长,平台 GMV 连续三个季度的平均环比增速超过 150%,同时用户日活、用户数量、流水相较 2016 年度分别增长了 8 倍、10 倍、30 倍。

　　腾讯课堂是腾讯公司所拥有的 B2B2C 商业模式在线教育平台[159],拥有信息技术、语言、艺术、职业资格、升学和爱好共计 6 方面内容,每一类又分为若干二级类目。经过 4 年的发展与运营,已有超过三亿学生对平台上十万门课进行学习。

　　网易云课堂(2018)自 2012 年正式投入运营,提供的课程数量已超过一万门,课时量汇总达十万[160],拥有语言、职业考试、少儿教育等 10 大类目。到 2017 年,平台注册学习者超过五千万,入驻的网师和企业超过五千家。表 3-5 为典型平台的比较分析。

表 3-5　典型平台的比较分析

	CCtalk	腾讯课堂	网易云课堂
上线时间	2016 年 10 月	2014 年	2012 年 12 月
用户规模	超过 1000 万人	3 亿用户	已经突破 5500 万
课程数量	85 万节	10 万网络教育课程	课程数量已超 1 万门
课程体系	语言类、职业教育、中小幼、兴趣爱好 4 个分类	信息技术、语言、艺术、职业资格、升学和爱好共 6 方面内容	拥有语言、职业考试、少儿教育等 10 大类目
平台优势	16 年行业经验，工具全面且创新，课程前、中、后服务完整，社群化学习	课程体系全面，流量大，资质及质量控制严格	将小众专业、教育系统和企业模块作为亮点内容，使教育质量精细化
盈利模式	课程收入佣金，工具类收费，收费云软件服务	课程销售佣金	课程销售佣金

3.4　本章小结

　　本章对在线教育、在线教育商业模式和全球的在线教育发展概况进行了阐述。B2B2C 在线教育平台作为专业性电子商务网站，也应具备在线教育和电子商务平台所具备的特性。本章先对在线教育进行阐述，再对在线教育平台的商业模式进行分类，整理归纳其所具备的特点，描述了其发展历史与未来发展趋势。本章内容对产业背景进行了研究评述，为之后开展中国 B2B2C 在线教育平台用户课程购买影响因素研究打下坚实的基础。

Chapter 3　An Overview of
B2B2C OEP Industry

3.1　An Overview of Online Education

Miltiadou (2001) considered online learning to be a rich and dynamic way of learning. It provides attractive learning programs that rely on the Internet and computers and provides lifelong learning opportunities for many people who cannot go to college. Piccoli, Ahmad, and Ives (2001) argued that online learning is an open system that emphasizes the important role of technology, interactivity, and self-control throughout the online learning process. Harasim (1995) pointed out that online learning is a learning method that uses the Internet to provide learning content that breaks the time and place constraints.

He (2005) reviewed the history of the development of educational technology: in the early 1990s, the American education community raised the question of whether "a traditional university with walls will be replaced by a network university without walls in the near future", which sparked a heated debate for several years. The two sides who agreed that it would be replaced, and those who thought it would not be replaced had their own opinions and reasons that they could not reach a unified conclusion. This debate about the way of education in the future has gradually sprawled from the United States to the rest of the world, attracting the participation of many scholars and educators in the United States and the rest of the world. However, the two opposing views failed to reach an agreement. However, after nearly 10 years of online education exploration and experience accumulation, American educators and international education professionals have summarized the profound advantages and disadvantages of online education, reaching some practical basis about whether the traditional brick-and-mortar schools will be replaced in the future. Both sides realize that there is no absolute substitution or non-replacement. Instead, online education and traditional education in brick-and-mortar schools enjoy high complementary, just like that e-books and paper books can co-exist and complement with each other.

United States Department of Education (USDE, 2014) pointed out that "e-learning" can achieve some of of educational goals on the condition of appropriate pedagogy and curriculum design, but the not able to replace the teaching effect brought by traditional classrooms; e-learning will not replace the traditional education model, but it will greatly improve and enhance the teaching experience and teaching methodology. USDE defined "e-learning" in a more comprehensive manner, which is at the outset of education and related services through the Internet; secondly, it provides learners with a new way of learning and a carrier of learning anytime anywhere; thirdly, the combination use of information plans and various tools can achieve some of the educational goals to help improve the teaching effect, but it cannot replace the traditional brick-and-mortar teaching, nor the traditional school education. These lay the foundation for the new terminology, e-learning, to be popularized and widely accepted in the United States and even the world in the future.

"10 Best Teaching Technology Application Projects in the United States in 2003" were selected in 2003 (Mao, 2003). From the teaching technology application projects selected by this event, it can be seen that many teaching projects use online information technology to develop and implement their online educational behaviors. It also fully shows that the development of information technology and the popularity of the Internet have promoted a great upsurge in producing online educational content and further catalyzed the development of upstream and downstream industries in the online education sector.

Moallem (2003) suggested that only online communication tools cannot promote learning, but they can be turned into practial online learning tools through careful design. Carson and Margulies (2004) surveved online education in MIT and concluded that most online education users in MIT are from North America, but the internationalization trend is becoming prominent. Self-learners usually have a bachelor's or master's degree.

In 2008, Canadian professors Stephen Downes and George Simens first proposed the concept of massive open online courses (MOOC). MOOC emphasizes learning from human-machine interaction, making full use of social interaction tools such as Facebook, Wikipedia, blogs, and forums to provide online teaching resources, teaching processes, and learning discussions. This new teaching model and teaching organization are entirely different from traditional teaching in a classroom. It has two notable features. Firstly, the group of learners is open. The courses allow students on campus to register and students outside the school to register. Secondly, there is no time-space limitation. MOOC breaks through the time and space constraints of traditional ways of teaching, making teaching and learning more flexible, and expanding classroom teaching to accommodate more participants.

Dong (2015) analyzed China's online education business model, finding that online education content can be described in the following four aspects. Firstly, online education is supported by the Internet, breaking the time and space restrictions. It allows users to be educated and learn at any time and any place, creating a good learning environment for learning. Secondly, with the popularity of mobile terminals and technology upgrading, online education is no longer limited to traditional PCs, but can also be readily accessible through mobile devices such as mobile phones, tablets, and smart TVs. Mobilization, fragmentation, and intelligence have become three characteristics of online education.

Thirdly, online education is not just a simple education informationization or educational equipment updating, but it is about changes in the whole process of educational content, educational forms, educational themes, etc. If users have specializations, they can become teachers of the OEP, which also refreshes the traditional definition of teacher. Fourthly, thanks to the convenience of Internet communication, OEPs can pool and aggregate individualized learning needs that used to be scattered around the world into the OEP, providing personalized and customized education through the matching of big data. This learning method can improve the educational results that enhance education segmentation, thus teaching students according to their different learning abilities and aptitudes. It bids farewell to the traditional standardized teaching content of the past, offering targeted education while further enhancing the learning experience.

Allen and Seaman (2016) defined the traditional face-to-face education, online education, and mixed education, stating that courses with more than 80% content learned online can be classified as online education. IResearch (2018) considered the popularization and application of PCs and the Internet and the widespread adoption of digital multimedia technology in education and training, providing new channels for accessing educational resources, and officially promoting online education development. Before the birth of online education, education informatization promoted the modernization drive of education. The teaching forms such as slides, projectors, radio, television, audio, and videotapes accelerated the process of information transmission and improved the efficiency of education, laying a solid foundation for the emergence of online education.

ERCICI (2019) divided the development of online education into three stages: the late 20th-2009, 2010-2014, and 2015 to date, are respectively defined as the germination period, the outbreak period and maturity period. It also pointed out that 2013 is the first year of the online education era, and the development of new technologies such as artificial intelligence, big data, cloud computing, and augmented reality (AR), has been promoting online education to thorough and impeccable human-computer interaction.

Since the introduction of online education, Chinese scholars have published many theses on online education from various angles. Yu and Lin (2003) analyzed application cases of education informatization in China, pointing out that China has a vague definition of the development of online education, the content of online courses is broad, the construction of learning environment lacks a good design and the form of teaching performance is monotonous and lacks feedback mechanisms for interaction and evaluation. Ding (2004) put forward opinions on accelerating the key discipline construction of distance education and how promoting the long-term development of online education. He also encouraged innovative content of subjects and teaching forms to promote the innovation-driven development of online education. Fang and Liu (2006) studied the OEP of Marshall University in the United States, concluding that OEPs should consider five management dimensions: teachers, curriculum development, curriculum evaluation, organizational efficiency, and external relationship.

Peng and Zhou (2006) divided online education into two categories according to the infrastructure: Internet-based online education and campus network-based online education, suggesting that the enhancement of the service level of the OEP should guarantee five achievements: developing more high-quality online courses, increasing research of technology platforms, providing better interaction, building an evaluation feedback mechanism, and providing personalized learning services. Gao (2008) proposed a leading online learning model by studying foreign OEPs, advocating learning through interpersonal interaction on online platforms, thus solving some problems in the independent and self-directed learning mode. Jiang, Zhang, and Huang (2008) conducted a case study and validated that tutors' active participation and effective organization have a significant correlation with the completion of homework; the teaching and discussion organized by tutors have a significant correlation with the level of knowledge collaboration in group; and the tutors' emotional support has a significant correlation with the level of knowledge collaboration in a group, and the building of a good communication atmosphere.

Li and Jiang (2009) used the content analysis method to conduct a statistical analysis on the posting behavior of teachers in the online course, Distance Education Research Method jointly established by the School of Professional and Continuing Education of the University of Hong Kong and the Peking University School of Continuing Medical Education found that a sufficient sense of presence in online teaching generates an excellent way to ensure teaching efficiency. Hu, Han, and Wu (2010) suggested that the curriculum design of online courses should focus on the nature and characteristics of the curriculum through the study of mathematics and culture courses, online teaching should also create a pleasant learning environment, and the active participation of teachers can boost learners' confidence in learning. Therefore, the curriculum design needs to highlight interactive to enhance the fun of the course. Zhang (2018) investigated the advantages and disadvantages after researching China's rapidly developing online universities, and believed that online universitives convenience, cost-effectiveness and sharing characteristics provide new channels for educational resources Howerer, because the teaching activities are entirely taking through the network, which may cause insufficient interpersonal skills, collectivism, team collaboration ability, and value education of students, and online education cannot supervise and remind students.

Chen (2010) took online adult higher education as the research focus, carrying out empirical research on the problems Chinese adult higher education foces, combining with the limitations of online education, such as low time and space restrictions, rich learning resources and flexible learning forms. He recognized the role of online education in China's adult higher education, suggesting that it should continue to increase innovation and reform. Qi (2012) elaborated some common misunderstandings of online education from the aspects of users suitable for online learning, the number of students in an online cours, online teaching costs, education quality, learning environment, suitable course content, learning consciousness, and computer literacy, then he objectively argued the advantages and disadvantages of online education to achieve the teaching goals of online education surely. Han (2012) made a new exposition of the new online education model in the web 2. 0 era, emphasizing that the online learning environment built by the web 2. 0 OEP can realize socialized and humanity-orientation, ultimately improving the effectiveness and experience of online learning.

Wang and Xu (2012) believed that adult education, online education, and self-taught higher education examinations are three essential components of Chinese adult education. In 2010, the number of students enrolled in adult education in China reached 5. 36 million, the number of students enrolled in online education was 4. 53 million, and the number of students enrolled in courses for self-taught higher education examinations was 595,000. The three models of adult education show a complementary and integrated development trend. They suggested that the development of adult higher education should be supported by changing educational concepts, optimizing the curriculum system, improving methodology, and strengthening the building of teaching staff. China Industry Research Institute (2019) pointed out that online education uses knowledge technology and Internet technology for knowledge dissemination and course learning. CINIC (2019) found that the rapid development of live broadcast, cloud computing, big data, cloud storage, and other technologies has created a good learning atmosphere for online classrooms, and one-on-one teaching methods that can meet the individualized teaching needs and break the time and space constraints to provide a great convenience for teaching and learning. Su (2019) believed that online education brings together more high-quality resources, offers transparent curriculum content, breaks through time and space restrictions, saves costs, and meets the needs of using the fragmented time to learn, so it has been developing rapidly.

Chinese scholars began to research on MOOCs since 2012. Li (2013) pointed out that a MOOC provides an innovative source of ideas for traditional teaching methods. There are also many differences between MOOC and previous online open classes. MOOC pays more attention to who participates, how participants are evaluated, and what problems and ideas participants have. MOOC has been an essential inspiration for changing the traditional teaching model in the classroom for hundreds of years. A MOOC also brings more possibilities and space for innovation in education. Based on the theory of destructive innovation and sustaining innovation, Yuar, Powell and Ma (2014) research identifying MOOCs provide a new exploration channel for colleges and universities to seek funding, ensure quality and recognize students' credit. Additional, it fully recognizing the contribution of MOOC to higher education that includes promoting higher education institutions to ponder over new teaching methods, business models, and learning flexibility. Li (2013) proposed that the rise of MOOC challenges the traditional market where universities sell academic qualifications in a package, using the enterprise boundary theory and information economics of new institutional economics, and found that MOOC helps to improve the quality of Chinese higher education courses and eliminate inferior quality. The MOOC brings excellent courses to China, brings opportunities for China to offer excellent courses to the world in the MOOC format.

Gu, Hu, and Cai (2013) proposed the differences between MOOCs and traditional online education in terms of technology platforms, teaching methods, knowledge, copyright of resources, learning, and technology through analyzing the development history of MOOCs and their international development background, and comparing them with the development environment and possibilities in China. Wang (2013) found that many well-known institutions of higher learning in the world began to embrace MOOCs and believed that they should have an open view of

MOOCs. However, whether MOOCs will be integrated with higher education in the future requires further development of MOOCs technology. If MOOC technology in the future can help users analyze what they want to learn and make learning fun and efficient, perhaps the future MOOC will replace the current higher education system as the main way of learning. Jiao and Jia (2011) researched the movement of open educational resources worldwide, which sheds light on the construction and application of higher education resources in China, and its feasible ways contain mechanism innovation, resource creation and sharing, and application of quality resources.

Through literature and research, it was found that there are multiple versions and definitions of online education. China Business Research Institute (2019) pointed out that there are some slight differences among online education, online learning, online training, online education, e-learning, etc. After nearly 30-year development of new technologies and new models, it also verifies that there is no substantial difference between the connotation and essence of theses above-mentioned terminologies. Therefore, this study defines online education as a learning behavior based on Internet knowledge acquisition. It is an educational and learning activity in which the students and teachers use the Internet as the medium of communication. Thanks to online courseware, online video, web audio, online Q&A and other online tools, students can learn at any time and any place. Different from traditional education in school, it breaks the time and space constraints. The advantages of online education are: exceeding the limitations of time and space, and human and material resources, maximizing the use of resources, conducting learning behaviors at any time and any place, interacting with teachers and students, learning independence, mastering learning progress, obtaining immediate feedback, innovating the form of teaching, the adoption of new educational tools, and automatic online teaching management.

3.2　Business Model of Online Education

3.2.1　OEP Classification and Business Model

China Business Research Institute（2019）classified Internet online education into ten categories：preschool education，maternal and child，adults，foreign language，vocational skills，children's English，hobbies，international students，college students，primary and secondary school students，and vocational examinations. CIT & SLI（2017）pointed out that the demand for vocational skills training，English training，and tutoring in primary and secondary schools is relatively high in the OEI in China，while civil servant examinations，postgraduate examinations，and foreign language are also hot areas of online education. However，the content of online education is not limited to these topics. Each OEP has launched a variety of paid online learning services，covering a wide range.

IResearch（2018）classified OEPs into a comprehensive platform，vertical platform，and MOOC platform. The specific classification refers to the following table：

In the current market-oriented OEI，online education services cover a wide range of forms，and there are many types of companies involved in the OEI，including traditional training companies，emerging training companies，and Internet business giants. The OEI has two main ways to charge consumers. One is to pay for courses and studying materials，which are mainly used by suppliers who provide high-quality digital and original course content. The other way is used by online education institutions that charge users by providing relevant examination services，online testing services，educational consulting services，and related professional services.

IResearch（2018）believed that the current online education business model mainly relies on course sales to make profits where the platform acts as an intermediary. One end is connected to teachers who provide online education resources, and the other connects students with educational needs. Currently, the main profit model is that students pay course fees to online teachers through the platform, and OEPs charge commissions for course fees as a source of income. Various profit models can be explored in the future. In the process of teaching, the platform can operate in a similar way to live broadcasts. Students can reward teachers online, and the platform can also extract commissions from rewards. After teachers and suppliers entering the platform, they still need to carry out publicity and promotion. The enrollment, teaching, management, and service tools provided by the platform can also improve the efficiency of teaching work. As a result, future platforms can charge some additional fees on inventory and web tool resources. There are many ways to increase the income of OEPs in the future, but the sales of online courses still dominate the current source of income for them.

3.2.2　Comparison of B2B2C OEPs, B2C Online School, and Knowledge-based Pay

Jiguang Big Data (2017) summarized the mainstream knowledge paid APP after research: knowledge-based payment has certain universality and systemicity in publishing, education, and training. The knowledge paid by the public mainly refers to the soft knowledge that is the knowledge products that the consumers consider to be valuable and non-standardized by the users themselves, such as the practice summary and experiences of the knowledge cognizers.

IResearch (2018) conducted a comparison of B2B2C OEP, B2C online school, knowledge-based payment platform and found that B2B2C OEP and B2C online school both consider education realization as their ultimate goal, B2B2C OEP is an open carrier aggregating curriculum in multiple fields, B2C online school is a network carrier that focuses on self-operation education. The B2B2C OEP and the B2C online school platform aim to carry out skills training and online education, moving the traditional teaching scene to the online classes classes. The difference between these two is that as an open carrier platform, the B2B2C OEP is responsible for the function of the educational carrier via a role in the aggregation and distribution of various vertical courses. The B2C online school is the network carrier for the self-management of the education subject. Generally, its main course products are relatively vertical education fields, such as language training, vocational training, and skills training.

The B2B2C OEP and knowledge-based pay platform are both open content and resource aggregated platforms. Pang (2018) pointed out that the B2B2C OEP mainly focuses on the model of education service based on platform, while the knowledge-based pay platform focuses on sharing and disseminating fragmented and light knowledge. It was believed that the B2B2C OEP and the knowledge-based pay platform are all open platforms for the aggregation of third-party knowledge and content. As an intermediary role of the education carrier, they link the content provider and the content receiver at two ends. Both can provide delivery channels, information system function, and other supporting service in the process of education (knowledge) sharing and dissemination, and in the meanwhile of implementation, knowledge can be sold off. However, there are some differences between the two. The B2B2C OEP focuses on providing structured and systematic professional education services as the main content, often in a business model combining multiple education types with courses as its core products. Paid platforms are often based on services sharing and delivering fragmented light knowledge. The sharing and dissemination methods are relatively simple and convenient. Generally, text, images, audio, video, and other light multimedia transmission methods are used as the carrier to achieve the goal of knowledge transmission.

3.2.3　An Introduction of B2B2C OEPs

Pang (2018) defined the OEP as an Internet third-party education platform that links the educational resources at both the supply and demand sides, provides online technology, information system functions, and services for all aspects in the teaching process, and accomplishes the realization of educational resources.

IResearch (2018) defined the B2B2C OEP as a third-party educational services platform that provides supporting service for online education and the profit realization of educational resources and contents. From a macro perspective, the B2B2C OEP refers to the Internet third-party education platform that aims to achieve quality education and links both educational content providers and the demand side. As a service provider, the platform does not produce and provide curriculum resources. The bulk of its responsibility is to assume the role of the carrier platform for education on the Internet, providing multi-faceted support and Internet technology services needed in all aspects of the teaching process. The B2B2C OEP helps the education content providers to realize the productization, commercialization, and branding of the curriculum to achieve the goal of realizing the profit of the educational content while providing primary conditions to implement education.

TRI (2019) argued that the OEP of the B2B2C business model refers to online education training institutions and individuals provide services of a large number of educational curriculum for individual users through entering the OEP. The content of B2B2C OEP is more comprehensive, and relying on the platform'colossal data advantage, it can provide accurate matching for course providers and course demanders.

Table 3-1　Comparison of B2B2C OEP, B2C online school, knowledge-based pay

	B2C online school	B2B2C OEP	Knowledge-based pay
Definition	A carrier where institutions focuses on self-operated education.	An open carrier that aggregates courses in multiple fields	A third-party platform focuses on the aggregation of content and fragmented light knowledge sharing.

Continuation

	B2C online school	B2B2C OEP	Knowledge-based pay
Generality	To carry out skills training and online education, move the traditional teaching scene online.		
		An aggregation and intermediary platform for open third-party knowledge content, linking both content providers and content receivers.	
	Belong to information consumption; the whole process involves purchasing and using information products and services (State Information Center, 2017).		
Teaching entity	Teaching and research team of the platform	Independent teachers, educational institutions, Internet celebrated teachers	Internet celebrated teachers
Scope of knowledge	Relatively vertical education	A wide range of courses in the vertical field.	Light knowledge of various social experiences and opinions
Course consumption	Platform is in charge of pricing, so course fees are direct income. The course price is higher.	The platform assists in pricing, and relatively high commission income, and unit price.	Relatively low per customer transaction
Ways of dissemination	Heavy models, combine multiple forms of education with the live/recording course as the core, and some combined with offline education services.	Heavy models, combine multiple forms of education with the live/recording course as the core.	Light mode, simply use some form of education, such as text, images, community, audio, etc.

	B2C online school	B2B2C OEP	Knowledge-based pay
Course system	Mature and structured curriculum.	Mature and structured curriculum.	Fragmented way of transferring knowledge.
Learning purposes	Targeted education investment, which is aimed at users who need to achieve their educational purposes.	Targeted education investment, which is aimed at users who need to achieve their educational purposes, while some users need light knowledge.	Diverse needs for knowledge, but there are also users who need light knowledge.

The differences and identification of these three kinds of OEP have been clarified in Table 3-1. In this study, the B2B2C OEP is defined as the third-party education platform on the Internet that links the educational resources to both the supply and demand sides to provide technical support and services for online education implementation and content realization. At the same time, educational content demand is referred to as "users", and the B2B2C OEP is referred to as "platforms" in short. Online education, the development of new technologies on the Internet, the transformation of educational concepts, the escalation of user education needs, and lifestyle changes are closely related. With the continuous expansion of Internet education, and the increasingly stable business model, the deepening of user learning needs, the awakening of consumer awareness, and the improvement of spending power, China's online education (online learning) has ushered in the era of intelligent education featuring vertical segmentation of learning content, the diversification of learning methods, open and sharing learning content, and the the realization of the profits of educational resources.

3.3　Overview of Global OEI Development

3.3.1　Overview of Foreign Global OEI Development in the United States, the United Kingdom

Docebo (2016) showed that by the end of 2016, the value of the online learning market in the United States exceeded 27 billion US dollars. The concept of online learning is beginning to be accepted by users. In addition, as the network and mobile terminal devices become popular, the online education market will continue to grow in the next few years. All the above factors positively impact market size, boosting the growth of online education demand and the industry growth in the next few years.

BestColleges.com (2018) indicated that 40% of respondents plan to increase the online education expenditure in the near future, 79% of online education students and 76% of alumni believe that online education is "better than" or "equal to" traditional school education, while 57% of schools say employers have similar feelings, and online education shows an upward trend in the United States.

Table 3-2　History of online education development

Time	Stage	Representation	Characteristics
Before 1990	Traditional education	Correspondence, slide/projector, radio/television, recording/video-tape	Education informationization and new teaching methods are applied in offline education, which improves teaching efficiency.

Continuation

Time	Stage	Representation	Characteristics
1990—2000	Digitized education	Electronic computer, multimedia courseware, internet, distance learning	The popularity of PC computers and the Internet, digital technology is applied to the process of education and teaching. China has approved 68 universities to become pilots for modern distance education.
2000—2010	Internet + education	Learning community, video courseware, online school	The Internet learning community, teaching videos and other methods have developed rapidly. New Oriental, Hujiang and other network schools are running their business online.
2010—2013	Mobile + education	Recording/live class, MOOC, mobile education, big data application	Recorded and courses that needs to be paid form a stable business model. Live courses appear. Mobile education begins to develop. MOOC with high-quality in universities rises in China.
2013 till now	Intelligence + education	Knowledge payment platform, B2B2C platform, artificial intelligence application	A knowledge-based payment platform with "light knowledge" emerged. B2B2C OEPs, which integrates online schools, MOOC, live broadcast, and knowledge payment, has become a new model.

Source: iResearch (2018) and FIRI (2019)

The forms of online education in the United States include MOOC, distance education, and Open University. The MOOC market in the United States nearly, equal to China's OEPs. In terms of selecting nouns, "online education" and "e-leaning" depict online education from different angles. This study uses the OEP as the research object, and since the meaning of the above nouns is not fundamentally different, synchronized searching with these keywords were also done.

Table 3-2 indicates the history of online education development. Born in the United States, the form of online education, MOOC, has registered 160,000 users (Li, 2014) in more than 190 countries in 2011. Professor Sebastian at Stanford University developed *Introduction to Artificial Intelligence*, which gained popularity rapidly. It also gave birth to the Udacity online course. Shortly after, professors Wu Enda and Daphne at Stanford University co-founded the online free course Coursera in 2012. In April, the number of students reached more than 1 million. Later, more than 100 famous universities, including Princeton University, Stanford University, California Institute of Technology, University of Michigan and the University of Pennsylvania joined the Coursera OEP and offered free online courses. In May 2012, MIT and Harvard University jointly launched the edX, network online teaching program. The first Electronics and Circuits course they initiated had more than 120,000 students registered. By the end of the autumn in 2012, over 370,000 students registered for the courses, and hundreds of well-known universities around the world have joined edX. In 2012, various MOOC courses were rapidly spread and developed. The *New York Times* called 2012 the "MOOC first year". MOOC began to rise on a global scale. The arrival of MOOCs has made people realize that the combination of network and education is easier and faster than ever. It is firmly believed that this imposes a considerable impact on the development of higher education and even changes higher education's pattern. In the past, only a few outstanding students had the opportunity to participate in world-class universities because of the soaring tuition fees and the limited number of students enrolled. Now, with the advent of the MOOC, as long as the Internet is connected, anyone can enjoy the quality education content of the world's top universities for free anywhere and anytime. Therefore, MOOC quickly attracted both higher education and the general public

(Shu, 2016).

USDE (2014) pointed out that there would be more valuable explorations of online learning communities to promote professional learning, and three stories about using online communities to improve educational outcomes have been listed. For example, Sherri mentioned that as a middle school teacher, she used to offer day-to-day teaching, and then she always feels distrought and helpless when she encounters some of the problems in teaching. Then she was glad to join some online math forums and found some teaching methods that were valuable to her. Finally, she solved the problems that she encountered in teaching. The report also describes more explorations in the future on how to use information tools and OEPs to enhance teaching effectiveness (USDE, 2014).

Shah (2019) mentioned that the size of the MOOC in the United States has grown to more than 9,400 courses, with more than 500 certificates based on MOOC courses, and more than a dozen master's degrees. According to data collected by Class Central, approximately 23 million new students enrolled in their first MOOC course in 2017. This number is similar to the 23 million new students enrolled in the MOOCs in 2016. According to statistics, the total number of MOOC students is currently about 81 million.

Founded on April 23rd, 1969, the Open University of the UK is a leading world-class university that is flexible and innovative. The unique system there helps the Open University to have a better understanding of the needs of part-time students, so students can better balance their work and study. More than 2 million students have been educated at the Open University of the UK, including more than 300,000 graduate students. Now it is the largest university in the UK 250,000 students at university (Open University, 2019).

Docebo Research Institute (2016) indicated that half of India's population is less than 25 years old. It is expected that India will face a shortage of 250 million skilled workers by 2022, so it is considered that

India's education will rely heavily on online education. By 2015, India was already the second—largest online education market after the United States. Google and KPMG (2017) calculated that India's online education market would grow from approximately 1.6 million users in 2016 to 9.6 million users in 2021. Latin America is expected to achieve significant growth between 2016 and 2020. The share of the online education market in Latin American is estimated at approximately 2.1 billion US dollars in 2016 and may continue to grow at a compound annual growth rate of over 14% in the next few years. According to Ambient Insight, revenue from mobile learning products and services in Brazil reached 333.3 million US dollars in 2014, a growth rate of 25.7%. By 2019, revenues surged to more than 1 billion US dollars. Brazil is also the fastest-growing mobile learning market in Latin America. In recent years, some countries in Latin America have adopted MOOCs on a larger scale. Mexico and Brazil are 2 of the 10 countries with the highest usage rates of MOOCs. Veduca is a Brazilian MOOC platform offering more than 300 free online courses in 21 areas. According to Ambient Insight, by the end of 2016, the US e-learning market exceeded $27 billion, and the US is also the largest consuming country of online education, followed by Japan, South Korea, China, and India. According to data from Ambient Insight, the online education market in western Europe in 2016 was about 8 billion US dollars, while the eastern European market was about 1 billion US dollars. The largest consuming country in Eastern Europe is the Russian Federation, while the one in Western Europe is the United Kingdom.

3.3.2　Overview of China's OEI

In September 1998, the Chinese Ministry of Education officially approved Tsinghua University, Beijing University of Posts and Telecommunications, Zhejiang University and Hunan University as the first batch of pilots for online distance education. Since then, China's online distance education has entered a period of rapid development, and online education in Chinese universities has also taken off, catalyzing the development of China's OEI.

Shu (2016) proposed that China's online distance education usher in a period of rapid development after 200: firstly, educational information technology, multimedia technology, including online video courseware, system for web-based online questions and answers, were started to be applied, significantly improving the efficiency of education; secondly, the Ministry of Education officially approved 68 colleges and universities as pilot institutions for the national modern distance education, the establishment of online education colleges, and issuing both online education qualification and degree certificate for students who meet the graduation requirements. The total scale of distance education accounts for more than 90% of the online market share of online education in China; thirdly, the online school represented by New Oriental was officially launched in 2000, marking the beginning of the traditional training school to enter the online education market and enriching the type of content provider in the online education sector.

In 2012, MOOCs swept the world, and Chinese universities began to join the MOOC building and practice in early 2013. Tsinghua University, Peking University, the University of Hong Kong, and Hong Kong University of Science and Technology have joined the edX OEP. In 2014, Peking University, Fudan University, Shanghai Jiaotong University, National Taiwan University, The Chinese University of Hong Kong, and the Hong Kong University of Science and Technology joined the Coursera platform. In June 2014, Fudan University, Shanghai Jiaotong University and Future Learn signed a memorandum to cooperate in building MOOC in London, according to which they provided quality courses on the platform. On the one hand, China has introduced foreign MOOC, and on the other hand, China is also trying to build a local MOOC OEP. For example, Xuetangx of Tsinghua University signed a cooperation agreement with edX to become the sole authorized partner of edX in China's mainland. Currently, Xuetangx has more than 120 MOOCs offered by universities on edX.

CINIC (2019) released that the number of online education users in China reached 201 million. In 2018, it continued to grow at a rate of 29% compared with that in 2017. ERCIEI (2019) calculated that the market size of China's OEI in 2018 exceeded 300 billion, at a growth rate of 45% comparing with that number in 2017. With the gradual maturity of the OEI and the rationality of venture capitals, it has become increasingly difficult for traditional offline education institutions to transform into online ones and new knowledge sharers who join education institutions quickly to seek growth online. However, the B2B2C OEP provides opportunities and space for development for the above-mentioned two groups.

Since 2018, the investment and financing situation in China's online education market has been booming. Ni (2018), a reporter at Guangzhou Daily, put forward that despite the prospering financing situation of OEP, many online platforms are at a loss. Su (2019) pointed out that the New Oriental Net School, which was listed on the stock exchange 2019, still faces the urgent need to solve the problem of high customer costs, and its net profit was 36.2 million yuan from June to November 2018, a year-on-year increase of -59.9%. The prospects of online education in China are not optimistic.

Although many companies in China's OEI are still losing money, five factors are still giving impetus to China's OEI entering motorway and these five factors are the popularity of the Internet, the continuous growth of the number of Internet users, the development of habits in electronic payment, favorable policies, optimistic views owned by venture capitals, and the continuous growth of demand. ERCIEI (2019) pointed out that the per capita consumption of online education in China is far less than the per capita investment in developed countries, such as Europe and America. Therefore, online education in China is still in the growing stage. With the increase in China's household disposable income, coupled with China's huge population base and the government's encouragement of fertility, China's online education market has an inclusive space for development.

3.3.3   Analysis of Typical China's OEP Enterprises

Torch Center of China Ministry of Science and Technology (2017) pointed out that the concept of "unicorn enterprise" refers to start-ups that have fast development, few counterparts, and are investors' enthusiasm. The threshold is that the company's valuation needs to be larger than 1 billion US dollars after ten years of development. If the valuation exceeds 10 billion US dollars, the company will be called "super unicorn". Since the concept of "unicorn" was put forward, it has quickly gained recognition from many organizations in the global science and technology and investment communities, such as *Wall Street Journal*, *Fortune*, *Tech Crunch*, and *CB Insights*. The Torch Center (2017) also clarified the standards of Chinese unicorn enterprises:

(1) Enterprises registered in China with legal person status.

(2) The establishment time is not more than ten years (established in 2007 and after).

(3) Obtain private equity investment and has not been listed by IPO.

(4) A unicorn needs to meet the conditions of (1) (2) (3) and whose valuation exceeds 1 billion US Dollars.

(5) A super unicorn needs to meet the conditions of (1) (2) (3) and whose valuation exceeds $10 billion.

According to the statistics of the online education "unicorn" by ERCIEI (2019), 11 "unicorns" were born in the OEI in China. CCtalk is a real-time OEP of Hujiang. It provides independent online education tools and platforms for independent knowledge instructors and sharers, providing users (knowledge seekers) with rich content and an online community environment for learning. The meaning of CC is the combination of "content" and "community". It is a B2B2C OEP overlapping with knowledge sharing and online education. There are four major categories of education, language, vocational education. Education for students in kindergarten, primary and middle schools, and art. It covers more than 50 sub-categories, including English, Japanese, Korean, civil service examination, vocation, biology, Olympics, physics, music, overseas study tour, cooking, and IT training. The model of an online live classroom on CCtalk can be used to communicate online with students worldwide. The learning community restrains students from learning alone. CCtalk (2019) claimed that there were more than 30,000 online teachers and thousands of high-quality content and teaching institutions on CCtalk, with a total of 850,000 courses and more than 10 million students. In 2017, the business volume of CCtalk achieved exponential growth. The average growth rate of platform gross merchandise volume exceeded 150% for three consecutive quarters. At the same time, the number of daily active users, the number of users, and the flow of users increased by 8, 10, and 30 times compared with those figures in 2016 (CCtalk, 2019).

Tencent Classroom is a B2B2C OEP owned, controlled, and operated by Tencent. Tencent Classroom is a neutral platform and service provider that provides course publishers with neutral network services such as information storage and links to neutral technical support services for course publishers to publish, operate and promote independently on a neutral platform, and at the same time, the platform can meet the users' demand for learning online and knowledge acquisition. At present, Tencent Classroom has six significant categories on its website, IT Internet, design, and creation, language and studying abroad, vocational certification, higher school education and entrance examination for post-graduation, and interest and daily life. Each category is divided into different segments. After more than four years of hard work and development, Tencent has provided more than 100,000 online education courses to 300 million users.

NetEase Cloud Classroom is an online practical skill learning platform created by NetEase. The platform was officially launched in December, 2012. It provides many high-quality courses for learners. Users can arrange their learning plan and design according to their level. The purpose of NetEase Cloud Classroom is to provide a thoughtful one-stop learning service for every learner who wants to learn practical knowledge and skills. Based on practical requirements, NetEase Cloud Classroom selects various courses and cooperates with several authoritative education and training institutions. The number of courses on this platform has exceeded 10,000, and the total number of course hours has exceeded 100,000, covering more than ten categories, such as practical software, IT and Internet, foreign language learning, living and home, hobbies, workplace skills, financial management, exam certification, primary and secondary schools, parent-child education, etc. In this way, a practical platform has been created for users, covering their life, career, entertainment, and other dimensions. By the end of December, 2017, the number of users on NetEase Cloud Classroom has exceeded 55 million (NetEase, 2018). At present, the paid courses on NetEase Cloud Classroom account for 70% of all their online courses, and there are more than 5,000 lecturers and institutions partnering with the platform (NetEase, 2018).

3.4   Chapter Summary

This chapter describes online education, its business models, and an overview of online education development around the world. This research aims at studying factors influencing online PI, and the B2B2C OEP is a professional e-commerce website, so the B2B2C OEP should also have the characteristics of online education and e-commerce. The chapter first describes online education, then classifies the business model of the OEP, summarizes its characteristics, and depicts its development history and future trends. This chapter reviews the industry background and lays a solid foundation for researching the factors affecting user courses on China's B2B2C OEP.

第4章 研究设计与数据收集

4.1 模型建立

网经社(2019)指出,无学习地点和时间局限并允许学生可以自主地安排学习的时间[6],已成为在线教育的重要优势。因此,本文作者构念出"时空自主性"情景变量,来考察课程学习在时间空间方面的自主性是否会影响用户购买在线教育平台课程的决策。

"购买意愿"为因变量,以反映顾客消费倾向;感知价值、感知有用性、时空自主性、免费试听、感知易用性、用户感知成本、用户感知风险和在线课程口碑8个变量为潜在影响用户购买意愿的解释变量。此外,基于中国B2B2C在线教育平台用户课程购买消费情景的特殊性,本文选取了年龄、教育水平和收入水平作为控制变量来研究其对用户课程购买意愿的影响。

根据以往的研究成果,并基于相关理论,联系特定消费场景,建立了本研究模型,如图 4-1 所示。

4.2 变量构念与研究假设

本研究模型变量由四部分组成,"购买意愿"为因变量;自变量为感知有用性、时空自主性、感知易用性、课程免费试听、感知风险、感知成本等 6 项;模型的中介变量是感知价值;此外,将调节变量定为在线课程口碑。本研究将年龄、教育水平、收入水平列为控制变量。

具体的变量如表 4-1 所示。

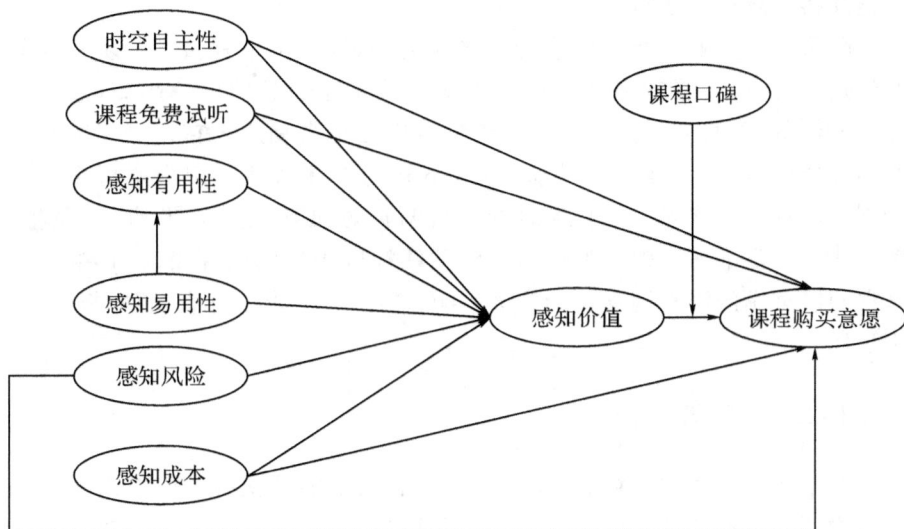

图 4-1　在线教育平台用户课程购买意愿模型

表 4-1　本研究涉及的变量汇总

模块组成	变量
因变量	课程购买意愿
中介变量	感知价值
自变量	感知有用性、时空自主性、感知易用性、课程免费试听、感知风险、感知成本
调节变量	在线课程口碑
控制变量	年龄、教育水平、收入水平

4.2.1　课程购买意愿

　　购买意愿是用户购买相关产品或服务的可能性,是预测用户购买行为的关键性衡量标准(Fishbein,1975;Bagozzi 等,1979;Dodds 等,1991;冯建英等,2006;许亚楠等,2018;林婷婷、曲洪建,2019)[9,11,15,16,18,33]。在本文的研究情景中,B2B2C 在线教育平台用户课程购买意愿是指购买 B2B2C 在线教育平台课程的概率,是本研究模型的核心因变量,其他因素都是通过购买意愿间接影响用户的行为。

购买意愿是购买行为付诸行动之前的决定因素,也是做下一步行动的必经过程,购买意愿越强烈的用户未来购买相应商品的概率越高,反之亦然。Kim 等(2012)通过研究发现,价格和信任是影响用户在线网络购买决策的重要因素[161]。在以往的研究中,不同的消费情境下用户购买意愿会受到不同的因素影响,其中感知价值与购买意愿存在正向影响(王茂彬,2018)[162]。洪菲等(2019)通过对在线问答社区用户的研究发现,影响用户付费问答意愿的潜在因素包括社会影响、任务压力、求知好奇、感知趣味、技术易用[163]。

4.2.2 感知价值

在本研究情境中,感知价值是指消费者处于消费抉择的时候对所选购标的物感知利益部分与感知成本部分开展权衡,若消费者主观感受到的所得更大,说明顾客对所选商品的感知价值为正,也代表了消费者对所选购产品或服务的购买意愿更加强烈(Monroe,1973)[25]。

关于用户感知价值和用户购买意愿两者之间的关系,众多学者在以前的研究中就确认了用户感知价值的正向作用(Zeithaml,1988)[59]。何海英(2015)通过研究得出综合类 B2C 电子商务店铺的在线用户,其用户感知价值会对在线环境下的购买意愿产生显著且正向的作用[164]。庞玉玮(2018)得出用户主观感受到的感知价值部分会对其购买意愿产生潜在的积极作用[23]。洪菲等(2019)发现了网络评论的质量、数量、效价和资信度皆对大学生在网络环境下的购买意愿产生显著且正向的影响[163],指出网络评论可读性和帮助越大,则用户感知到的价值会越高,得出感知价值显著且正向地作用于用户的购买意愿,同时也发现了用户的感知价值部分中介网络评论与网络购买意愿。

基于上述分析,本研究提出如下假设:

假设 1(H1):感知价值对在线课程的购买意愿有积极正向的作用。

4.2.3 在线口碑

在线课程的口碑是用户对相关课程、执教讲师两方面的在线点评信息对潜在消费者购买在线课程决定的影响。同时,在线口碑这一变量被众多研究者认为是会影响潜在用户购买决策的关键点(陈超等,2017;王建军等,2019)[47,68],在线口碑通过传递信息来影响顾客的消费行为。

Park 等(2007)[35]指出网络点评的数量和质量都有可能对消费者的购买意愿产生积极的影响。Lee 和 Youn(2009)[36]提出正面的在线点评对用户选购相关产品和服务拥有正面的影响,而负面信息会有负面的作用。

中国学者在相关研究中也证实,正面的在线口碑对用户的在线消费决策有较为正面的帮助(李佳,2015;储林,2018)[40,165],互联网的负向点评则不利于用户的在线消费意愿(毕继东,2010;张景,2015)[43,44]。王小丽(2017)发现感知价值的 3 个纬度都正向影响用户对模仿品牌的购买意愿[166]。庞玉玮(2018)发现课程的评价与口碑对用户的购买意愿拥有正向的影响[23]。

基于上述分析,本研究提出如下假设:

假设 2(H2):在线课程的口碑对用户感知价值与课程购买意愿的关系有正向调节作用。

4.2.4 感知风险

在本研究情境中,感知风险是指用户购买课程时,由于购买行为在课程使用和学习之前,用户并不能对课程有更全面的了解,且在线教育平台的课程不支持 7 天无理由退货而存在的潜在风险,一方面,由于对课程质量和内容的未知,缺乏对课程具体内容与课程质量的了解可能会给用户带来风险。另一方面,用户出于对具体课程内容的不明确,会担心课程是否能够达到预期的学习效果,从而对所花费的货币成本是否有等价甚至超值的回报存在顾虑。此外,因为教育课程属于不可退货的虚拟产品,加上用户是否能够有充足的时间、精力完成整个课程存在未知,由此可能造成所花费的时间和货币转变为沉默成本。

Bauer(1960)认为感知风险的概念是指顾客决定购买后带来的对未知不确定感[78]。众多学者在研究中也发现了感知风险会对潜在消费者的购买意愿带来负面且消极的作用(季文静,2013;王睿,2013;王英迪,2016)[88,167,168]。王小丽(2017)以感知价值为基础理论,将采用品牌模仿策略的企业列为研究对象,发现感知成本同感知风险都负向作用于潜在消费者的购买意愿[166]。向云峰(2018)得出用户在主观上感到风险的概率越小,其购买机会就越大;反之亦然[169]。崔剑峰(2019)在网络冲动购买意愿研究中把感知风险细分成 5 种,发现感知风险的 5 个纬度对网络冲动购买意愿都为负向影响[55]。

基于上述分析,本研究提出如下假设:

假设 3(H3):用户感知风险对课程购买意愿有负向影响。

假设 4(H4):用户感知风险对感知价值有负向影响。

4.2.5 感知成本

感知成本是指当用户做出最终购买决定时,对在线课程的货币价格和在线学习花费成本的感知。

Zeithaml(1988)指出用户所感受的感知成本是潜在消费者处于购买、学习使用产品时所主观感受的付出[59]。Rabinovich 等(2007)强调了感知成本取决于交易过程中花费的努力程度以及关联的活动[170]。王英迪(2016)认为在 WeChat 使用环境中,产品完善与技术优化有助于用户降低主观感受的成本,提升购买意愿[88]。王晰巍等(2017)基于用户价值接受模型,在研究后得出信息感知成本负向影响感知价值[81]。宋金倩(2018)基于感知价值理论和期望确认理论,探究后验证了感知成本会对感知价值产生负面影响[171]。董庆兴等(2019)从感知收益和感知成本来衡量用户的感知价值,研究得出更好的隐私安全和反馈及时有利于降低感知成本而提升用户的感知价值[172]。

基于上述分析,本研究提出如下假设:

假设 5(H5):用户感知成本对课程购买意愿有负向影响。

假设 6(H6):用户感知成本对感知价值有负向影响。

4.2.6 感知有用性、感知易用性

在本研究情境中,感知有用性是指用户购买在线课程的主观利益判断,感知易用性则指用户对在线教育平台是否易用的感知评估。

Davis(1986)提出的技术接受模型中包含了感知易用性和感知有用性,并用该模型来对用户持续使用信息系统进行解释和预测[105]。刘晓庆(2016)发现感知有用性、感知易用性两个变量都会正向作用于用户在网络教育产品方面的购买意愿[173]。杨秀云等(2017)基于感知价值的视角,以

消费者对网络文化产品的购买意愿为研究对象,也发现了类似的研究结论[174]。方爱华等(2018)在虚拟社区用户知识付费意愿实证研究中发现用户感知有用性正向影响感知价值[69]。李梦吟和王成慧(2019)对社会化媒体促进在线消费行为展开探究,发现感知有用性对潜在用户的购买意愿存在正向作用,感知易用性会对潜在用户的感知有用性存在正向作用,同时也部分证实了感知易用性对网络环境的购买意愿拥有积极作用[56],该结论也与相关 TAM 研究结果类似。

基于上述分析,本研究提出如下假设:

假设 7(H7):感知有用性对感知价值产生积极效果。

假设 8(H8):感知易用性对感知价值产生积极效果。

假设 9(H9):感知易用性对感知有用性产生积极效果。

4.2.7 课程免费试听

在本研究情境中,课程免费试听用于研究其对用户做出消费行为的影响(李雅筝,2016)[10]。蒋晓茜(2018)建议在线培训平台提供课程免费试听的机会,可以获得更多销售机会[175]。在线课程的免费试听也会进一步传导并最终影响到用户的消费决定(高晨璐,2018;许亚楠等,2018)[11,176]。李正峰等(2019)通过研究得出有吸引力的试用信息有助于提升用户的购买意愿[177]。综上所述,提供免费的在线课程试听机会,使用户获得优质的试听体验,可以提高用户付诸购买行为的可能性。

基于上述分析,提出如下假设:

假设 10(H10):课程免费试听对课程购买意愿有正向显著影响。

假设 11(H11):课程免费试听对感知价值有正向显著影响。

4.2.8 时空自主性

在本研究情境中,时空自主性是指在线教育平台给用户提供了一种不受时间、空间局限的使用环境,即可以随时随地学习购买的课程。Lee(2005)在研究后得出移动商务中的无处不在这一特性对提升用户的感知信任拥有积极作用[178]。杨永清等(2012)也发现移动互联网打破时间和空间的便利性对用户的感知价值影响显著[179]。傅颖(2013)认为微博这样的在线平台以其自主性赢得了众多网民的追随[180]。用户在使用移动互联网时,可享受这种自主学习的便利(杨根福,2016;李雅筝,2016)[10,181],可节省时间和精力。玄海燕等(2018)发现 APP 营销中跨时空这一项对青少年购买行为的促进作用较大[182]。腾讯研究院(2019)发布的《2019 中国在线职业教育市场发展报告》中提及自主选择时间、空间给用户带来了巨大的便利[4],用户可以借此充分利用碎片化的时间进行学习,报告中还指出时空自主性是用户选择的关键原因之一。

基于上述分析,本研究提出如下假设:

假设 12(H12):时空自主性对在线课程的购买意愿存在正向的影响。

假设 13(H13):时空自主性对用户的感知价值存在正向的影响。

4.2.9 控制变量与课程购买意愿关系

不同个体对在线教育平台课程购买意愿可能存在差异,本研究也将探讨不同用户属性对在线教育平台课程购买意愿是否存在显著的差异。范琳琳(2015)通过问卷调查和实证分析得出不同年龄阶段、不同教育水平的用户对拥有慈善捐赠行为企业的商品的购买意愿有显著差异[183]。陈芳草(2018)通过对越南消费者在线购买意愿的研究发现,用户收入正向影响购买意愿,而用户年龄负向影响在线购买意愿[184]。腾讯研究院(2019)发布的《2019 中国在线职业教育市场发展报告》中提出高学历的用户对课程的选择有明确的目标和判断能力[4],因此高学历用户对在线职业教育平台产生的价值也更加明显,同时发现年龄大于 40 岁的用户比例明显低于年龄小于 40 岁的用户占比。

基于上述分析,本研究提出如下假设:

假设 14(H14):不同的用户属性对课程购买意愿存在差异。

1)假设 H14a:用户的年龄对课程购买意愿有负向影响。

2)假设 H14b:用户的教育水平对课程购买意愿有正向影响。

3)假设 H14c:用户的收入状况对在线课程的购买意愿存在正向的影响。

综上所述,本文共提出 16 个研究假设,并建构了假设模型,如图 4-2 所示。

本研究所提出的假设汇总如表 4-2 所示。

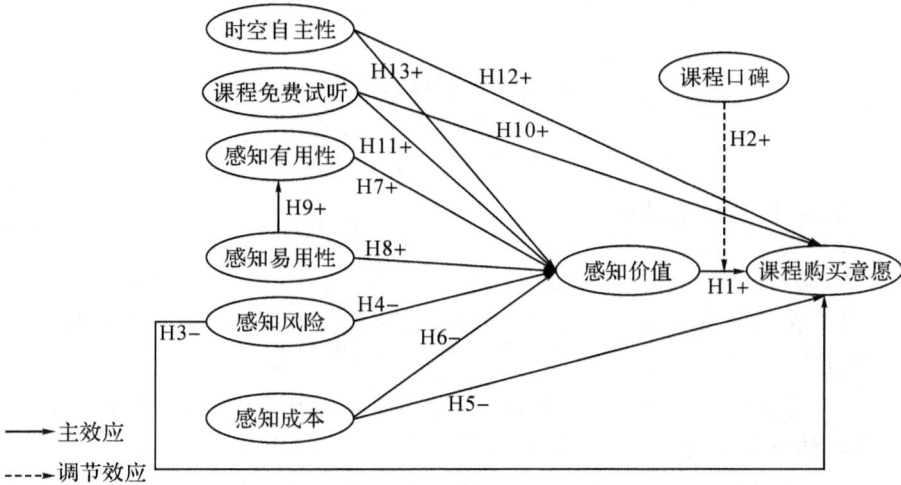

图 4-2　B2B2C 在线教育平台用户课程购买意愿的影响因素研究假设模型

表 4-2　本研究所提出的假设汇总

假设序号	研究假设内容
H1	用户感知价值对课程购买意愿有正向影响。
H2	在线课程的口碑存在正向调节从用户感知价值到课程购买意愿的关系。
H3	用户感知风险对课程购买意愿有负向影响。
H4	用户感知风险对感知价值有负向影响。
H5	用户感知成本对课程购买意愿有负向影响。
H6	用户感知成本对感知价值有负向影响。
H7	感知有用性对感知价值产生积极效果。
H8	感知易用性对感知价值产生积极效果。
H9	感知易用性对感知有用性产生积极效果。
H10	课程免费试听对课程购买意愿有正向显著影响。
H11	课程免费试听对感知价值有正向显著影响。
H12	时空自主性对课程购买意愿有正向影响。
H13	时空自主性对用户的感知价值存在正向的影响。
H14a	用户的年龄对课程购买意愿有负向影响。
H14b	用户的教育水平对课程购买意愿有正向影响。
H14c	用户的收入状况对在线课程的购买意愿存在正向的影响。

4.3　研究设计

4.3.1　问卷设计

本研究问卷的设计步骤如下。

(1)在检索大量相关文献的基础上,整理出与本研究具体研究变量相一致的量表。

(2)考虑到本研究的特殊情境,先开展了小范围的用户访谈,以了解研究环境的真实情况。而后开始相应的问卷设计与优化。

(3)在初步制定问卷后,作者拟邀请经验丰富的在线教育行业从业者、相关研究专家提出改善问卷的相关意见。该研究还邀请少数用户进行正式问卷发放前的预测试,以保证问卷的可靠可信。

(4)考虑到 B2B2C 在线教育平台的特殊研究背景,本次调研活动全程采用网络调查工具来完成。

4.3.2　问卷结构

调查问卷共分三部分。

第一部分为在线教育平台使用情况。包括用户对在线教育平台的使用情况,常用的在线教育平台。

第二部分的内容为受访用户基本特征情况。

第三部分是在线教育平台课程用户购买意愿的因素调查。调查问卷这一部分中的测度项反映了模型的概念变量。

4.4　量表开发与问卷设计

4.4.1　量表开发

本研究结合 B2B2C 在线教育平台课程购买的特殊情境,使用文献检索回顾和内容分析的方法,首先回顾了学者以前的相关研究成果,研制了本书的问卷。

在完成初步测量量表的开发后,作者邀请了五位做过类似实证研究的博士和研究学者,三位从事在线教育公司经营的行业专家,以及五位B2B2C 在线教育平台的用户,建立了一个测量尺度设计专家团队。结合当前设计的测量主题,认真对每个潜在变量的概念、定义和测量指标的范围进行推敲,并讨论了初始尺度的测量内容、措辞和问题描述,通过多轮讨论和总结,根据专家组成员反馈的意见修改了存在歧义的问题,谨慎删除了一些无法有效反映潜在变量构造的项目,形成了最终的测量量表,见表 4-3。调查问卷以李克特七个分级的形式编制,从很不认可到很认可依次给予 1 分到 7 分的值。

表 4-3 B2B2C 在线教育平台用户对课程购买意愿影响因素测量模型及测量题项

潜在变量名称	编号	测量题项	量表参考文献
感知价值 Perceived Value	PV1	与我花费的货币相比,在线课程是值得购买的	Sirdeshmukh 等(2002)
	PV2	相比我付出的时间,购买在线课程是值得的	
	PV3	与我花费的精力相比,在线课程是值得购买的	
	PV4	我认为购买在线课程是具有价值、意义的	
课程口碑 Word of Mouth	WM1	购买在线课程前,我会参考课程的相关评论	Park 等 (2007)、Lee (2009)、钟凯 (2013)
	WM2	在线课程评论区的点评信息比较真实	
	WM3	在线课程评论区的点评信息比较可靠	
	WM4	在线课程评论区的点评信息比较客观	
	WM5	课程的评论会影响我购买付费课程	

续表

潜在变量名称	编号	测量题项	量表参考文献
感知风险 Perceived Risk	PR1	我在购买在线课程时,会担心课程质量无法达到预期	Shim(2001)
	PR2	我在购买在线课程时,会担心课程达不到学习的目的	
	PR3	我在购买在线课程时,会担心自己不能坚持完成课程学习	
	PR4	我在购买在线课程时,会担心售后服务无法保证	
感知成本 Perceived Cost	PC1	我认为在线课程的定价相对较高	Kankanhalli 等(2010)
	PC2	过高的价格是我购买在线课程的障碍	
	PC3	购买在线课程会让我花费更多金钱	
	PC4	在线课程没有缩短我掌握知识的时间或节省我的精力	
感知有用性 Perceived Usefulness	PU1	我认为在线课程能提升学习效率	Davis(1989)、欧阳映泉(2014)
	PU2	我认为在线课程能提高我的学习效果	
	PU3	我认为在线课程能帮助我完成学习目标	
	PU4	我认为在线课程能使我学习变得更轻松	
感知易用性 Perceived Ease of Use	PEU1	我能轻松地通过在线教育平台找到所需的课程	Davis(1989)、季文静(2013)
	PEU2	我能轻松地使用在线教育平台进行课程学习	
	PEU3	我能轻松地联系到在线课程的供应商	
	PEU4	我能轻松地使用在线教育平台的新功能、新版本	
课程免费试听 Course free trial	CFT1	支持免费试听的在线课程能帮助我进行更理智的购买决策	李雅筝(2016)
	CFT2	试听的在线课程若达到我的预期,我的购买意愿会增强	
	CFT3	试听的在线课程老师授课形式能吸引我,我的购买意愿会增强	
	CFT4	在线课程是否支持试听会影响我的购买意愿	

续表

潜在变量名称	编号	测量题项	量表参考文献
时空自主性 Time and space autonomy	TSA1	在线课程学习时,我可以自主决定学习内容	杨根福(2016)
	TSA2	在线课程学习时,我可以自主决定学习进度	
	TSA3	在线课程学习时,我可以自主决定学习时间	
	TSA4	在线课程学习时,我可以自主决定学习地点	
购买意愿 Purchasing Intention	PI1	未来,我会尝试购买在线课程	Kim（2012）、 王茂彬(2018)
	PI2	未来,我会继续购买在线课程	
	PI3	如果在线课程是我需要的,我很愿意购买	
	PI4	我愿意将优质的在线课程推荐给朋友	

4.4.2　问卷设计与预调研

本次调研主要是用在线问卷调研的方式进行,预调研的环节共收集了来自武汉大学、电子科技大学等大学的学生的 70 份答卷,并对不合理和无效的数据进行清洗,最终获得了 63 份合理答卷,本次调查的回收率达到了90%。为了检测是否获得用户一贯性和稳定性的真实反馈,使用了信效度指标来分析回收的样本。

信度分析结果显示,从模型的 37 个项目中提取了 9 个共有因素,其中 $\alpha > 0.75$,说明该问卷信度状况良好。

效度部分通过分析发现各变量的 KMO 值均在 0.7 以上,在进行数据分析环节时,发现课程口碑中测量题项"购买在线课程前,我会参考课程的相关评论"的公因子方差提取值小于 0.7,为保证问卷最终的信度和效度,对因子载荷比较低的问项进行了删除。

此外,本研究对用词和说明做了优化。最终形成了 B2B2C 在线教育平台用户课程购买意愿影响因素调研问卷,详见附录。

4.5　数据收集与整理

4.5.1　样本容量确定

Schumacker 和 Lomax(1996)提出 Structural Equation Model 的研究，其样本数值应该以 200 至 500 为宜[185]。孙晓军和周宗奎(2005)指出用于研究的样本容量应超过潜在观测变量数值的十倍[186]。本研究共包含了 37 个测量题项，考虑问卷数据收集过程中可能存在无效问卷，因此本研究的样本容量目标数量在 370 份。

本研究将没有使用过在线教育平台的受访者视为不符合目标样本要求。因此本研究将在线问卷的第一题设置为筛选题项，没有使用过在线教育平台的受访者会直接结束问卷调查，这样将有效排除不符合条件的受访者，留下符合目标样本要求的问卷数据。

4.5.2　数据收集方法

结合预调研结果对初始问卷调整后，使用问卷星制作了大规模调查的问卷。经过 DC 学院、喜马拉雅 FM、脉脉 APP、在线教育平台用户学习 QQ 群送达在线教育平台的使用者。在 DC 学院用户运营部门的协调帮助下，网络问卷得以通过 DC 学院微信公众号、DC 学院官方通知邮件、站内信、学习用户的微信群等多种渠道同步发布。

DC 学院(https://www.dcxueyuan.com)定位于专业的大数据在线课程学习平台，为鼓励该平台的用户参与调研活动，DC 学院平台的运营者还特地策划了针对本次调研的优惠券奖励，以此号召更多用户参与本次调研。在本次调研活动中针对 DC 学院用户共计发送 7416 次邮件和累计 51697 封站内信邀请。

此次问卷调研从开始投放到回收总共历经 3 个月(2019 年 1 月 24 日—2019 年 4 月 23 日)，累计收到 997 份回复，其中通过微信提交的有 698 份，通过手机端提交(或直接通过链接访问)的有 299 份。在 997 份问卷中，拥有在线教育平台使用经验的用户有 729 位，没有相关平台使用经验的共

268 位。本次问卷调查还对拥有在线教育平台使用经验的用户设置了是否有购买在线教育平台课程的经历进行了询问,729 位用户中有 436 人曾经购买过在线教育平台的课程,293 位未购买过在线课程。

4.5.3 数据整理

在调研结束后,笔者从问卷星平台下载了 997 份样本数据,以方便对数据的进一步处理与分析。由于本次调研的第一个问项就询问了用户是否具有在线教育平台的使用经验,选择没有相关使用经验的用户会直接结束本次调研,有相关使用经验的用户才能继续进行问卷的填写,进一步保证了填写质量。在 997 份问卷中,一共得到了 729 位拥有在线教育平台使用经验的用户的反馈,另外 285 位没有相关平台使用经验的用户则直接提交了问卷。

问卷星平台的问卷收集系统自带只有完成问卷中所有题项才能提交问卷数据的功能,因此 729 份有在线教育平台使用经验的问卷完整反馈均为完整问卷数据,并不存在数据缺少。为保证数据的质量,开展了数据清洗工作。

因为本次调研一般情况下需 3 至 10 分钟才能完成,因此先对回答时间少于 120 秒和部分作答时间明显过长(多于 720 秒)的样本数据,通过问卷星平台的问卷填写时间统计功能筛选出来,共发现 18 份用时较短和较长的答卷,经人工排查,发现其中 15 份并不理想,进行了剔除。随后,通过对数据样本逐一检验,又从剩余的 714 份中去除了 45 份回答完全一致的问卷。从 729 份答卷中清洗出 669 份有效问卷,最终回收的有效率达到了91.77%。

4.6 本章小节

本章为本书的第四部分内容,主要包括了六部分内容。

(1)通过借鉴前人成果,构建了研究模型。用"在线课程的购买意愿"反映用户购买课程的意愿,并设其为因变量,同时包含了 8 个潜在的解释变量。此外,根据中国 B2B2C 在线教育平台消费者购买情景的特点,本研究选取了年龄、教育水平和收入水平作为控制变量来研究其对用户课程购买意愿的影响。

（2）在借鉴前人研究成果的基础上，以中国 B2B2C 在线教育平台为研究情景，研究了相关的变量与概念。

（3）在本研究过程中，笔者制定了调查问卷的编制原则，确定了调查问卷的内容、结构和程序。

（4）在变量测量方面，本研究参照了国内外的成熟量表，结合 B2B2C 在线教育平台课程购买的特殊情境，设计和开发了潜在变量测量的量表。

（5）本研究问卷采用了 Linkert 七级量表形式设计调研问卷，从非常不认同到非常认同分别赋值 1～7 分，而后形成了本研究的预调研问卷。通过本次预调研收到 63 份有效问卷，借助信效度分析和反映的意见优化了相关内容，完成了本研究的正式调研问卷。

（6）根据结构方程模型进行模型假设检验，确定了本次研究所需的样本容量。使用问卷星制作了大规模调查的问卷。经过数据城堡、喜马拉雅FM、脉脉 APP、在线教育平台用户学习 QQ 群将调研问卷送至在线教育平台的使用者。本次问卷调研过程中共收集到 997 份问卷，通过数据清洗删除无效问卷后共获得用于实证分析的 669 份有效数据样本。

Chapter 4   Research Design and Data Collection

4.1   Factors Influencing Users' PI

The construction of the model of factors influencing users' intention to purchase courses on OEP. This study was based on the related theories of PV and PR, taking PU and PC as the consideration factors for the perceived benefits and perceived loss of buying online courses. This research also learned from previous researches results and introduced time and space autonomy (TSA), course free trial (CFT), PEU, and PR as the key factors that directly affect the users' intention in purchasing online courses.

ERCIEI (2019) pointed out that no limitation of the place and time of the study becomes an notable advantage of online education. This advantage breaks the limitation of time and space restrictions, better saving users time and cost, and allowing students to be independent in scheduling their time of the study. Therefore, this research constructed a context variable of TSA to examine whether the autonomy of time and space of the course affects users' decision in purchasing courses on OEP.

"Purchase Intention" in buying an online course is the core dependent variable of the model, which is used to reflect the user's willingness to purchase the course. PV, TSA, FCT, PU, PEU, PR, PC, and WM are eight explanatory variables that potentially affect the willingness of users to purchase courses. In addition, due to the particularity of buying online courses on China B2B2C OEP, this study selects age, education and income level of users as control variables to study their impacts on the user's intention in purchasing online courses.

Therefore, utilizing the PV theory and previous research results, as well as combining the courses consumption scenarios on Chinese B2B2C OEP, he builds a model of users' intention in purchasing courses on OEP with eight factor variables, which is shown in Figure 4-1.

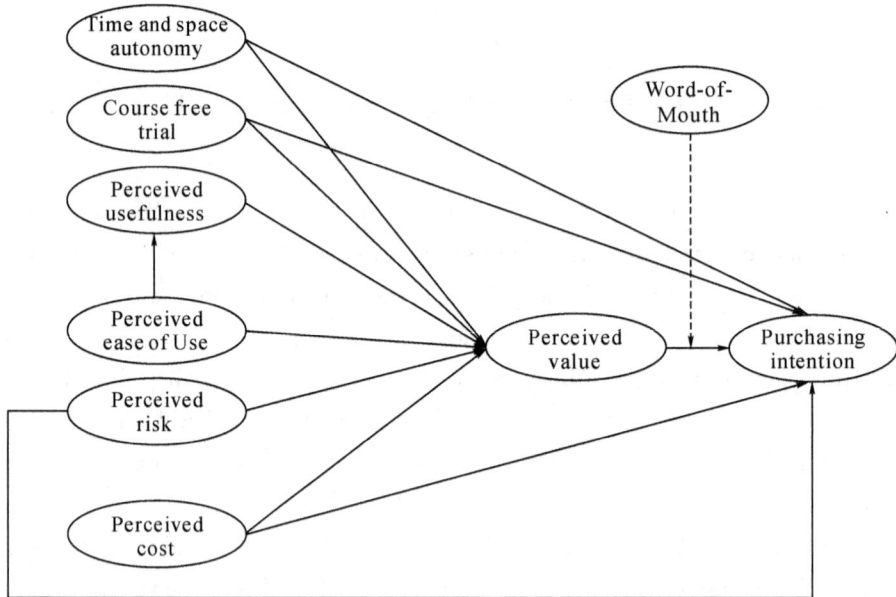

Figure 4-1   The model of PI of users on B2B2C OEP to buy courses

4.2   Variable Constructs and Research Hypotheses

"Purchase Intention" is the dependent variable of this model in which the model variable consists of four parts, including the independent variable, the mediation variable, the dependent variable, and the moderation variable. The independent variables are TSA, CFT, PU,

PEU, PR, and PC; the mediation variable is PV, and the moderation variable is WM. Due to the particularity of the course consumption scenarios on the Chinese B2B2C OEP, this study includes user' characteristics and demographic attributes on Chinese B2B2C OEP as control variables, which are age, education background, and income level of users.

The specific variables are shown in Table 4-1.

Table 4-1   Summary of variables of this research

Type	Variables
Dependent variable	PI
Mediator	PV
Independent variable	TSA, CFT, PU, PEU, PR PC
Moderator	WM
Control variables	Age, education, income

4.2.1   Course PI

"Purchasing Intention" is considered as the decision-making process and refers to the possibility that consumers have purchased or attempted to purchase a product or service (Fishbein & Ajzen, 1975; Bagozzi & Burnkrant, 1979; Dodds, Monroe, & Grewal, 1991; Feng, Mu, & Fu, 2006; Xu, Zhang, & Dong, 2018; Lin & Qu, 2019). In this research, PI of users on B2B2C OEP to buy courses refers to the probability of purchasing the course on B2B2C OEP, which is the core dependent variable of this research model since all other factors indirectly affect the user's behavior through PI.

As the decisive factor before putting purchase behavior into action, PI is the necessary process for the follwing action stop. The stronger the PI is, the higher the probability will be that the user will purchase the corresponding product or service in the future, and vice versa. Through their research Kim, Xu, and Gupta (2012) found that price and trust are signficantly influence users' online purchasing decisions. Previous studies concluded that users' PI in different consumption scenarios was affected by different factors, and most studies confirmed that there was a significant positive correlation between PV and PI (Zeithaml, 1988; Ravald & Grönroos, 1996; Han & Tian, 2005; Feng, Mu, & Fu, 2006; He, 2015; Wang, 2018). PC, PR, perceived trust, and other factors also affects the user's PI. Hong, Zheng, and Zhou (2019) found that users that the potential factors affecting users' intention to pay for answering questioned they have proposed include social impacts, task pressure, curiosity, perceived interest, and ease of technology use through the research on online Q&A community.

4.2.2 PV

In the context of this study, PV refers to the comparison conducted by users between the perceived benefit and PC that the product or the service brings. When the perceived benefit is greater than PC, the customer has positive PV (Monroe, 1973). Positive PV increases consumers' willingness to buy. Similarly, when the benefit perceived by the consumer is greater than PC, the customer will have a willingness to purchase, and the greater the PV is, the higher PI will be.

In terms of the relationship between PV and PI, many researchers have confirmed the positive impacts of PV on consumers' PI in previous studies (Zeithaml, 1988; Grewal, Monroe, & Krishnan, 1998; Wang, 2007; Zhong, 2013). Therefore, when constructing the theoretical model of the factors influencing the PI of courses on the education platform, he regards the user's PV of the paid course as a key factor affecting the user's PI. He (2015) found that the PV of consumers on the comprehensive B2C online shop has a significant and positive impact on their PI. From the research on the relationship between the two dimensions of PV and PI, it could be found that: both the functional value and the emotional value have a significant and positive impacts on the consumers' PI. From the perspective of the level of impacts, the functional value is the priority in consumers' consideration with the emotional value next to it. It can be explained that for cyber consumers, the first purpose of online shopping is to purchase goods, and the second purpose is to enjoy the fun brought by online shopping. Consumers' PI depends on the perception of value. When purchasing goods or services in an online store, the greater PV the customer has, the greater PI the customer will have, and vice versa. It can be illustrated that improving the functional perception of online products or services that the consumers can access increases their PI, and the improvement of emotional perception also increases their PI. Pang (2018) concluded that PV also positively affects the user's willingness to pay. Hong, Zheng, and Zhou (2019) found that the quality, quantity, valence of online reviews, and the credibility of online reviewers have a positive impact on college students' PI, indicating that the quality of online reviews of higher quality delivers greater PV to users. It was also found that the PV significantly and positively affects users' PI, and PV partially mediates the online comment and PI. Therefore, improving both the functional and emotional value of online products and services perceived by consumers is an effective way to enhance consumers' PI.

Based on the analysis above, the hypothesis proposed in this study is as follows:

Hypothesis 1 (H1): PV has positive impacts on PI.

4.2.3 WM

In the context of this study, WM refers to the user's perceptions of the course, the online comments of the instructor, and the impacts of WM on PI. WM regards as an important factor to affect marketing and consumer buying behavior (Huang & Zhu, 2003; Chen, Wu, & Zhang, 2017; Wang, Li, & Wang, 2017). WM delivers relevant information of products and services to the consumer, and it helps other consumers make purchasing decisions.

Park, Lee, and Han (2007) believed that online commentary plays a vital role in affecting consumer decision-making through their empirical research. The quality and quantity of online reviews positively impact consumers' PI. Lee and Youn (2009) argued that positive reviews have positively impact consumer' willingness to recommed and purchase, while negative reviews have a negative impact. During the study of the consumer's reading motivation and the search for online WM on online consumption platform, Hennig-Thurau and Walsh (2003) found that consumers read other consumers' evaluations of relevant products while they shop online, and they help them save time and make better decisions.

Chinese scholars have also confirmed that online WM has a significant impact on consumers' purchasing behavior in relevant researches, and positive online WM of goods or services have positive impacts on customers' PI in the context of online shopping (Bi, 2009; Huang & Lao, 2013; Li, 2015). Negative online WM harms purchasing intention (Bi, 2010; Guo, 2015; Zhang, 2017). Wang (2017) divided the PV into three dimensions, social value, emotional value and functional value in the research of the PI of imitation brand, and it can be found that all the three dimensions of PV positively affect the user's PI of imitation brand. Pang (2018) found that the evaluation and WM of the course has a positive impact on the user's PI. Chu (2018) divided customer PI into three dimensions: social value, emotional value and functional value, and concluded that PI of consumers of the legacy brand is positively affected by PV.

Based on the analysis above, the hypothesis proposed in this study is as follows:

Hypothesis 2 (H2): WM positively moderates the impacts of PV on the PI.

4.2.4 PR

In this study, PR refers to the potential risks that buying the course brings to the consumer. Since the purchasing behavior is prior to learning the course, the potential risks may be caused due to the lack of comprehensive understanding of the course, the absence of the policy of return of goods for no reason within seven days, and the lack of understanding of the content and quality of the course. On the one hand, without fully understanding the quality and content of the course, users may worry that learning the course cannot help them achieve their learning expectation, causing their concern that spending money to buy the course may not be worthy. On the other hand, because the course is usually a non-returnable virtual product, and the user may not have enough time and energy to complete the entire course, users may worry that the time and money they devote the courses can be converted into sunk costs.

Bauer (1960) was the first one to establish the concept of PR, often referring to the subjective judgment of the individual on the risk characteristics and the severity of the risk, which is the uncertainty about the results of the decision-making, and severity of the possibility of making wrong decisions. Ji (2013) argued that perceived benefits, purchase costs and PR are factors directly influencing user's PI, and PR harms the user's PI in the study of consumers' intention to purchase in the context of online consumption. Zhong (2013) took perceived product quality, perceived website service quality, purchase cost, and PR as antecedent variables of online consumers' PV, and this empirical study found that all these four factors have an impact on consumers' PV and PI. Wang (2013) studied factors influencing users' intention in buying APPs at App store, and in the empirical analysis, it is also found that users' PR has a significantly negative impact on PI. Wang (2016) divided PV into functional social and situational values to explore the relationship between PV and use intention. After verification, it is found that both social and situational value positively affect use intention, while PR negatively impacts users' situational value, functional value, and use intention. Wang (2017), based on PV theory, took imitative brands as research object, and found that both PC and PR negatively affect PV, while PC and PR have a negative impact on PI of imitation brands. Xiang (2018) found that users' PI and perceived financial risks, service risks, time risks, social risks, and functional risks have negative impacts, which means that when consumers perceive all more signifiant risks, their PI will be undermined. On the contrary, when consumers perceive milder risks, their PI will be more robust. When researching on online impulsive PI, Cui (2019) divided PR into product risk, financial risk, psychological risk, service risk, and system risk finding that the five dimensions of PR all impose negative impacts on an online impulsive PI.

Based on the analysis above, the hypotheses proposed in this study are as follows:

Hypothesis 3 (H3): PR has negative impacts on PI.

Hypothesis 4 (H4): PR has negative impacts on PV.

4.2.5　PC

In the context of this study, PC refers to the perceptions of the course price of OEP and the cost of online learning when the user of OEP makes the final purchasing decision.

When conducting the PC study, Zeithaml (1988) proposed that perceived loss includes the PC, which refers to things users have to pay and can be perceived when using a product. Dick and Basu (1994) divided the PC, which refers to the cost perceived by the consumers in the payment process mainly into time cost, money cost, and cognitive cost. The time cost refers to the amount of time that the consumer perceives for the payment. The money cost refers to the amount of money that the consumer perceives for the payment. The cognitive cost refers to the amount of cognitive resource that the consumer perceives for the payment. The cognitive cost is mainly due to the unskilled mobile payment operation (accepted by new technology) or the risk during the payment process. Rabinovich, Knemeyer, and Mayer (2007) suggested that PC depends on the efforts spent in the transaction and all transaction-related activities.

Wang (2016), in the research of factors influencing the users' willingness of WeChat payment, found that improving product technology is in favor of reducing PC and increasing PI. Wang, Li, and Wang (2017), based on the user value acceptance model is under the automobile new media environment, the empirical analysis of the questionnaire and the structural equation model shows that the information PC negatively affects the PV. Song (2018) based on the theory of PV and expectation confirmation theory to explore the internal mechanism that affects the continuous use of online knowledge payment by users, and finally found that the hypothesis of PC negatively affects PV is verified. Dong, Zhou, and Mao (2019) measured the PV of users from perceived benefit and PC. The study shows that better privacy security and feedback are timely helps to reduce PC and enhance user's PV.

Based on the analysis above, the hypothesis proposed in this study are as follows:

Hypothesis 5 (H5): PC has negative impacts on PI.

Hypothesis 6 (H6): PC has positive impacts on PV.

4.2.6   PU and PEU

In this study, PU is primarily used to measure the perceived benefit of a user when purchasing a paid course. It refers to the usefulness of the paid courses perceived by users compared to free courses. PEU refers to the perceived assessment of whether the OEP is easy to use.

Davis (1986) proposed the TAM that consists of six variables: external variables, PU, PEU, attitude toward using, behavioral intention to use, and actual use. TAM is mainly used to explain and predict the acceptance of users' continuous use of information systems. Based on the theory of rational behavior, TAM proposes two concepts, PEU and PU. PEU mainly refers to the user's subjective ease of using the information system, and PU mainly refers to the subjective performance improvement of using the information system. At the same time, Davis (1986) believed that PU and PEU could replace "subjective norms", so the model excludes "subjective norms" and its corresponding influencing factors "normative beliefs" and "compliance motivation". Davis (1989) further proposed that whether the user adopts the new system depends on the user's behavioral intention to use that is affected by the attitude toward using that is determined by PEU and PU together. In her research, Liu (2016) discussed the factors affecting the intention to pay for online education, stating that PU and PEU positively affect the user's PI. Yang, Jiang, and Ma (2017) took consumers' intention to purchase online cultural products as the research object based on PV, discovering that users' PU significantly and positively affects PV and PI, and PEU significantly and positively affects users' PV. Fang, Lu, and Liu (2018) found that users' PU positively affects PV in the empirical study of users' intention to pay for knowledge in a virtual community. Li and Wang (2019) studied how social media promote online purchase behavior based on TAM, from which it was found that PU positively affects PI, and PEU positively affects PU. At the same time, the positive impacts of PEU on PI has also been partially confirmed, and this conclusion is similar to the results of TAM-related studies.

Based on the analysis above, the hypothesis proposed in this study are as follows:

Hypothesis 7 (H7): PU has positive impacts on PV.

Hypothesis 8 (H8): PEU has positive impacts on PV.

Hypothesis 9 (H9): PEU has positive impacts on PU.

4.2.7 CFT

In this study, CFT is a new factor variable combined with online education to reflect the user's perceived impacts of the CFT on OEP on their purchasing decisions (Li, 2016). Jiang (2018) suggested that the online training platform provides opportunities for CFT to gain more attention and sales opportunities. Whether the OEP supports course trials and the user's evaluation of the course trial affects the users' trust and purchase decision. (Gao, 2018; Xu, Zhang, & Dong, 2018). Li, Zhang, and Hu (2019) argued that attractive trial information positively impacts the user's intention to purchase. Based on this, this study believes that if the paid course of the OEP supports CFT and the quality of CFT can meet the user's expectations, their PV and PI will be enhanced, and the probability that the course will be purchased may be higher.

Based on the analysis above, the hypothesis proposed in this study are as follows:

Hypothesis 10 (H10): CFT has positive impacts on PI.

Hypothesis 11 (H11): CFT has positive impacts on PV.

4.2.8   TSA

In this research, TSA refers to OEP provides users an environment where the time and space of learning are not restricted, Therefore, the course that can be purchased anytime anywhere. TSA is a unique advantage of the mobile Internet. Lee (2005) also confirmed that the ubiquitous nature of mobile commerce has a positive correlation with consumer perception trust. Yang, Zhang, and Man (2012) also found that mobile Internet breaks time and space restrain. The convenience of the user has a significant impact on their PV. Fu (2013) proposed that the online platform, such as Weibo, has many users due to its autonomy. Users can enjoy the convenience of self-learning when using the mobile Internet (Yang, 2016; Li, 2016), saving their time and effort. Xuan, Dai, and Lin (2018) found that the feature of beyond the limits of time and space have more signficant effect on promoting the purchasing behavior of young people in APP marketing. TRI (2019) mentioned that the independent choice of time and space had brought great convenience to users to make full use of their fragmented time to learn. It was also reported that TSA is an essential factor in choosing an online vocational education platform for course learning (TRI, 2019).

Based on the analysis above, the hypothesis proposed in this study are as follows:

Hypothesis 12 (H12): TSA has positive impacts on PI.

Hypothesis 13 (H13): TSA has positive impacts on PV.

4.2.9   Relationship between Control Variables and PI

In this research model, individuals with different situations have a gulf in their willingness to purchase OEP courses. Therefore, this study also explored whether users with different attributes have significant differences in their intention to purchase OEP courses. Fan (2015) concluded that users of different ages and education levels have significant differences in their intention to donate to charity through questionnaires and empirical analysis. Chen (2018) found that the user's income positively affects their PI while the user's age negatively affects their PI through studying Vietnam users' intention to purchase online. TRI (2019) proposed that highly educated users have clear goals and judgments of course choosing so that high-education users can generate prominent and pronounced value for an online professional education platform. At the same time, it was also proposed that the proportion of users aging over 40 years old is significantly lower than the proportion of users younger than 40 years old.

Based on the analysis above, the hypothesis proposed in this study are as follows:

Hypothesis 14 (H14): Users with different attributes have differences in their intention to purchase courses.

(1) Hypothesis 14 (H14a): Users' age has negative impacts on PI.

(2) Hypothesis 14 (H14b): Users' education has positive impacts on PI.

(3) Hypothesis 14 (H14c): Users' income has positive impacts on PI

In summary, this study proposes sixteen research hypotheses and constructs hypothetical model figures is shown in Figure 4-2.

In order to better verify the scientificity and hypothesis of this research model, a total of sixteen research hypotheses were proposed in this study is shown in Table 4-2.

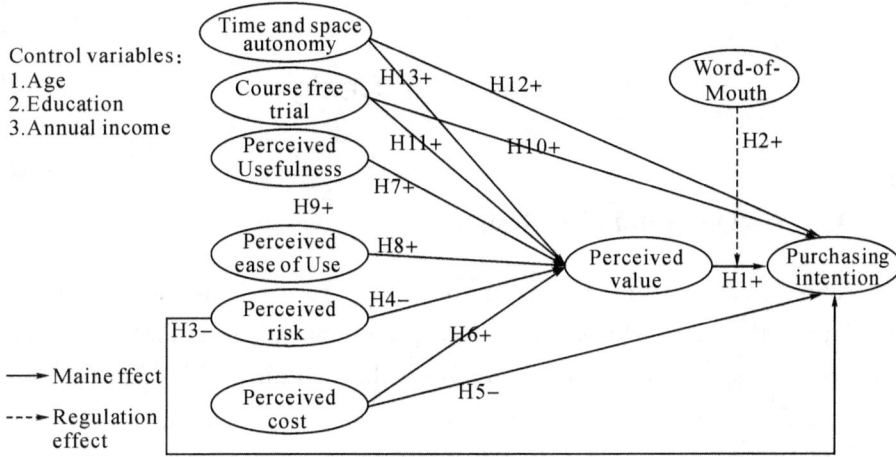

Figure 4-2　The whole mode l of PI of users on B2B2C OEP to buy courses

Table 4-2　Hypotheses summary

Hypothesis No.	Research hypothesis
H1	PV has positive impacts on PI.
H2	WM negatively moderates the impacts of PV on PI.
H3	PR has negative impacts on PI.
H4	PR has negative impacts on PV.
H5	PC has negative impacts on PI.
H6	PC has positive impacts on PV.
H7	PU has positive impacts on PV.
H8	PEU has positive impacts on PV.
H9	PEU has positive impacts on PU.
H10	CFT has positive impacts on PI.
H11	CFT has positive impacts on PV.
H12	TSA have positive impacts on PI.
H13	TSA have positive impacts on PV.
H14a	Users' age has negative impacts on PI.
H14b	Users' education has positive impacts on PI.
H14c	Users' income has positive impacts on PI.

4.3 Research Design

4.3.1 Questionnaire Design

This research study adopts the empirical research method to obtain the data of the interviewees through a questionnaire survey, so as to test the hypothesis model. In order to ensure the reliability and validity of the questionnaires issued, the steps for designing the questionnaire are as follows.

(1) Based on the research questions and research purposes, this study is based on the constructed theoretical model, he extensively read domestic and foreign literature in related fields for scales consistent with the meaning of the conceptual variables involved in this research model. Since scales used in this study are mainly from the English literature which needs to be translated into Chinese at the outset and then translated back into English to avoid tampering with the original meaning measured by original items.

(2) Considering the specific research background of users on OEP, he was the one who first conducted small-scale interviews with some users to understand the uniqueness of the specific research background. The relevant measurement items were adjusted to fit specific research, scenarios based on the matured scales and pre-investigation interviews.

(3) After formulating the initial questionnaire, he invited several experts experienced in online education, scholars in a relevant field, mentors and students to evaluate the measurement items in the questionnaire, so that the problem statement is more in line with academic norms and life practices. The author also invited a small number of interviewees to conduct a formal questionnaire survey before issuing the questionnaire to confirm that the questionnaire has good reliability and effectiveness.

（4）Taking into account the special research background of the B2B2C OEP, this study issued and recycled the formal questionnaires in the form of electronic questionnaires.

4.3.2   Questionnaire Structure

The questionnaire consists of three parts.

The first part is a survey of the basic information of users on OEP. Questions in this section were designed for information, including their frequently used OEPs and the condition of how they used them.

The second part is the characteristics of the essential demographic variables of the interviewees, such as gender, age, education level, monthly income, occupation. Information of this part can reflect the individual and group characteristics of the research object and the control variables of the model more comprehensively and intuitively.

The third part is the investigation of the factors influencing users' intention in purchasing courses on OEP. Measurement items in the part are meant to reflect conceptual variables in the model, such as TSA, CFT, PEU, PU, PR, PC, PV and PI.

4.4   Scale Development and Questionnaire Design

4.4.1   Scale Development

In order to validate the path hypotheses about factors that affect users' intention in purchasing courses on B2B2C OEP, he based on the literature review and previous researches, and considered the situation of buying courses on the B2B2C OEP, as a result of which he decided to adopt the method of literature review and content analysis to design and develop scales for the measurement of latent variables.

The author first reviewed the results of previous researches about factors affecting PI of paid courses on OEP, summarized mature measurement scales related to the latent variables in the theoretical model, and combined the situation of OEP. A mature measurement scale including potential variables containing PV was finally readily accessible.

After completing the development of the preliminary measurement scale, he invited five doctors or scholars who have done similar empirical research, three industry experts engaged in online education companies, moreover, five users with experience with B2B2C OEPs to form an expert team of measurement scale design. The expert team weighed and studied the concept, definition and scope of each potential variable elaborately after several rounds of discussion, and thought over the measurement content, wording and problem description of the initial scale. According to their feedback, the scale was revised to avoid ambiguity in meaning, and some items that could not effectively reflect the construct of latent variables were deleted after careful consideration. As a result, the final measurement scale was finalized, which can be seen in Table 4-3. This questionnaire used the 7-point Linkert scale to conduct the survey that extends from one end of the spectrum, an extremely positive attitude to the other, an extremely negative attitude.

Table 4-3　The models of the factors affecting PI of the course for B2B2BC OEP users and measurement scales

Potential variables	No.	Measurement scales	Reference
Perceived Value	PV1	Purchasing an online course is worthwhile compared to the money I pay.	Sirdeshmukh, Singh and Sabol (2002)
	PV2	Purchasing an online course is worthwhile compared to the time I spend.	
	PV3	Purchasing an online course is worthwhile compared to the energy I spend.	
	PV4	I think purchasing online courses is valuable and meaningful.	

140

Continuation

Potential variables	No.	Measurement scales	Reference
Word-of-Mouth	WM1	I will refer to the relevant comments of the course before purchasing the online course.	Park, Lee, and Han (2007); Lee and Youn (2009); Zhong (2013)
	WM2	The review information of the online course in comment area is more realistic.	
	WM3	The review information of the online course in comment area is more reliable.	
	WM4	The review information of the online course in comment area is more objective.	
	WM5	The review of the course will affect whether I purchase a paid course.	
Perceived Risk	PR1	When I purchase an online course, I will worry that the quality of the course cannot meet expectations.	Shim, Eastlick, and Lotz (2001)
	PR2	When I purchase an online course, I will worry that the course cannot achieve the purpose of learning.	
	PR3	When I purchase an online course, I will worry that I cannot stick to the course.	
	PR4	When I purchase an online course, I will worry that the after-sales service cannot be guaranteed.	
Perceived Cost	PC1	I think the online course is relatively expensive.	Kankanhalli, Tan, and Wei (2005)
	PC2	High price is a barrier to my online course purchase.	
	PC3	Purchasing an online course will cost me more money.	
	PC4	Online courses do not shorten the time and energy of my knowledge learning.	

Continuation

Potential variables	No.	Measurement scales	Reference
Perceived Usefulness	PU1	I think online courses can improve my learning efficiency.	Davis （1989）; Ouyang (2014)
	PU2	I think online courses can improve my learning result.	
	PU3	I think online courses can help me achieve my learning goals.	
	PU4	I think online courses can make my learning easier.	
Perceived Ease of Use	PEU1	I can easily find the courses I need through the OEP.	Davis （1989）; Ji （2013）
	PEU2	I can easily use the OEP for course learning.	
	PEU3	I can easily contact the provider of the online course.	
	PEU4	I can easily use the new features and new versions of the OEP.	
Course Free Trial	CFT1	Online courses that support free trials can help me make more informed purchasing decisions.	Li (2016)
	CFT2	If the free trial of the online course reaches my expectations, my willingness to purchase will increase.	
	CFT3	If the form of teaching can attract me during the free trial, my willingness to purchase will increase.	
	CFT4	Whether the online course supports free trial will affect my willingness to purchase.	

Continuation

Potential variables	No.	Measurement scales	Reference
Time and Space Autonomy	TSA1	When I study online, I can decide the learning content on my own.	Yang (2016)
	TSA2	When I study online, I can decide the learning progress on my own.	
	TSA3	When I study online, I can decide the learning time on my own.	
	TSA4	When I study online, I can decide the learning place on my own.	
Purchasing Intention	PI1	In the future, I will try purchasing a paid course on the OEP.	Kim, Xu, and Gupta (2012); Wang (2018)
	PI2	In the future, I will continue to purchase paid courses on the OEP.	
	PI3	If the online course is what I need, I am willing to purchase it.	
	PI4	I am willing to recommend high quality online courses to friends.	

4.4.2   Questionnaire Design and Pre-investigation

Linkert (1932) improved the original scale and proposed the Likert scale. After designing the measurement index of each latent variable, the 7-point Linkert scale was used to design the questionnaire for each measurement index of the influencing factors of the B2B2C OEP user course PI. The initial survey questionnaire consisted of two parts: (1) the primary purpose of the course and experience of purchasing the course; (2) the 7-point Linkert survey of 37 index items about the 9 potential variables.

The survey was conducted mainly by employing an online questionnaire survey. The pre-investigation section collected 70 questionnaires from Wuhan University, University of Electronic Science and Technology, Zhejiang Vocational College of Business and Technology, and after cleaning unreasonable and invalid data, 63 valid questionnaires were obtained, with an effective recovery rate of 90%. In order to ensure the reliability and validity of the final data measuring the factors affecting users' PI of the OEP, the reliability analysis, and exploratory factor analysis of IBM SPSS V24 was used to verify the reliability of the data after the pre-survey. In order to verify whether the research obtained real feedback on consistency, consistency and stability from users, the Alpha model was used to obtain the cloned Bach coefficient.

The reliability analysis used Cronbach's alpha value as an indicator. It is generally considered that if the total correlation coefficient of an item is less than 0.5 and deleting the item can significantly increase the Cronbach's alpha of the entire scale, it is rational to delete the item. The analysis results showed that 9 common factors were extracted out of the 37 measures items, and the reliability test of the 9 factors is more incredible than 0.75, which indicates that the questionnaire has good reliability.

Validity analysis mainly refers to KMO, exploratory factor analysis, and confirmatory factor analysis. Through analysis, it was found that the KMO values of each variable were above 0.7. When the data analysis was been done, it was found that the common factor variance extraction value of the WM measurement item, "I will refer to the relevant comment of the course before purchasing it," was less than 0.7. In order to ensure the final reliability and validity of the questionnaire, the remove factors with a lower load.

In addition to the reliability and validity, he also revised and improved the wording and description of items based on the feedback, and then formed a questionnaire containing 36 measurement items about factors that impose impacts on PI of courses on the B2B2C OEP, which can be seen in the Appendix.

4.5　Data Collection and Processing

4.5.1　Determination of Sample Capacity

This study used the SEM to test the proposed hypothesis model. Determine sample size, Schumacker and Lomax (1996) suggested that when using SEM to conduct a study samples should be between 200 and 500. Mueller (1997) considered that the mumber of samples for SEM should be over 200. Sun and Zhou (2005) believed that the sample capacity of at least 10 times that of each observed variable. A total of 36 measurement items were included in the study. Considering that there may be invalid questionnaires during the data collection process, the sample size of this study is more than 360.

The main research subjects of this research are the users who have experience in using OEP in China. Respondents who have not used the OEP are considered to be ineligible for the target sample. Therefore, this study sets the first question of the online questionnaire as the screening item. For the respondents who never used the OEP, the questionnaire was directly ended after question one, filtering the ubjects who do not meet the requirements, and selecting out the target topics that meet the questionnaire needs. In this way, enough valid questionnaires can be obtained, laying a scientific foundation for further data analysis. Whether the respondents have experience in using OEP is also considered to ensure the accuracy of the research object.

4.5.2　Methods of Collecting Data

After adjusting the initial questionnaire based on the results from the preliminary survey, he designed the finalized web-based questionnaire on the Questionnaire Star platform. The completed questionnaire is mainly issued to users through QQ learning groups of OEP users, such as DC Academy, Himalayan FM, Maimai APP. With the coordination and assistance of the operation department of DC Academy, the online questionnaire was distributed through various channels such as the WeChat official account of DC Academy, official notification email of DC Academy, station letter of DC Academy, and its users' WeChat groups.

The DC Academy is positioned as the professional big data online learning platform. To encourage users on the platform to participate in the research, the operators of DC Academy have precisely planned and carried out coupons for this survey as rewards in order to attract more users to participate in this survey. In this research, a total of 7,416 emails and a total of 51,697 station letters were sent to invite users in DC Academy.

The question issuing and collection period lasted more than three months (from January 24th, 2019 to April 23rd, 2019). Due to the different rules on each platform, issuing the questionnaire on different platforms was slightly different. There were 997 responses involved, including 698 were submitted via WeChat, and 299 were submitted via mobile (or directly through the link). Among the 997 questionnaires, 729 users have experience using the OEP, and 268 users have no experience using the platform. In this survey, users who have experience in using the OEP have also been asked whether they have purchased courses on the OEP. 436 of 729 users have purchased courses on the OEP, and 293 have not purchased any online course.

4.5.3   Data Cleaning

After the investigation, he downloaded 997 sample data from the Questionnaire Star platform to facilitate further data processing and analysis. Since the first question of the questionnaire asks users whether they have experience in using the OEP, users without relevant experience are not allowed to proceed with the survey at the first question, and users with relevant experience can continue to fill out the questionnaire, so as to further guarantee the quality of the data from questionnaires. In 997 questionnaires, a total of 729 users with experience in using the OEP were received, and 285 users who did not have experience in using the platform automatically submitted the questionnaire right after the first question.

The function of the Questionnaire Star platform mandate that questionnaires are not eligible for submission unless all questions are responded. This function automatically guarantees that the 729 questionnaires done by users with experience in OEP are completed without any missing item. In addition to that, he cleaned the 729 original questionnaire data to exclude non-applicable sample data to ensure that the sample data used for empirical analysis were filled in with high quality.

Since this survey questionnaire contains two parts with a relatively high number of questions, it usually takes 3 to 10 minutes to complete the questionnaire. Therefore, the questionnaires responded with less than 120 seconds and more than 720 seconds were deemed unsatisfactory. Questionnaires filled in with too little time are not taken seriously by users. Therefore, according to the time taken by the preliminary investigation, he cleaned some samples that were completed with are too short time (less than 120 seconds) and those with obviously too long time (more than 720 seconds). With the timing statistics function on the Questionnaire Star platform, 18 questionnaires with short and long answering time were pinpointed and excluded. Then with the manual investigation, it was determined that 15 samples were not filled with high quality and were considered invalid questionnaires to be deleted. Subsequently, to further ensure the validity of the data of other questionnaires, 45 questionnaires without the discrepancy in answering (options are all consistent or homogeneous) were removed from the remaining 714 questionnaires through manual indentification. Finally, after data cleaning, 669 valid data samples for empirical analysis were obtained from 729 respondents, and the sample valid rate of the questionnaire was 91.77%.

4.6　Chapter summary

This chapter is the fourth part of the thesis, which mainly includes the establishment of research models, research hypotheses, questionnaire design, scale development, preliminary investigation, data collection and rearrangement.

(1) Based on the literature research and the determination of variables, this study built the "hypotheses model of factors influencing users' PI" based on PV, PR, and TAM, as shown in Figure 4-2. "Purchase Intention" is the dependent variable of the research model to reflect the user's willingness to purchase the course. PV, TSA, CFT, PU, PEU, PR, PC and WM are eight explanatory variables that potentially affect user's willingness to purchase the course. In addition, according to the characteristics of the Chinese B2B2C OEP, this study selected age, education and income level as control variables to study their impacts on the user's willingness to purchase the course.

(2) Based on previous research results, the Chinese B2B2C OEP is used as the research scenario to study the relevant factors affecting the user's PI on B2B2C OEP in China and the impacts of various factors influencing PV. At the same time, this study also proposed that PV is used as a mediator and the hypothesis that WM plays a moderator role between PV and PI. In order to better verify the scientific nature of the research model, a total of sixteen research hypotheses were proposed in this study, as shown in Table 4-2.

(3) In the process of this study, he developed the principles for the preparation of the questionnaire and determine the content, structure, and procedures of the questionnaire.

(4) In terms of variable measurement, this study has designed and developed a scale for measuring latent variables with the reference to domestic and international maturity scales and under the exceptional

circumstances of B2B2C OEP.

(5) The questionnaire was designed using the Linkert 7-point scale. Extreme disagreement to radical agreement is represented by 1 and 7, respectively, based on which the preliminary investigation of this study was formed. Through this preliminary investigation, 63 valid questionnaires were received. Based on the reliability and validity analysis, the questionnaires were adjusted and optimized according to the feedback, and the formal questionnaire of this study was finally formed.

(6) According to the requirements of using SEM to test the hypothesis, the sample capacity required for this study was determined. This study used the Questionnaire Star platform as the carrier of the final platform to issue questionnaires that were later sent to the users of OEPs through QQ learning groups of the DC Academy, Himalayan FM, Maimai APP. A total of 997 questionnaires were collected during the survey, and 669 valid data samples for empirical analysis were obtained through data cleaning and deletion of invalid questionnaires.

第5章　数据统计与分析

5.1　数据分析方法和工具

近期的一些研究中,结构方程模型获得了长足的发展,许多人文社科类的实证研究文章都采用了这一种建模方法(刘金兰等,2005;李梦莹,2018)[187,188]。偏最小二乘(PLS)分析方法最早由 Wood 和 Albano 于 1983年提出,相比较其他的研究方法而言,PLS 具有的以下优势更利于本研究的开展:

● PLS 对样本数量的要求更少;

● PLS 允许非正态分布的数据内容,十分适合对由李克特量表所采集数据开展的研究,适合本研究采用李克特量表所采集的数据;

● PLS 适合构念较多的复杂型结构方程模型,本研究的模型包含 9 个构念,构念数量相对较多且模型复杂;

● 相比理论测试,PLS 更适合用于理论的发展,本研究的模型进行了理论整合创新,更加适合采用 PLS 进行分析;

● PLS 更加有利于预测,本研究期望为商业的在线教育平台提供模型预测与参考,所以 PLS 分析更加适用。

综合上述分析,本研究将使用 PLS-SEM 技术来开展之后的实证分析(张军,2007;赵耀华,韩之俊,2007;Urbach, Ahlemann, 2010; Ringle, et al.,2012)[189,190,191,192,193],使用软件为 IBM SPSS V24.0 和结构方程模型软件,其版本为 SmartPLS 3.2.8。

5.2　描述性统计分析

5.2.1　人口统计特征相关分析

本研究的调查问卷全部采用网络问卷进行,通过在线教育平台用户聚集的网络社区、社交软件等进行邀约填写完成,关于人口统计分析的内容参考了中国互联网络信息中心(2019)[154]在 2019 年公布的分析报告、百度指数(2019)[194]中 2013 年 07 月 01 日至 2019 年 05 月 03 日且关键词为"在线教育"的人群画像数据。表 5-1 为样本人口统计特征信息汇总表。表 5-2 为样本代表性。

表 5-1　样本人口统计特征信息汇总表

变量名称	类型描述	样本数量	样本百分比
性别	男	329	49.2%
	女	340	50.8%
年龄	18 岁以下	19	2.8%
	19~25 岁	239	35.7%
	26~35 岁	261	39.0%
	36~45 岁	110	16.4%
	46 岁以上	40	6.0%
学历	高中(中专)及以下	27	4.0%
	大学专科	113	16.9%
	大学本科	304	45.4%
	硕士研究生	175	26.2%
	博士研究生	50	7.5%

续表

变量名称	类型描述	样本数量	样本百分比
职业	在校学生	201	30.0%
	企业职员	252	37.7%
	事业单位工作人员	114	17.0%
	公务员	17	2.5%
	社会团体工作人员	3	0.4%
	企业主、个体从业者	55	8.2%
	其他	27	4.0%
年收入	3 万元以下	191	28.6%
	4 万元~10 万元	152	22.7%
	11 万元~20 万元	170	25.4%
	21 万元~30 万元	73	10.9%
	31 万元以上	83	12.4%

表 5-2　样本代表性

性别	整体(中国整体网民情况)		样本	
	单位:万	百分比	单位(个)	百分比
男性	43688.3	52.7%	329	49.2%
女性	39211.7	47.3%	340	50.8%
总计	82900	100%	669	100%

由表 5-1 可知,在性别方面,性别为男的人数是 329 人,性别为女的受访对象是 340 人,男性和女性在整体中占有的百分比各自为 49.2%、50.8%。受访对象中女性的人数略多于男性,但男女性别的占比没有太大的差别。

从报告中的性别内容可以得出:到 2018 年 12 月,当前中国整体因特网用户男女比例为 52.7∶47.3。由此可知我国因特网用户的性别中男性的百分比为 52.7%,女性的百分比为 47.3%。从表 5-2 中可以得出,报告中的性别分布与样本数据的分布基本一致,没有过大的偏差。

在年龄方面,由表 5-1 可知受访对象中 26~35 岁的人群占据绝大多数比例,其人数为 261 人,在总样本中占到的比例为 39.00%;其次是年龄在 19~25 岁之间的受访对象,为 239 人,占比达到了 35.70%,从中可以得出 19~35 岁的受访对象占到了总被调查者的 74.70%,年轻人群成为在线教育平台的主要用户群体。

百度指数的数据显示,在 2013 年 07 月 01 日至 2019 年 05 月 03 日且关键词为"在线教育"的人群画像中,20~29 岁人群占比 17%,30~39 岁年龄段所占比例为 57%,40~49 岁年龄段所占比例为 18%,20~49 岁用户人群占比为九成,与受调查对象大多数人介于 19~45 岁较为一致。受访对象中大多数用户年龄在 19~45 岁之间,与报告中提及的 65.9% 年龄层次居于 20~49 岁的现象一致。本次样本所表现出的年龄特征,与以上报告指出的"中国因特网用户年龄分布以年轻用户为主,并有持续向中高龄人群渗透的迹象"的相关论断相符。

由表 5-1 可知,在学历方面,在调查样本中大学本科人数最多,为 304 人;所占比例最少的为高中(中专)及以下学历,数量仅为 27 人,占到总样本的 4.00%;大学专科人数为 113 人,占到总被调查者的 16.90%;硕士研究生的人数为 175 人,占到总样本的 26.20%;高学历人群中博士研究生人数为 50 人,占到总被调查对象的 7.5%。

从中可知在线教育平台用户中高学历人群所占比例较高。受访用户多为在校学生群体、企事业单位的相关人员,这部分人群使用电脑和移动上网设备较为频繁,理解能力较强,所填写的问卷质量也相对较高。综上所述,本次调查样本中学历分布情况与在线教育平台的使用情景较为符合,具有一定的合理性。

由表 5-1 可知,在职业方面,所占比例最大的为企业职员,人数为 252 人,占到总被调查者的 37.70%;在校学生共计 201 人;事业单位的相关人员合计为 114 人。从职业分布方面进行分析,本次受调查者覆盖的职业面较广泛,分布也相对合理,所填写的网络调查问卷质量也相对较高。

从表 5-1 可知,在年收入方面,年收入在 3 万元以下的受访对象为 191 人,占总样本的 28.60%;年收入在 4 万~10 万元的受访对象为 152 人,占总被调查对象的 22.70%;年收入在 11 万~20 万元的受访对象为 170 人,占总样本的 25.40%。本次受访对象的年收入大多数在 20 万元以下,所占比例超过了 76%,符合职业方面企业职员、在校学生、事业单位人员所占比例较多的分布情况。从年收入分布情况分析,本次调查问卷所获得的数据较为合理,符合在线教育平台用户的收入结构情况。

5.2.2 在线教育平台使用情况描述性统计分析

本研究在网络问卷调查阶段,还对受访对象在线教育平台使用情况的数据进行了收集,包括受访对象使用过哪些在线教育平台、是否购买过在线教育平台的付费课程等。

表 5-3 显示,本研究的受访对象中使用人数最多的在线教育平台为网易云课堂(有道精品课),使用人数达 360 人,占总受调查对象的 53.81%;其次是未列入问卷选项中的其他类在线教育平台,使用人数为 204 人,占到总体样本的 30.49%;再次是腾讯课堂和沪江网校(含 CCtalk),使用的比例占总受访人数的 29.00%和 24.36%。

表 5-3 受调查对象所使用的在线教育平台描述性统计分析

题项	类型描述	样本数量	百分比
您使用过哪些在线教育平台	网易云课堂(有道精品课)	360	53.81%
	沪江网校(含 CCtalk)	163	24.36%
	淘宝教育(淘宝大学)	118	17.63%
	腾讯课堂	194	29.00%
	百度传课	60	8.97%
	YOUKU 学堂(优酷教育频道)	46	6.88%
	YY 教育	32	4.78%
	多贝网	7	1.05%
	淘客网	39	5.83%
	新浪公开课	100	14.95%
	其他	204	30.49%
您是否购买过在线教育平台的付费课程	不打算购买	170	25.41%
	正在打算选购	99	14.80%
	已购买正在学习	228	34.08%
	曾经购买已学完	172	25.71%

题项	类型描述	样本数量	百分比
学习的课程内容	证书获取	180	26.91%
	职业技能	396	59.19%
	专升本、考研课程	59	8.82%
	公务员考试培训	44	6.58%
	英语培训	184	27.50%
	兴趣爱好	341	50.98%
	其他	65	9.72%

相比之下,多元化互联网企业如网易、腾讯、淘宝、新浪所运营的在线教育平台的使用人数相对较多,这与互联网企业自身拥有庞大的用户人群密不可分。但是未列入问卷选项中的其他类在线教育平台的使用比例也占到了总体受访对象的 30.49%,间接说明中国在线教育平台的数量众多,符合当前中国在线教育平台快速发展的情景。

由表 5-3 可知,受访对象中不打算购买的人数为 170 人,占到受访者的比例达 25.41%;正在打算选购 99 人,占到受访者的比例达 14.80%;已购买正在学习为 228 人,占到受访者的比例达 34.08%;曾经购买已学完为 172 人,占到受访者的比例达 25.71%。从中可以得知已经拥有在线教育平台课程购买历史的用户为已购买正在学习和曾经购买已学完两类用户,而不打算购买和正在打算选购则是没有在线教育平台课程购买历史的用户。

从表 5-3 中学习的课程内容显示的情况可知,占总受调查用户比例最高的为职业技能提升的受访对象,人数为 396 人,占总人数比例高达 59.19%;其次是为了个人兴趣和爱好,占总人数比例达 50.98%;英语培训和证书获取的人数分别为 184 人和 180 人,占总人数比例分别为 27.50% 和 26.91%。从表 5-3 可知,职业技能和兴趣爱好的两类相关课程最受用户欢迎,而英语培训和证书获取则较为接近,成为除职业技能和兴趣爱好两类课程外受到用户青睐最多的在线课程类型。

5.2.3　模型变量描述性统计分析

本研究采用 IBM SPSS V24.0 运算每一个测量题项的极小值、极大值、平均值、偏度、峰度和标准差共 6 项内容,其运算的最终结果见表 5-4。

表 5-4 变量测度项描述性统计

变量	题项	N	极小值	极大值	均值	标准差	偏度	峰度
时空自主性	TSA1	669	1	7	5.492	1.308	−0.783	0.326
	TSA2	669	1	7	5.501	1.297	−0.745	0.326
	TSA3	669	1	7	5.658	1.264	−0.867	0.415
	TSA4	669	1	7	5.716	1.269	−0.931	0.475
课程免费试听	CFT1	669	1	7	5.649	1.324	−0.920	0.370
	CFT2	669	1	7	5.713	1.301	−1.195	1.535
	CFT3	669	1	7	5.701	1.255	−0.971	0.725
	CFT4	669	1	7	5.511	1.322	−0.843	0.481
感知有用性	PU1	669	1	7	4.994	1.362	−0.524	0.109
	PU2	669	1	7	4.934	1.324	−0.422	−0.106
	PU3	669	1	7	5.260	1.286	−0.663	0.338
	PU4	669	1	7	4.934	1.335	−0.424	−0.025
感知易用性	PEU1	669	1	7	4.822	1.390	−0.344	−0.202
	PEU2	669	1	7	5.070	1.319	−0.495	0.013
	PEU3	669	1	7	4.451	1.479	−0.256	−0.459
	PEU4	669	1	7	4.857	1.378	−0.388	−0.170
感知风险	PR1	669	1	7	5.326	1.491	−0.779	0.067
	PR2	669	1	7	5.294	1.447	−0.707	0.005
	PR3	669	1	7	5.202	1.597	−0.748	−0.093
	PR4	669	1	7	5.112	1.528	−0.674	−0.075
感知成本	PC1	669	1	7	4.719	1.437	−0.359	−0.074
	PC2	669	1	7	4.398	1.508	−0.175	−0.337
	PC3	669	1	7	4.274	1.528	−0.149	−0.572
	PC4	669	1	7	4.344	1.609	−0.217	−0.611

变量	题项	N	极小值	极大值	均值	标准差	偏度	峰度
感知价值	PV1	669	1	7	5.076	1.446	−0.661	0.150
	PV2	669	1	7	5.123	1.464	−0.652	−0.023
	PV3	669	1	7	5.138	1.432	−0.749	0.301
	PV4	669	1	7	5.139	1.424	−0.740	0.430
课程口碑	WM1	669	1	7	5.381	1.483	−0.847	0.205
	WM2	669	1	7	4.688	1.329	−0.242	−0.153
	WM3	669	1	7	4.710	1.322	−0.274	−0.121
	WM4	669	1	7	4.641	1.305	−0.254	−0.060
购买意愿	PI1	669	1	7	5.350	1.505	−0.977	0.619
	PI2	669	1	7	5.184	1.475	−0.733	0.250
	PI3	669	1	7	5.572	1.397	−1.025	0.710
	PI4	669	1	7	5.432	1.438	−0.882	0.435

有效的 N（列表状态）：669

由表 5-4 可知，本研究的模型中包含的变量有用户感知价值、在线课程口碑、用户感知风险、课程免费试听、用户感知成本、时空自主性、感知有用性、用户感知易用性和购买意愿，各个变量中所包含的测量题项数量为 4 个，满足 IBM SPSS 软件统计分析的要求。

如表 5-4 所示，所有涉及变量的测量题项峰度的绝对值都小于 8 且偏度绝对值都小于临界值 3，该结果显示本次样本符合正态分布要求，适合本研究即将采用的结构方程模型（SEM，Structural Equation Model）进行后续数据分析。表 5-5 为变量描述性统计。

表 5-5　变量描述性统计

变量	变量代码	N	均值	标准差
时空自主性	TSA	669	5.592	1.115
课程免费试听	CFT	669	5.643	1.062
感知有用性	PU	669	5.031	1.132
感知易用性	PEU	669	4.800	1.166

续表

变量	变量代码	N	均值	标准差
感知风险	PR	669	5.234	1.266
感知成本	PC	669	4.433	1.255
感知价值	PV	669	5.119	1.180
课程口碑	WM	669	4.855	1.176
购买意愿	PI	669	5.385	1.236

有效的 N（列表状态）：66

由表 5-4 和表 5-5 可知，感知价值变量的平均值为 5.119，标准差值为 1.180。感知价值变量中测量题项平均值最高的是测度项 PV4"我认为购买在线课程是具有价值、意义的"，平均值为 5.139；平均值次高的是 PV3"相比我付出的精力，购买在线课程是值得的"，其余的测量题项均在 5.0 及以上，说明在线教育平台用户普遍认为购买在线课程价值较高，感觉是价值较高的在线教育商品。

口碑变量的平均值为 4.855，标准差值为 1.176。其中测量题项平均值最高的是 WM1"购买在线课程前，我会参考课程的相关评论"，平均值为 5.381；其余测量题项的平均值都低于 4.8，说明在线教育平台用户对在线课程的相关口碑普遍感觉一般。

感知风险变量的平均值为 5.234，标准差值为 1.266。其中测量题项平均值最高的是 PR1"我在购买在线课程时，会担心课程质量无法达到预期"，其平均值为 5.326；平均值最小的是 PR4"我在购买在线课程时，会担心售后服务无法保证"，其平均值为 5.112；其他题项的平均值也都超过了 5。以上说明了在线教育平台用户比较担心在线课程不能达到预期的质量，这也是制约在线教育平台用户购买在线课程的重要因素。

感知成本变量的平均值为 4.433，标准差为 1.255。其中测量题项均值最高的是 PC1"我认为在线课程的定价相对较高"，其平均值为 4.719；平均值最小的是 PC3"在线课程没有缩短我掌握知识的时间或节省精力"，其平均值为 4.274；其他题项的平均值也都超过了 4。从整体上看，在线教育平台用户认为在线课程的定价相对较高，从而影响了在线教育平台用户对在线课程的购买意愿。

感知有用性变量的平均值为 5.031，标准差值为 1.132。其中测量题项平均值最高的是 PU3"我认为在线课程能帮我获得更多的知识",其平均值为 5.260;平均值最小的是 PU2"我认为在线课程能提高我的学习效果"和 PU4"我认为在线课程能使我学习变得更轻松",其平均值为 4.934。说明在线教育平台用户普遍认为在线课程能帮助自己获得更多的知识。

感知易用性变量的平均值为 4.800,标准差值为 1.166。其中测量题项平均值最高的是 PEU2"我能轻松地使用在线教育平台进行课程学习",其平均值为 5.070;平均值最小的是 PEU3"我能轻松地联系到在线课程的供应商",其平均值是 4.451。说明在线教育平台用户认为能轻松地使用在线教育平台提供的系统进行在线课程的学习。

课程免费试听变量的平均值为 5.643,标准差值为 1.062。其中测量题项平均值最高的是 CFT2"试听的在线课程若达到我的预期,我的购买意愿会增强",测量题项的平均值都为 5.713;平均值最小的是 CFT4"在线课程是否支持试听会影响我的购买意愿",其平均值是 5.511;其他题项的平均值也都超过了 5.5。表明在线教育平台用户认为课程的免费试听可以提高消费者的购买意愿,并且试听的效果如果达到预期会加强消费者的购买意愿。

时空自主性变量的平均值为 5.592,标准差值为 1.115。其中测量题项平均值最高的是 TSA4"在线课程学习时,我可以自主决定学习地点",其平均值为 5.716;平均值最小的是 TSA1"在线课程学习时,我可以自主决定学习内容",其平均值为 5.492;其他题项的平均值也都超过了 5.4。以上表明在线教育平台用户普遍认为时空自主性对自身学习在线课程有重要影响。

购买意愿变量的平均值为 5.385,标准差值为 1.236。其中测量题项平均值最高的是 PI3"如果在线课程是我需要的,我很愿意购买",其平均值为 5.572;平均值最小的是 PI2"未来,我会继续购买在线教育平台的付费课程",其平均值为 5.184;其余测量题项的平均值也都超过了 5.1。说明在线教育平台用户对购买在线课程的意愿依然较高。

5.3 信度、效度与数据检验

5.3.1 信效度分析

信度采用 α 系数进行判断,Alpha 值越高则说明问卷内各个项目的结果越趋于一致,即表明问卷的信度越高(刘春艳,2016;侯军利,2018)[195,196]。运行 IBM SPSS 软件对 9 个变量的信度进行统计学分析,结果见表 5-6 所示。

表 5-6 变量 Cronbach's Alpha 值汇总

变量	变量代码	项数	Cronbach's Alpha
课程免费试听	CFT	4	0.834
感知成本	PC	4	0.844
感知易用性	PEU	4	0.859
购买意愿	PI	4	0.871
感知风险	PR	4	0.855
感知有用性	PU	4	0.876
感知价值	PV	4	0.836
时空自主性	TSA	4	0.891
课程口碑	WM	4	0.886
整体内部统一性		36	0.861

由表 5-6 可知,整体 α 数值是 0.861,由此可得调研问卷拥有较高的信度水平。其余 9 个变量的 α 值都大于 0.8,表明每个变量都具有良好的可靠性。说明问卷整体具有很好的信度。

在问卷信度水平达标的情况下,为了保证问卷题目的设置能真实有效地反映本次研究变量的含义,获取 KMO 值并进行 Bartlett 球形度测验,如果 KMO 值大于 0.8,则有效性非常高(方艺文,2016)[197]。

从表 5-7 可以看出,KMO 的数值为 0.917,说明效度非常高。在 Bartlett 球形度检验的项目中近似卡方的数值是 12988.833,显著度的数值是 0 并且小于 0.001,则进一步表明本次调研问卷很显著,因此本研究问卷的数据结构具有很好的效度(孟佳佳,2013;刘晓琴,2017)[198,199]。

表 5-7 KMO 值

KMO 取样适切性量数		0.917
Bartlett 球形度检验	近似卡方	12988.833
	自由度	630
	显著性	0

5.3.2 模型信度与效度分析

本研究将使用 SmartPLS 的 PLS Algorithm 与 Bootstrapping 功能来运算出测量模型中的内部一致性系数,并同时得出组合信度情况、收敛效度和区分效度。Bootstrapping 中的数量设置为 669。表 5-8 为因子负荷量和交叉因素负荷量表。表 5-9 为测量模型的运算结果。

表 5-8 因子负荷量和交叉因素负荷量

	CFT	PC	PEU	PI	PR	PU	PV	TSA	WM
CFT1	0.815	−0.109	0.191	0.244	−0.179	0.195	0.199	0.208	0.286
CFT2	0.813	−0.081	0.239	0.270	−0.215	0.240	0.234	0.234	0.241
CFT3	0.834	−0.145	0.206	0.259	−0.209	0.214	0.222	0.186	0.304
CFT4	0.805	−0.052	0.244	0.263	−0.189	0.209	0.191	0.200	0.257
PC1	−0.110	0.826	−0.126	−0.195	0.148	−0.154	−0.342	−0.141	−0.101
PC2	−0.108	0.798	−0.110	−0.152	0.118	−0.136	−0.267	−0.085	−0.097
PC3	−0.094	0.842	−0.117	−0.186	0.138	−0.143	−0.334	−0.146	−0.082
PC4	−0.081	0.831	−0.098	−0.188	0.184	−0.123	−0.311	−0.082	−0.122
PEU1	0.203	−0.110	0.824	0.278	−0.236	0.300	0.309	0.271	0.239
PEU2	0.216	−0.081	0.855	0.300	−0.259	0.276	0.314	0.244	0.191
PEU3	0.236	−0.136	0.832	0.272	−0.248	0.289	0.330	0.210	0.204
PEU4	0.247	−0.129	0.840	0.333	−0.276	0.304	0.362	0.291	0.186
PI1	0.278	−0.202	0.290	0.856	−0.345	0.316	0.491	0.457	0.372
PI2	0.308	−0.202	0.319	0.890	−0.388	0.310	0.496	0.464	0.409
PI3	0.236	−0.164	0.296	0.804	−0.343	0.278	0.484	0.430	0.307
PI4	0.253	−0.178	0.297	0.848	−0.352	0.323	0.451	0.452	0.322
PR1	−0.203	0.164	−0.279	−0.360	0.836	−0.257	−0.431	−0.302	−0.218

续表

	CFT	PC	PEU	PI	PR	PU	PV	TSA	WM
PR2	−0.206	0.124	−0.233	−0.306	0.808	−0.221	−0.383	−0.248	−0.194
PR3	−0.196	0.168	−0.256	−0.382	0.871	−0.280	−0.433	−0.257	−0.206
PR4	−0.209	0.138	−0.246	−0.351	0.823	−0.273	−0.398	−0.261	−0.181
PU1	0.252	−0.134	0.250	0.300	−0.239	0.828	0.426	0.312	0.186
PU2	0.200	−0.127	0.303	0.303	−0.279	0.838	0.463	0.287	0.193
PU3	0.243	−0.164	0.300	0.328	−0.295	0.899	0.476	0.287	0.211
PU4	0.207	−0.151	0.334	0.301	−0.243	0.850	0.447	0.287	0.214
PV1	0.206	−0.318	0.357	0.467	−0.379	0.422	0.831	0.361	0.234
PV2	0.237	−0.286	0.324	0.457	−0.409	0.442	0.823	0.373	0.273
PV3	0.182	−0.329	0.291	0.462	−0.430	0.393	0.798	0.347	0.190
PV4	0.224	−0.319	0.316	0.466	−0.398	0.480	0.821	0.359	0.262
TSA1	0.215	−0.153	0.268	0.488	−0.277	0.311	0.425	0.885	0.267
TSA2	0.240	−0.146	0.263	0.480	−0.303	0.300	0.386	0.887	0.269
TSA3	0.248	−0.098	0.275	0.432	−0.261	0.299	0.353	0.818	0.253
TSA4	0.179	−0.084	0.252	0.438	−0.270	0.279	0.359	0.883	0.216
WM1	0.303	−0.076	0.225	0.353	−0.222	0.184	0.253	0.248	0.894
WM2	0.305	−0.107	0.252	0.406	−0.243	0.236	0.293	0.263	0.902
WM3	0.289	−0.138	0.194	0.334	−0.205	0.201	0.244	0.238	0.862
WM4	0.249	−0.102	0.166	0.338	−0.152	0.191	0.217	0.251	0.794

表 5-9　测量模型的运算结果

潜在变量	题项数	收敛效度		信度	
		AVE	communality	Composite Reliability	Cronbach's Alpha
课程免费试听	4	0.667	0.667	0.889	0.834
感知成本	4	0.680	0.680	0.895	0.844
感知易用性	4	0.702	0.702	0.904	0.859
购买意愿	4	0.722	0.722	0.912	0.871
感知风险	4	0.697	0.697	0.902	0.855
感知有用性	4	0.729	0.729	0.915	0.876
感知价值	4	0.670	0.670	0.890	0.836
时空自主性	4	0.754	0.754	0.925	0.891
课程口碑	4	0.747	0.747	0.922	0.886

由表 5-8 和表 5-9 可以得知:(1)所有因子的因素负荷量都>0.5 且水平较高;(2)9 个潜变量的组合信度值皆大于等于 0.8;(3)各潜变量的 Cronbach's Alpha 系数都>0.7。综合上述分析,认为该模型信度良好(Straub 等,2004;罗红霞,2014;王磊,2017)[200,201,202]。

模型的效度通常采用内容效度、收敛效度和区分效度来衡量。每个测量题项来自或者改编自之前学者发表的成果,大规模调查开始前已经展开过预测试确保了本次调研内容具有有效性,所以认为本研究量表是清晰的和准确的,并具备内容效度。表 5-10 为潜变量间相关系数、AVE 平方根。

表 5-10　潜变量间相关系数、AVE 平方根

	CFT	PC	PEU	PI	PR	PU	PV	TSA	WM
CFT	0.817								
PC	−0.119	0.825							
PEU	0.270	−0.137	0.838						
PI	0.317	−0.220	0.354	0.850					
PR	−0.243	0.179	−0.304	−0.421	0.835				
PU	0.263	−0.169	0.349	0.361	−0.310	0.854			
PV	0.260	−0.383	0.393	0.566	−0.493	0.531	0.818		
TSA	0.254	−0.140	0.304	0.530	−0.320	0.343	0.440	0.868	
WM	0.332	−0.122	0.244	0.416	−0.240	0.236	0.293	0.290	0.864

表 5-9 显示模型的 AVE 数值都>0.6,说明本研究的模型收敛效度表现良好(周驷华,2014;上官彩霞,2015;刘春艳,2016)[196,203,204]。

区分效度可由对应的 AVE 值开平方根同其他变量间相关系数对比进行检验得出(Fornell and Larcker,1981;曾薇,2013;张辉,2012;郁玉兵,2015)[205,206,207,208]。从表 5-10 可知该研究模型每一个潜变量的 AVE 平方根数值均比两者变量的相关系数要大,则模型的区分效度较好。

因子负荷量和交叉因素负荷量表可以用于检验测量模型的内部性和区分性。由表 5-8 可知,每个测量变量与其潜在变量间都有较高的相关系数,潜在变量的所有测量项的因子载荷远比与其他潜变量之间的交叉因子载荷更大,上述结论证明该模型拥有较好的内部一致性,也同时拥有了较好的区分性(姜岩,2013;陈志明,2015;梁乙凯,2017)[209,210,211]。

5.3.3 共同方法偏差检验

本研究的问卷调查全部采用单一的网络问卷调查方式进行,都是通过受访对象自陈式量表(self-report study)方式收集调查样本,这种人为导致的共同方法的偏误存在让分析论断造成较大误差的可能性,甚至误导本研究的最终研究结论(Doty and Glick,1998;杜建政等,2003;周浩、龙立荣,2004;朱海腾、李川云,2019)[212,213,214,215]。根据以往的研究结果,本研究将会从调查程序的控制、研究统计控制这两项来减小由共同方法偏误所带来的误差(Podsakoff and Organ,1986)[216]。

在程序控制方面,实施了以下四个方面的策略以减少共同方法偏差所带来的影响。

第一,在调查过程中,受访用户被告知调研数据将用于学术目的,不会挪作他用。第二,调研问卷采用不记名方式进行回答,不包含隐私类内容。第三,本研究问卷中所有变量都采用多个测量题项进行测量。第四,在前期的深度访谈和预调查的基础上对量表项目进行优化,通过对测量题项相关措辞进行更加清晰准确的描述,从而减少表述的模糊性。

共同方法偏误的统计方法控制运用 Harman 的单因素检测方法[210]。通过 IBM SPSS 内探索性因子的分析功能,将本研究问卷的全部测量题项进行检验后得出,第一因子的方差解释量小于 40% 则判断共同方法偏误影响程度较小(崔瑜,2010;杨明远,2017;邓稳根等;2018)[217,218,219]。所有题项的因子都做提取,得到 8 个其特征值>1,因子数值最高一个方差的解释达 28.18%,没有任何 1 个因素可以解释大多数偏离情况,有理由相信,共同方法上的偏误不会对研究产生重大影响。

5.3.4 多重共线性检验

Hair 等(2016)认为研究模型中的容差低于 0.20 或方差膨胀因子值>5,说明有重大的共线性问题[220]。

通过 SmartPLS 运算得出各变量的 VIF 值都小于 5,因此,认为该模型没有多重共线性。表 5-11 和表 5-12 为模型多重共线性的运算结果。

表 5-11 内部模型的 VIF 值(Inner VIF Values)

	PI	PU	PV
AGE	1.733		
CFT	1.191		1.159
EDUCATION	1.408		
INCOME	1.733		
PC	1.191		1.056
PEU		1.000	1.259
PR	1.389		1.241
PU			1.291
PV	1.758		
TSA	1.333		1.257
WM	1.222		
PV * WM	1.012		

表 5-12 外部模型的 VIF 值(Outer VIF Values)

题项	VIF	题项	VIF	题项	VIF
CFT1	1.864	PI1	2.197	PV1	1.905
CFT2	1.713	PI2	2.633	PV2	1.832
CFT3	1.917	PI3	1.771	PV3	1.686
CFT4	1.744	PI4	2.210	PV4	1.816
PC1	1.782	PR1	1.930	TSA1	2.586
PC2	1.804	PR2	1.830	TSA2	2.648
PC3	1.951	PR3	2.267	TSA3	1.916
PC4	1.911	PR4	1.889	TSA4	2.716
PEU1	1.898	PU1	2.076	WM1	2.956
PEU2	2.210	PU2	1.993	WM2	2.910
PEU3	1.941	PU3	2.857	WM3	2.426
PEU4	1.933	PU4	2.133	WM4	1.736
income	1.000	PV * WM	1.000	age	1.000
				education	1.000

5.4 模型检验分析

5.4.1 结构方程模型验证

本研究采用 SmartPLS 进行模型的构建。根据 Sarstedt 等(2011)关于 samples 数量设置的建议,本研究使用自助方法选择 5000 个重新采样的样本以分析路径系数的显著性[221]。在线教育平台用户课程购买意愿的 PLS 结构方程模型如图 5-1 所示。

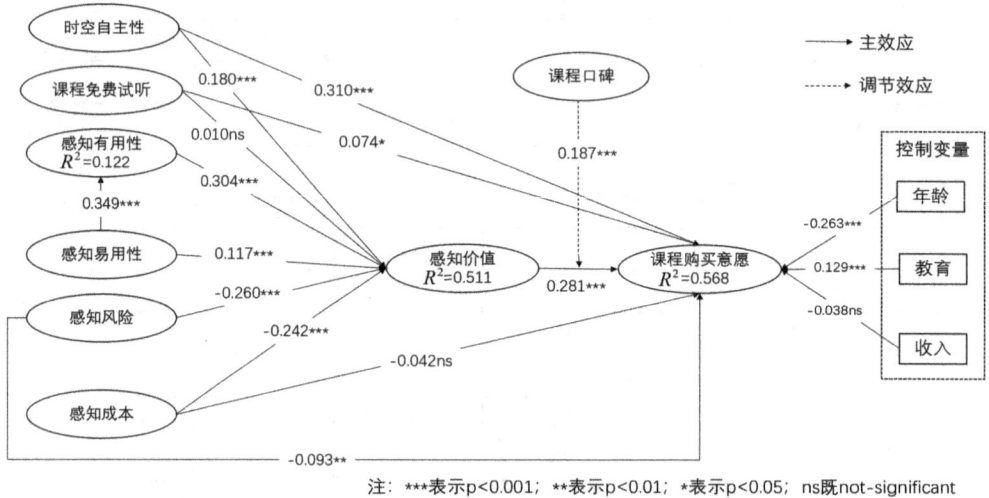

注: ***表示p<0.001; **表示p<0.01; *表示p<0.05; ns既not-significant

图 5-1 在线教育平台用户课程购买意愿的 PLS 结构方程模型

若 T 值大于 1.96 则说明 α 值在 0.05 水平上达到显著,用 * 来示意;当 T 值大于 2.58 时,则表明 α 在 0.01 水平上达到显著,用 * * 来示意;当 T 值大于 3.29 时,α 在 0.001 水平上达到显著,用 * * * 示意(谢佳琳、张晋朝,2014)[222]。

模型最终运算的结果表明,CFT→PV 和 PC→PI 的 T 值都小于 1.96,假设 H5、H11 影响作用并不显著,因此假设 H5 和 H11 并没有成立;在控制变量中 Income→PI 的 T 值未达到显著水平,则表明假设 H14c 不成立。

其余假设 H1、H2、H3、H4、H6、H7、H8、H9、H10、H12、H13、H14a、H14b中,假设 H1、H2、H4、H6、H7、H8、H9、H12、H13、H14a、H14b 已经达到 α 值为 0.001 的显著水平,假设 H3 达到了 α 值为 0.01 的显著水平,而 H10 达到 α 值为 0.05 的显著水平。

假设 H1 中,用户感知价值到课程购买意愿的路径系数为 0.281,T 值为 8.073,P 值为 0,表明 0 水平上的显著,表明用户感知价值显著正向影响课程购买意愿。这表明在线教育平台用户感知价值越大,则用户对在线教育平台课程的购买意愿也会越大。

假设 H2 中,课程口碑调节用户感知价值到在线课程购买意愿的 P 数值是 0,表明 0 水平上的显著,表明课程口碑显著正向调节感知价值对课程购买意愿的影响。假设 H2 的成立说明在线教育平台的课程口碑水平较高的情况下,感知价值越大则用户的购买意愿越强烈,用户的感知价值与用户的购买意愿之间有显著的正向相关作用。

假设 H3 中,用户感知风险到课程购买意愿的路径系数为 -0.093,T 值为 3.145,P 值为 0.002,表明 0.01 水平上的显著,说明用户感知风险对课程购买意愿有显著的负向影响。表明了在线教育平台用户感知风险越大,对课程的购买意愿会越低。

假设 H4 中,用户感知风险到用户感知价值的 P 数值是 0,表明在 0 水平上的显著,说明用户感知风险对感知价值有负向影响。假设 H4 成立说明在线教育平台用户感知风险会显著负向影响用户感知价值。

假设 H5 中,用户感知成本到课程购买意愿的路径系数为 -0.042,T 值为 1.523,P 值为 0.128,表明显著性并未得到验证,这说明用户感知成本对课程购买意愿有负向影响的假设并不成立。假设 H5 未成立说明在线教育平台用户感知成本并不会显著影响购买意愿。

假设 H6 中,用户感知成本到用户感知价值的 P 数值为 0,表明 0 水平上的显著,表明了用户在感知成本方面会显著负向影响感知价值。即说明在线教育平台用户感知成本越高,用户对课程的感知价值越低。

假设 H7 中,用户感知有用性到用户感知价值的 P 数值为 0,表明 0.001水平上的显著,表明用户感知有用性显著正向影响感知价值。即说明在线教育平台用户感知有用性越大,用户的感知价值也会越大。

假设 H8 中,感知易用性到感知价值的 P 数值为 0,表明 0.001 水平上的显著,表明用户感知易用性对感知价值存在显著的正向影响。这说明当在线教育平台用户感知易用性越高时,用户会认为该课程包含的感知价值也越高。

假设 H9 中,从感知易用性到用户感知有用性之间的标准化路径系数大于 0.2,说明影响水平较高,T 值为 10.135,P 值为 0,表明 0.001 水平上的显著,由此说明用户感知易用性对感知有用性具有显著的正向影响。假设 H9 得到支持说明了在线教育平台用户感知易用性越高,用户的感知有用性也会越高。

假设 H10 中,课程免费试听到课程购买意愿的检验结果表明,在线教育平台课程提供免费试听的服务和用户在试听后的体验越好,则用户的课程购买意愿会越强烈。

假设 H11 中,课程免费试听到感知价值的路径系数为 0.010,T 值为 0.335,P 值为 0.738,显著性并未得到证明,这表明课程免费试听对感知价值有正向影响的假设并不成立。由此说明课程提供免费试听的相关服务和用户所获得的试听体验,并不会显著影响用户的感知价值。

假设 H12 中,时空自主性到课程购买意愿的路径系数为 0.310,T 值为 9.756,P 值为 0,表明 0.001 水平上的显著,表明时空自主性显著正向影响课程购买意愿。当在线教育平台用户感知到的时空自主性越强烈,则表现出来的课程购买意愿会更加强烈。

假设 H13 中,时空自主性到感知价值的路径系数为 0.180,T 值为 5.739,P 值为 0,表明 0 水平上的显著,表明时空自主性显著正向影响用户的感知价值。由此说明在线教育平台用户感知到的时空自主性越强烈,则用户的感知价值也会越大。

假设 H14a 中,用户的年龄到课程购买意愿的路径系数为 -0.263,T 值为 7.123,P 值为 0,表明 0 水平上的显著,表明用户的年龄显著负向影响课程购买意愿。即表明在线教育平台用户年龄越大,则表现出来的课程购买意愿越低。

假设 H14b 中,用户的教育水平到课程购买意愿的路径系数为 0.129,T 值为 4.299,P 值为 0,表明 0 水平上的显著,表明用户的教育水平显著正向影响课程购买意愿。这说明在线教育平台用户教育水平越高,用户的购买意愿也会愈加强烈。

假设 H14c 中,用户的收入水平到课程购买意愿的路径系数为 -0.038,T 值为 1.106,P 值为 0.269,说明显著性未得到验证,表明用户的收入水平对课程购买意愿有正向影响的假设并不成立。假设 H14c 未得到证明。

5.4.2 模型适配度检验

R^2 (Coefficient of determination)可以在结构方程模型的框架内测量模型的解释力和模型预测能力的准确性。R^2 值从 0 到 1 不等,其值越高,则表明模型内各变量对因变量的解释能力越强 (Urbach and Ahlemann, 2010)[191]。

Chin(1998)认为 R^2 的取值大于 0.333,则为平均水平以上[223]。从图 5-1 中可知感知价值($R^2 = 0.511$)、购买意愿($R^2 = 0.568$)和感知有用性($R^2 = 0.122$)。该模型总解释力达到 0.568,可知该模型预测效果较好(Straub 等,2004)[200]。

在 PLS-SEM 中,模型整体指标可以检验适配度(Goodness-of-Fitness,GoF)值,表示整个模型的预测效用(Tenenhaus 等,2005)[224]。GoF 值计算方法为平均共性方差与平均 R^2 两者乘积的平方根。若 GoF 值达到 0.36,就表示它的适配程度较好(Wetzels 等,2009;周驷华,2014)[204,225]。

由表 5-9 可知测量模型的共性方差(Communality)的平均数为 0.708,R^2 平均数为 0.401,进行计算后可得出 GoF 值为 0.533,由此得出本研究的整体模型的适配度表现良好。

SRMR 可用作模型适配度的衡量。SRMR 是计算模型的观测相关矩阵与隐含相关矩阵之间的差异,当 SRMR 数值<0.08 时,则表明模型具有良好的拟合性(Hu and Bentler,1998;Hair 等,2016;成升,2017;蔡杨等,2019)[220,226,227,228]。

通过 SmartPLS 运算得出 SRMR 值为 0.035,小于临界值 0.08,进一步说明本研究的整体模型具有良好的适配度,能够较好地解释在线教育平台用户课程购买意愿的影响因素。

5.4.3 模型预测力分析

本研究将使用 Blindfolding 功能来对研究模型的预测力进行分析,采用 Stone-Geisser 的 Cross-validation 方法计算(predictive relevance)Q^2 值来评价模型的预测力(姜岩,2013;Davadas and Lay,2017)[209,229]。Q^2 的计

算公式为 $Q^2 = 1 - SSE/SSO$。如果 $Q^2 < 0$，则表明模型没有预测力；若 $Q^2 > 0$，说明模型具有良好的预测力（Chin,1998；张辉,2012）[206,223]。

通过 SmarPLS 软件的运算得出本研究模型中的三个内生变量即感知价值、感知的有用性和在线课程购买意愿的 Q^2 值依次是 0.321、0.383 和 0.083，都大于 0，由此说明本研究所构建的在线教育平台用户课程购买意愿模型具有良好的预测力。

5.4.4　模型中介效应分析

通过相关中介效应检测方法的文献回顾，根据 Zhao 等（2010）[230] 和 Hair 等（2017）[231] 的建议，本研究最终使用拔靴法开展中介变量效应的检测与分析。

在 SmartPLS 软件中，PLS-SEM algorithm 和 bootstrap 两个功能的运算结果将包含直接效应、总效应和特定的间接效应。根据 Hair 等（2017）的建议，把 bootstrap 的样本数设在 5000[231]，其置信的区间以 95% 水平检测，运算结果如表 5-13 所示。

表 5-13　中介效应分析结果

路径	效应	初始样本 (O)	95% confidence intervals	T 值	显著性	中介类型
CFT→PV→PI	直接效应	0.074	[0.015, 0.129]	2.522	显著	无中介
	总效应	0.077	[0.014, 0.134]	2.511	显著	
	间接效应	0.003	[−0.015, 0.020]	0.333	不显著	
PC→PV→PI	直接效应	−0.042	[−0.094, 0.012]	1.523	不显著	完全中介
	总效应	−0.110	[−0.163, −0.054]	3.923	显著	
	间接效应	−0.068	[−0.094, −0.046]	5.672	显著	
PR→PV→PI	直接效应	−0.093	[−0.153, −0.038]	3.145	显著	部分中介
	总效应	−0.166	[−0.227, −0.111]	5.565	显著	
	间接效应	−0.073	[−0.100, −0.052]	6.118	显著	
TSA→PV→PI	直接效应	0.310	[0.244, 0.370]	9.756	显著	部分中介
	总效应	0.361	[0.300, 0.419]	11.842	显著	
	间接效应	0.051	[0.031, 0.077]	4.466	显著	

路径	效应	初始样本（O）	95% confidence intervals	T 值	显著性	中介类型
PEU→PU→PV	直接效应	0.117	[0.053,0.178]	3.658	显著	部分中介
	总效应	0.224	[0.158,0.285]	5.201	显著	
	间接效应	0.106	[0.079,0.137]	7.182	显著	

在中介效应分析中，(1)如果间接效应不显著，说明未存在中介效应；(2)如果间接效应显著性成立，但是直接效应不显著，表明中介效应为完全中介；(3)如果间接效应显著，并且直接效应也显著，表明中介效应为部分中介（Zhao 等，2010；Hair 等，2017；张亚运，2017；杨爽、郭昭宇，2018)[230,231,232,233]。

由表 5-13 可知，CFT 至 PI 的间接效应为 0.003，置信区间是（-0.015,0.020），包含 0，间接效应不显著；CFT 至 PI 的直接效应为 0.074，置信区间是（0.015,0.129），不包含 0，直接效应显著。因此，PV（感知价值）对 CFT（课程免费试听）与 PI（购买意愿）之间的关系表现为未产生中介效应。

PC 至 PI 的间接效应为-0.068，置信区间是（-0.094,-0.046），不包含 0，间接效应显著；PC 至 PI 的直接为效应-0.042，两者置信的区间是（-0.094,0.012），存在 0，则说明其直接效应并未达到显著。所以，PV（感知价值）对 PC（感知成本）和 PI（购买意愿）之间的关系表现为完全中介效应。

PR 至 PI 的间接效应为-0.073，置信区间是（-0.100,-0.052），不包含 0，间接效应显著；PR 至 PI 的直接效应为-0.093，置信区间是（-0.153,-0.038），不包含 0，直接效应显著。因此，PV（感知价值）对 PR（感知风险）与 PI（购买意愿）之间的关系表现为部分中介效应。

TSA 至 PI 的间接效应为 0.051，置信区间是（0.031,0.077），不包含 0，间接效应显著；TSA 至 PI 的直接效应为 0.310，置信区间是（0.244,0.370），不包含 0，直接效应显著。所以认为 PV（感知价值）对 TSA（时空自主性）与 PI（购买意愿）之间的关系表现为部分中介效应。

PEU 至 PV 的间接效应为 0.106，置信区间是（0.079,0.137），不包含 0，间接效应显著；PEU 至 PV 的直接效应为 0.117，两者的置信区间是

(0.053,0.178),未存在 0,则说明了其直接效应达到了显著。PU 对 PEU（感知易用性）和 PV（感知价值）之间的关系表现为部分中介效应。

综上所述,感知利得方面(感知易用性、时空自主性、感知有用性)与感知利失方面(用户感知风险、用户感知成本)通过用户感知价值这一中介变量作用于在线课程购买意愿,符合之前学者关于感知价值的相关研究成果(Zeithaml,1988；Butz and Goodstein,1996；Parasuraman and Grewal,2000；赵岩,2013；方爱华等,2018)[59,60,64,67,69]。

5.4.5 模型调节作用检验

使用 SmartPLS 建立在线口碑对用户感知价值与在线课程购买意愿关系调节的模型,导入获取的问卷数据,使用 PLS Algorithm 和 Bootstrapping 功能进行分层回归(Hierarchical Regressions)检验(Al-Gahtani 等,2007；周驷华,2014；张梦雪,2018)[204,234,235],调节作用的检验结果如表 5-14 所示。

表 5-14　调节作用的检验结果

假设路径	无调节变量			有调节变量			假设检验结果
	路径系数 β 值	T-value	显著性	路径系数 β 值	T-value	显著性	
PV→PI	0.288	7.899	* * *	0.281	8.703	* * *	
WM→PI				0.186	6.044	* * *	假设成立
PV * WM→PI				0.187	6.961	* * *	
R²	0.509	0.568					
f²		0.066					

注：* * * 表示 $p < 0.001$；* * 表示 $p < 0.01$；* 表示 $p < 0.05$；ns 即 not significant.

如表 5-14 所示,调节作用项 PV * WM 与 PI 的路径系数 β 值为 0.187,证明调节项对在线课程购买意愿具有正向且显著的影响。以在线口碑为参照点时,用户感知价值和在线课程购买意愿两个变量的关系数值为 0.281,但是在在线口碑增加的同时,用户感知价值和在线课程购买意愿两个变量的关系数值会随着调节作用的影响而变为 0.468(0.281+0.187),由此得出当口碑较高时,感知价值对购买意愿的解释力会加强。

以上结论的成立须建立在调节作用达到显著的前提下,表 5-16 的运算结果显示在有调节变量存在的情况下,感知价值与购买意愿的路径系数 β 值为 0.281,T-value 为 8.703；口碑与购买意愿的路径系数 β 值为 0.186,

T-value 为 6.044；调节作用项（WM * PV）与购买意愿的 β 值为 0.187，T-value 为 6.961；T-value＞1.96，证明具有显著性。因此在线课程的口碑评论对用户感知价值和在线课程购买意愿的关系存在显著且正向的调节作用，假设检验结果得到了证明。其对应的简单斜率可见图 5-2。

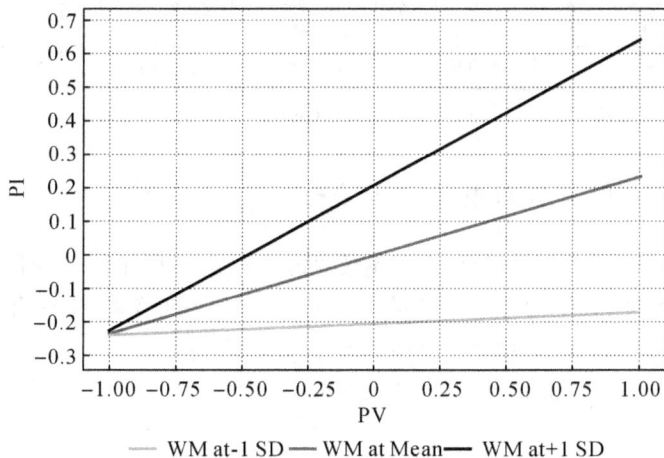

图 5-2　在线口碑调节作用

在加入课程口碑的调节变量后，R^2 的值从 0.509 增加到 0.568，说明购买意愿受到了课程口碑的调节影响（林峥峥，2018）[236]。其中 f^2 这一数值可以解释外因变量对内所产生的作用，在判断标准中：当 $0.02 < f^2 < 0.15$ 为弱的影响（姜岩，2013；Hair 等.2017）[209,231]。由表 5-14 中可知调节效应的 f^2 值为 0.066，表明课程口碑对感知价值和购买意愿的关系具有弱的调节效用。

5.4.6　控制变量影响分析

通过运行 SmartPLS 软件进行计算获取标准化路径系数 β 值和 T-value 来确认教育、年龄、收入这三个控制变量对模型是否具有显著影响（李洪琳，2015；林峥峥，2018）[236,237]。

从表 5-15 可知用户的年龄阶段（$\beta = -0.263$，T=7.123，$p < 0.001$）对课程购买意愿有负向影响的假设成立并具有显著性；用户的教育水平（$\beta = 0.129$，T=4.299，$p < 0.001$）对在线课程购买意愿存在正向并且显著作用

的假设成立；用户的收入水平对课程购买意愿有正向影响的假设不成立。

表 5-15 控制变量影响分析

路径	β 值	T-value	显著	结果
education→PI	0.129	4.299	＊＊＊	成立
age→PI	−0.263	7.123	＊＊＊	成立
income→PI	−0.039	1.106	ns	不成立

注：＊＊＊ $p<0.001$；＊＊ $p<0.01$；＊ $p<0.05$；ns：not-significant。

5.4.7 有调节的中介效应分析

为进一步探讨课程口碑在调节感知价值对购买意愿的中介影响中是否起到了调节效应，将使用 SPSS 的 Process 工具中的模型 14 展开存在调节变量中介效应的检测，拔靴法数量定在 5000（Hayes，2012；Leal-Rodríguez 等，2014；方杰等，2014；陈志明，2015）[238,239,240,241]，运算结果如表 5-16 所示。

表 5-16 具有调节的中介效应检验

中介路径	调节变量	高低组	Effect	Boot SE	Bias Corrected (95%)		Index of moderated mediation		
					LLCI	ULCI	Index	LLCI	ULCI
时空自主性—感知价值—购买意愿	课程口碑	低分组	0.041	0.015	0.015	0.072	0.049	0.032	0.067
		高分组	0.156	0.023	0.112	0.205			
课程免费试听—感知价值—购买意愿	课程口碑	低分组	0.012	0.007	0.001	0.027	0.014	0.001	0.027
		高分组	0.044	0.020	0.005	0.084			
感知成本—感知价值—购买意愿	课程口碑	低分组	−0.036	0.013	−0.063	−0.013	−0.043	−0.059	−0.028
		高分组	−0.137	0.020	−0.178	−0.100			
感知风险—感知价值—购买意愿	课程口碑	低分组	−0.044	0.016	−0.077	−0.016	−0.053	−0.071	−0.036
		高分组	−0.169	0.021	−0.212	−0.129			

由表 5-16 可知，时空自主性—感知价值—购买意愿路径在课程口碑调节效应下，存在调节变量的中介指数在 95% 的置信区间是 [0.032,0.067]，不存在 0，表明课程口碑在不同水平时，感知价值的中介效应存在显著差异。当课程口碑为低分组时，中介效应为 0.041，在 95% 的置信区间是 [0.015,0.072]，不存在 0，也进一步说明中介效应显著；当课程口碑为高分

组时,中介效应是 0.156,在 95％ 置信区间数值是[0.112,0.205],不存在 0,表明了中介效应显著。其中高分组的中介效应 0.156 高于低分组的中介效应 0.041,由此表明中介效应受到了正向的调节。

课程免费试听—感知价值—购买意愿在课程口碑调节效应下,具有调节变量的中介指数在 95％ 的置信区间为[0.001,0.027],未包含 0,表明课程口碑在不同水平时,感知价值的中介效应存在显著差异。当课程口碑为低分组时,中介效应数值是 0.012,在 95％ 的置信区间数值是[0.001,0.027],不存在 0,说明中介效应存在显著;当课程口碑为高分组时,中介效应是 0.044,在 95％ 的置信区间为[0.005,0.084],不包含 0,表明中介效应显著。其中高分组的中介效应 0.044 高于低分组的中介效应 0.012,由此表明中介受到了正向的调节。

感知成本—感知价值—购买意愿在课程口碑调节效应下,具有调节变量的中介指在 95％ 的置信区间为[-0.059,-0.028],未包含 0,表明课程口碑在不同水平时,感知价值的中介效应存在显著差异。当课程口碑为低分组时,中介效应数值是 -0.036,在 95％ 置信区间数值是[-0.063,-0.013],不含 0,说明中介效应显著;当课程口碑为高分组时,中介效应是 -0.137,在 95％ 的置信区间为[-0.178,-0.100],不包含 0,表明了中介效应显著。其中高分组的中介效应 -0.137 低于低分组的中介效应 -0.036,由此表明中介受到了负向的调节。

感知风险—感知价值—购买意愿在课程口碑调节效应下,具有调节变量的中介在 95％ 的置信区间为[-0.071,-0.036],未包含 0,表明课程口碑在不同水平时,感知价值的中介效应存在显著差异。当课程口碑为低分组时,中介效应数值是 -0.044,其 95％ 置信区间数值是[-0.077,-0.016],不含 0,说明中介效应显著;当课程口碑为高分组时,中介效应数值是 -0.169,其 95％ 置信区间数值是[-0.212,-0.129],不存在 0,表明中介效应显著。但是其中低分组的中介效应 -0.044 高于高分组的中介效应 -0.169,由此说明中介受到了负向的调节。

5.5　多群组比较分析

本研究使用 PLS-SEM 中多群组分析方法 MGA（Multi-group

analysis)检验已经具有在线教育课程购买经验的用户与没有购买经验的用户对在线课程购买意愿是否受共同的因素影响(Henseler 等,2009;Sarstedt 等,2011;)[221,242]。通过运行 SmartPLS 软件的多群组分析功能(MGA)后得到的运行结果如表 5-17 所示。

表 5-17　PLS-MGA 运行结果

	路径系数		T 值		显著性	
	bought	not purchased	bought	not purchased	bought	not purchased
AGE→PI	−0.325	−0.173	7.275	3.075	＊＊＊	＊＊
CFT→PI	0.007	0.205	0.174	4.809	ns	＊＊＊
CFT→PV	0.018	0.003	0.424	0.069	ns	ns
EDUCATION→PI	0.065	0.189	1.670	3.967	ns	＊＊＊
INCOME→PI	−0.021	−0.034	0.486	0.683	ns	ns
PC→PI	−0.036	−0.023	1.032	0.474	ns	ns
PC→PV	−0.314	−0.204	8.611	4.584	＊＊＊	＊＊＊
PEU→PU	0.183	0.544	3.768	12.035	＊＊＊	＊＊＊
PEU→PV	0.018	0.270	0.450	5.563	ns	＊＊＊
PR→PI	−0.052	−0.184	1.469	3.472	ns	＊＊＊
PR→PV	−0.172	−0.328	4.180	8.194	＊＊＊	＊＊＊
PU→PV	0.267	0.295	7.057	5.340	＊＊＊	＊＊＊
PV→PI	0.262	0.274	6.340	4.405	＊＊＊	＊＊＊
TSA→PI	0.389	0.197	10.624	3.901	＊＊＊	＊＊＊
TSA→PV	0.248	0.035	6.197	0.748	＊＊＊	ns
WM→PI	0.187	0.179	4.805	3.721	＊＊＊	＊＊＊
调节效应→PI	0.210	0.155	6.879	3.418	＊＊＊	＊＊＊

注:＊＊＊ 为 $p<0.001$;＊＊ 为 $p<0.01$;＊ 为 $p<0.05$;ns 即 not-significant。

表 5-17 显示,课程免费试听($\beta=0.205$,$p<0.001$)显著影响没有在线教育平台课程购买经验的用户的购买意愿,但拥有购买经验用户的课程免费试听($\beta=0.007$,$p>0.8$)并未显著影响其购买意愿,这说明课程免费试听对于没课程购买经验用户的购买意愿具有较大的影响。

无论是否拥有在线教育平台课程购买经验,课程免费试听对用户的感知价值都无显著影响。

拥有在线课程购买经验和没有购买经验的用户,他们的在线课程购买意向都没有被用户的感知成本显著影响。

拥有购买在线课程经验用户的感知成本($\beta=-0.314$,$p<0.001$)对感知价值产生显著影响,未购买过在线课程用户的感知成本($\beta=-0.204$,$p<0.001$)同样显著影响感知价值。

在没有购买在线教育平台课程的用户中,感知易用性($\beta=0.544$,$p<0$)显著且存在正向影响用户的感知有用性;另外,感知易用性($\beta=0.270$,$p<0$)显著影响感知价值。而在拥有购买在线教育平台课程经验的用户中,感知易用性($\beta=0.183$,$p<0$)显著且存在正向影响用户的感知有用性,感知易用性($\beta=0.018$,$p>0.6$)并未显著影响感知价值。因此得出没有在线教育平台课程购买经验的用户比拥有购买经验的用户更加看重在线课程的易用性。

在拥有在线教育平台课程购买经验的用户中,其感知风险($\beta=-0.052$,$p>0.1$)未显著影响购买意愿,感知风险($\beta=-0.172$,$p<0$)显著影响感知价值;在不拥有在线教育平台课程购买经验的用户中,其感知风险($\beta=-0.184$,$p<0$)显著且存在负向影响在线课程的购买意愿,感知风险($\beta=-0.328$,$p<0$)显著影响感知价值。

拥有购买在线课程经验用户的感知有用性($\beta=0.267$,$p<0$)显著影响感知价值,没有购买经验用户的感知有用性($\beta=0.295$,$p<0$)也同样显著影响感知价值。

在路径 PV(感知价值)→PI(购买意愿)上,在拥有在线教育平台课程购买经验的用户和不拥有在线教育平台课程购买经验的用户这 2 个群组中,其感知价值都显著影响购买意愿。

有在线教育平台课程购买经验的课程时空自主性($\beta=0.389$,$p<0$)显著影响用户购买意愿,不拥有购买经验用户的时空自主性($\beta=0.197$,$p<0$)也显著影响其购买意愿。拥有购买经验用户的 TSA→PI 的 T 值比没有购买经验用户的 T 值明显更大,表明了拥有购买经验用户受到时空自主性的影响更大。

拥有购买在线课程经验用户的时空自主性($\beta=0.248$,$p<0$)显著影响感知价值,但是没有购买经验用户的感知价值却未受到时空自主性($\beta=0.035$,$p>0.4$)的显著影响。

拥有购买在线课程经验用户的口碑($\beta=0.187$, $p<0$)显著影响购买意愿,没有购买经验用户的口碑($\beta=0.179$, $p<0$)同样显著影响感知价值。但在潜在消费者拥有购买经验的情况下,在线口碑显著作用于在线课程购买意愿;而没有购买经验的情况下也得到了同样的结果。

在年龄、教育、收入三个控制变量中,两个群组的年龄都呈现出显著影响购买意愿。但教育这一控制变量却在拥有不同购买经验的群组呈现出不同的结果,没有购买在线课程经验用户的教育($\beta=0.189$, $p<0.001$)显著影响购买意愿,但是拥有购买经验用户的购买意愿却未受到教育($\beta=0.065$, $p>0.09$)的显著影响。两个群组的收入这一控制变量都未显著影响购买意愿。

课程口碑这一调节变量在拥有不同购买经验的用户群组中呈现出相同的影响作用。有在线教育平台课程购买经验的课程口碑($\beta=0.210$, $p<0.001$)对感知价值与购买意愿具有显著正向调节作用,不拥有购买经验用户的课程口碑($\beta=-0.155$, $p<0.001$)对用户感知价值到在线课程购买意愿的路径存在正向且显著的调节影响。

5.6 本章小结

本章主要是对已经回收的数据进行统计与分析,以探讨在线教育平台课程用户购买意愿的影响因素,以及各个因素变量之间的路径关系。本章一共包含了五部分内容:数据分析方法与工具选择、描述性分析、信效度检测、假设验证、多群组比较分析。

为了检验本研究所提出的理论模型,选用了 IBM SPSS V24.0 和 SmartPLS 3.2.8 分析软件进行后期的数据分析。针对 669 份来自互联网的调查问卷开展了描述性的相关分析。之后的信度效度分析证明本研究的样本数据具有良好的信度效度,本次数据也不存在共同方法偏误和多重共线性。模型假设检验中显示本模型具有良好的适配度,16 个研究假设中共有 13 个得到了验证。

通过数据分析发现,感知价值、时空自主性、课程免费试听、感知风险成为直接影响购买意愿的关键因素;同时时空自主性、感知有用性、感知易用性、感知成本、感知风险会经用户感知价值而间接地作用于在线课程购买意愿,但是课程免费试听经用户感知价值而间接作用于在线课程购买意愿的假设并未通过检验。控制变量中年龄和教育也直接影响购买意愿,但是收入却并不显著影响购买意愿(假设检验未通过)。另外,本研究还发现课程口碑对感知价值与购买意愿具有显著正向调节作用。因而有理由认为课程口碑也是影响课程购买意愿非常关键的因素之一。

此外,本研究还进行了多群组的深层次分析,在拥有购买经验的用户群组中,时空自主性为感知价值的关键因素并通过假设检验,但是以上假设却没在未有购买经验的用户群组中得到验证。相反在没有购买经验的用户群组中,课程免费试听、感知风险、控制变量教育显著影响购买意愿并通过了假设检验,感知易用性也显著影响感知价值,同样这四个假设在拥有购买经验的用户群组中未得到验证。

Chapter 5   Data Statistics and Analysis

5.1   Data Analysis Methods and Tools

Structural Equation Modeling (SEM), a method based on linear statistical modeling technology, was proposed by Joreskog (1970). SEM has been dramatically developed in recent yrears, and many empirical pieces of research in the humanities and social sciences have adopted this modeling method. This method can be used for related studies of latent variables. Usually, latent variables refer to ones that cannot be accurately measured. In order to measure latent variables, some observable variables are used as "indicators" to measure the latent variables indirectly. The SEM is a multivariate statistical method to measure the relationship between visible and latent variables and the relationship between the latent variable and latent variable. Partial Least Squares (PLS) analysis was first proposed by Wood and Albano in 1983. Compared with other research methods, PLS has the following advantages that are more conducive to this research:

● PLS requires a relatively small sample size.

● PLS allows non-normally distributed data, which is suitable for the research that collects data by the Likert scale, and this study uses the Likert scale for data collection.

● PLS is ideal of relatively complex structural equation models with many constructs. The model of this study contains nine constructs, so the number of constructs is relatively large, and the model is complex.

● Compared with theoretical tests, PLS is more suitable for the development of theory. The model of this study has been innovatively integrated with many theories. Therefore, PLS is more suitable for the analysis of this research.

● PLS is more conducive to prediction. This study expects to provide model predictions and references for commercial OEPs, so PLS analysis is more applicable.

Based on the above analysis, this study used the PLS-SEM method for data analysis. IBM SPSS V24.0 was chosen as the data analysis tool and SmartPLS 3.2.8 was selected as the structural equation modeling software.

5.2　Descriptive Statistical Analysis

5.2.1　Descriptive Statistical Analysis of Demographic Characteristics of Sample Data

The questionnaires obtained in this study were all conducted using online questionnaires. Users were invited to complete the questionnaire via the online community of OEP and social software. CINIC (2019) revealed the data about demographic portrait according to the Baidu Index (2019) from July 1st, 2013 to May 3rd, 2019, with the keyword "online education".

Table 5-1　Demographic information summary of the sample

Variable	Description	Number	Percentage
Name	Male	329	49.2%
	Female	340	50.8%

Continuation

Variable	Description	Number	Percentage
Age	Below 18 years old	19	2.8%
	19~25 years old	239	35.7%
	26~35 years old	261	39.0%
	36~45 years old	110	16.4%
	Above 46 years old	40	6.0%
Education	Below high school (below technical secondary school)	27	4.0%
	Junior college	113	16.9%
Degree	Bachelor	304	45.4%
	Master	175	26.2%
	Doctor	50	7.5%
Job	Students	201	30.0%
	Staff in private sector	252	37.7%
	Staff in state-owned enterprises	114	17.0%
	Civil servants	17	2.5%
	Social organization	3	0.4%
	Business owner and self-employed individual	55	8.2%
	Others	27	4.0%

Variable	Description	Number	Percentage
Annual income	Below 30,000 RMB	191	28.6%
	40,000～100,000 RMB	152	22.7%
	110,000～200,000 RMB	170	25.4%
	210,000～300,000 RMB	73	10.9%
	Above 310,000 RMB	83	12.4%

Table 5-2　　Representativeness of the sample

Gender	Entirety (the overall situation of citizens in China)		Samples	
	Unit: million people	Percentage	Unit: people	Percentage
Male	436.883	52.7%	329	49.2%
Female	392.117	47.3%	340	50.8%
Total	829	100%	669	100%

Note: Figures in the "Entirety" column are from CINIC (2019).

As can be seen from Table 5-1, there were 329 male and 340 female respondents. The proportion of males and females in the total sample was 49.2% and 50.8% respectively. The number of female interviewees was slightly higher than that of male ones, but the proportion of males and females were similar.

The gender structure in CINIC showed that by the end of December 2018, the ratio of men and women Chinese netizens was 52.7 to 47.3. It can be seen that the proportion of males in Chinese netizens was 52.7% and that of women was 47.3%. It can be concluded from Table 5-2 shows that the ratio of male to female netizens in CINIC is roughly the same as than of male to female respondents in the sample without excessive deviation.

In terms of age, Table 5-1 shows that the majority of the respondents (261 respondents) were 26 to 35 years old, accounting for 39.00% of the total sample, followed by ages 19 to 25 (239 respondents), accounting for 35.70%. It can be concluded that the respondents aged 19 to 35 accounted for 74.40% of the total respondents. Young people became the primary users of the OEP, and this is in line with the fact that young people are active on the Internet.

According to the demographic portraits of the Baidu Index (2019) from July 1st, 2013 to May 3rd, in 2019, with the keyword "online education", the proportion of people aged 20 to 29 was 17%, the proportion of people aged 30 to 39 was 57%, the proportion of people aged 40 to 49 was 18%, and the banlance of users aged 20 to 49 was 90%, which is consistent with the fact that the majority of the subjects in this study are ages 19 to 45. Most of the respondents in this study were between 19 to 45 years old, which is consistent with the figure that the age of 65.9% of Internet users was 20 to 49 according to CINIC (2019). The age characteristics of the respondents in this study align with the argumentation in CINIC (2019) that "the age structure of Chinese netizens is mainly youth and the middle-age and there are signs of continuous penetration into middle-aged and high-aged population".

It can be seen from Table 5-1 that in the study, as for education background, the maximum number is undergraduate students (304 respondents), accounting for 45.40% of the total respondents and the lowest number (27 respondents) is high school (secondary school) and below, accounting for 4.00% of the total sample. There are 113 college students, accounting for 16.90% of the total respondents; 175 graduate students, accounting for 25.20%. Among highly educated respondents, the number of those with a doctoral degree is 50, accounting for 7.5% of the total respondents.

It can be seen that the proportion of users with advanced degrees in all OEP users is relatively high. This is due to the way that all the surveys were conducted using online questionnaires. Most of the respondents were students, employees in enterprises and institutions. These groups use computers and mobile Internet devices more frequently, and the quality of questionnaires completed by them is relatively high, thanks to their better understanding. In summary, the distribution of respondents' educational background is consistent with the using scenario of OEPs, so the results have certain rationality.

As can be seen from Table 5-1, in terms of occupation, the most significant proportion is employees in enterprises, and the number is 252, accounting for 37.70% of the total respondents. The number of students is 201, accounting for 30.00% of the total respondents. There are 114 respondents who work in public institutions, accounting for 17.00% of the total respondents. The competency and quality of staffs in private and public sectors, and students are relatively high. They are also reasonably familiar with the survey of online questionnaires, so the online questionnaires filled by them demonstrate relatively high quality. From occupational distribution, the respondents have covered a more comprehensive range of occupations and reasonably distributed.

As shown in Table 5-1, the most significant of respondents with annual income below 30,000 yuan is 191, accounting for 28.60% of the total sample. The number of respondents with annual revenue from 400, 000 to 100,000 yuan is 152, accounting for 22.70% of the total sample. 170 respondents have a year income from 120,000 to 200,000 yuan, accounting for 25.40% of the total sample. The annual income of the majority of the respondents is under 200,000 yuan, accounting for more than 76% of the total, which is in line with the distribution that the proportion of staffs in enterprises and public institutions, as well as students is relatively high. From the analysis of the annual income distribution, the data obtained in this questionnaire is fairly reasonable, in line with the income structure of users of OEPs.

5.2.2　Descriptive Statistical Analysis of the Use of OEPs

When issuing questionnaire online, this study also collected data on OEP used by the respondents, including OEPs which were used by the respondents, and whether they purchased paid courses on OEP.

Table 5-3 shows that the platform used by the most respondents (360 people) in this study is "NetEase Cloud Classroom (Youdao)", accounting for 53.81% of the total respondents; followed by "others education platforms not listed in the options" that have been used by 204 people, accounting for 30.49% of the total respondents. Tencent Classroom and Hujiang Network School (including CCtalk) rank the 3rd and the 4th, accounting for 29.00% and 24.36% of the total number of respondents respectively.

Table 5-3　Descriptive Statistical Analysis of OEPs Used by respondents

Item	Description	Number of observations	Percentage
What OEPs have you used?	NetEase Cloud Classroom (Youdao)	360	53.81%
	Hujiang Network School (including CCtalk)	163	24.36%
	Taobao Education (Taobao University)	118	17.63%
	Tencent Classroom	194	29.00%
	Baidu Chuanke	60	8.97%
	YOUKU Classroom (YOUKU education channel)	46	6.88%
	YY Education	32	4.78%
	Duobei.com	7	1.05%
	Taboke.com	39	5.83%
	Sina open class	100	14.95%
	Others	204	30.49%

Item	Description	Number of observations	Percentage
Have you ever bought any paid courses on OEP?	Not intend to buy.	170	25.41%
	I am choosing.	99	14.80%
	Yes and I am studying now.	228	34.08%
	Yes and I finished learning.	172	25.71%
The content of what you learned.	Certificates	180	26.91%
	Vocational skills	396	59.19%
	Top-up and postgraduate exam courses	59	8.82%
	Civil servant exam training	44	6.58%
	English training	184	27.50%
	Hobbies	341	50.98%
	Others	65	9.72%

By comparison, the number of users of OEPs operated by diversified Internet companies such as NetEase, Tencent, Taobao, and Sina is relatively high, which is inseparable from the large user base in these diversified Internet companies. However, the proportion of choosing the "other OEPs not listed in the questionnaire" option also accounts for 30.49% of the total respondents. It indirectly indicates that the number of OEPs in China is enormous, which is in line with the fact that OEPs are surging in China.

As shown from Table 5-3, the number of respondents who are not planning to purchase is 170, accounting for 25.41% of the respondents. 99 people are planning to purchase, accounting for 14.80% of the respondents. 228 people have bought courses and are learning, accounting for 34.08%. 172 once bought online courses and completed their learning, accounting for 25.71% of the respondents. It can be seen that the users with experience purchase courses on OEP consist of those who already have bought courses and are learning and those who once bought online courses and completed their learning. Users with experiences in buying courses on OEP consist of those who do not intend to buy and those who are selecting courses to purchase.

According to the situation of "the content of what you learned" in Table 5-3, the number of respondents who account for the highest proportion is "vocational skills", at 396, accounting for 59. 19% of the total number. The second largest proportion is for hobbies and personal interest, which number is 341, accounting for 50. 98% of the total number. The third largest proportion is for English training and certificates, which total 184 and 180 respectively, accounting for 27. 50% and 26. 91% respectively. As can be seen from Table 5-3, courses related to vocational skills and hobbies are the most popular courses among users, At the same time, English training and certificate acquisition enjoy a similar level of popularity, only next to vocational skills and hobbies.

5. 2. 3 Descriptive Statistical Analysis of Variables in the Model

In this study, the minimum, maximum, average, skewness, kurtosis, and standard deviation of each variable and specific item were calculated using, IBM SPSS 24. 0. The calculation results are shown in Table 5-4.

Table 5-4   Descriptive statistics of variable measure items

Variable	Item	N	Mini	Max	Avg	SD	Skewness	Kurtosis
TSA	TSA1	669	1	7	5. 492	1. 308	−0. 783	0. 326
	TSA2	669	1	7	5. 501	1. 297	−0. 745	0. 326
	TSA3	669	1	7	5. 658	1. 264	−0. 867	0. 415
	TSA4	669	1	7	5. 716	1. 269	−0. 931	0. 475

Continuation

Variable	Item	N	Mini	Max	Avg	SD	Skewness	Kurtosis
CFT	CFT1	669	1	7	5.649	1.324	−0.920	0.370
	CFT2	669	1	7	5.713	1.301	−1.195	1.535
	CFT3	669	1	7	5.701	1.255	−0.971	0.725
	CFT4	669	1	7	5.511	1.322	−0.843	0.481
PU	PU1	669	1	7	4.994	1.362	−0.524	0.109
	PU2	669	1	7	4.934	1.324	−0.422	−0.106
	PU3	669	1	7	5.260	1.286	−0.663	0.338
	PU4	669	1	7	4.934	1.335	−0.424	−0.025
PEU	PEU1	669	1	7	4.822	1.390	−0.344	−0.202
	PEU2	669	1	7	5.070	1.319	−0.495	0.013
	PEU3	669	1	7	4.451	1.479	−0.256	−0.459
	PEU4	669	1	7	4.857	1.378	−0.388	−0.170
PR	PR1	669	1	7	5.326	1.491	−0.779	0.067
	PR2	669	1	7	5.294	1.447	−0.707	0.005
	PR3	669	1	7	5.202	1.597	−0.748	−0.093
	PR4	669	1	7	5.112	1.528	−0.674	−0.075
PC	PC1	669	1	7	4.719	1.437	−0.359	−0.074
	PC2	669	1	7	4.398	1.508	−0.175	−0.337
	PC3	669	1	7	4.274	1.528	−0.149	−0.572
	PC4	669	1	7	4.344	1.609	−0.217	−0.611
PV	PV1	669	1	7	5.076	1.446	−0.661	0.150
	PV2	669	1	7	5.123	1.464	−0.652	−0.023
	PV3	669	1	7	5.138	1.432	−0.749	0.301
	PV4	669	1	7	5.139	1.424	−0.740	0.430

Continuation

Variable	Item	N	Mini	Max	Avg	SD	Skewness	Kurtosis
WM	WM1	669	1	7	5.381	1.483	−0.847	0.205
	WM2	669	1	7	4.688	1.329	−0.242	−0.153
	WM3	669	1	7	4.710	1.322	−0.274	−0.121
	WM4	669	1	7	4.641	1.305	−0.254	−0.060
PI	PI1	669	1	7	5.350	1.505	−0.977	0.619
	PI2	669	1	7	5.184	1.475	−0.733	0.250
	PI3	669	1	7	5.572	1.397	−1.025	0.710
	PI4	669	1	7	5.432	1.438	−0.882	0.435

effective N (status list): 669

As can be seen from Table 5-4, the variables included in the model of this study are PV, WM, PR, PC, PU, PEU, CFT, TSA, and PI. The number of items for each variable is 4, which meets the requirements of statistical analysis of IBM SPSS.

As shown in Table 5-4, the absolute value of the kurtosis of all the items is less than 8 and the absolute value of the skewness of all the items is less than 3. The results indicate that the sample data obtained in this study have met the requirements of normal distribution (Chen, 2017), and they are also suitable for the subsequent data analysis by SEM used in this study.

Table 5-5　Descriptive statistics of variables

Variables	N	Average	SD
TSA	669	5.592	1.115
CFT	669	5.643	1.062
PU	669	5.031	1.132
PEU	669	4.800	1.166
PR	669	5.234	1.266
PC	669	4.433	1.255

Continuation

Variables	N	Average	SD
PV	669	5. 119	1. 180
WM	669	4. 855	1. 176
PI	669	5. 385	1. 236

effective N (status list):66

As shown in Table 5-4 and Table 5-5, the average value of the PV variables is 5. 119, and the standard deviation is 1. 180. The item PV4 that is "I think that buying online course is valuable and meaningful" has the highest average that is 5. 139. The item PV3 that is "I think that buying online course is worthy compared with what I have paid out" has the second highest average value. The average value of the other items is all at 5. 0 or above, indicating that users of OEPs generally believe that the value of online courses is relatively high, and they are perceived as online education products remaining relatively high value.

The average value of the WM variables is 4. 855 and the standard deviation is 1. 176. The item WM1 is "before purchasing online courses, I will refer to the relevant comments of the course" has the highest average value, at 5. 381. The average of the remaining items is lower than 4. 8, indicating that users of OEPs generally do not score WM very high.

The average value of the PR variables is 5. 234 with a standard deviation at 1. 266. The item PR1 that is "I will wonder that the quality of the course will not meet my expectation when I bought online courses" has the highest average, at 5. 326. The item PR4 that is "I will worry that guarantee of after-sales service cannot be ensured when I bought online courses" has the smallest average, at 5. 112. The average of other items is also over 5. The above figures show that users of OEPs are worried that online courses cannot achieve the expected quality, which is also an important factor restricting users on OEP from buying online courses.

The average of PC variables is 4. 433 with a standard deviation at 1. 255. The item PC1 that is "I think the online course price is relatively high" has the highest average, at 4.719. The item PC3 that is "online course does not shorten my time and energy needed to grasp knowledge" has the lowest average, at 4.274. The average of other items also exceeds 4. Overall, users on OEP believe that the price of online courses is relatively high, which undermines users' willingness to purchase online courses.

The average of PU variable is 5.031 with a standard deviation at 1.132. The item PU3 that is "I think the online course can help me get more knowledge" has the highest average, at 5.260. The item PU2 that is "I think the online course can improve my learning effect" and the item PU4 that is "I think online courses make my learning easier" have the lowest average, at 4.934. It can be explained from these figures that users of OEP generally believe that online courses can help access to more extensive knowledge.

The average of PE variables is 4.800 with a standard deviation at 1.166. The item PEU2 that is "I can easily use the OEP for course learning" has the highest average, at 5.070 while the item PEU3 that is "I can easily contact the online course suppliers" has the lowest average, at 4.451. It can be explained that users of OEPs believe that it is easy to use the system provided by the platform to learn online courses.

The average of CFT variables is 5.643 and the standard deviation is 1.062. The item of CFT2 that is "If the CFT meet my expectation, my willingness to buy will increase" has the highest average, at 5.713. The item CFT4 that is "If the online course provides CFT will affect my willingness to buy" has the lowest average, at 5.511. The averages of other items also exceed 5.5. These figures indicate that users of OEPs believe that the CFT can increase consumers' purchase willingness, and if CFT can meet to consumers' need, their purchase willingness will be enhanced.

The average of TSA variables is 5.592 and the standard deviation is 1.115. The item TSA4 that is "I can decide where and when to study online" has the highest average, at 5.716, and the item TSA1 that is "I can decide the learning content when I am studying online" has the lowest average, at 5. 492. The other items have averages over 5. 4. The figures mentioned above indicate that users of OEPs generally believe that TSA has key impacts on their own learning online.

The average of PI variables is 5. 385 with the standard deviation at 1. 236. The item PI3 that is "If the online course is what I need, I am willing to buy it" has the highest average, at 5. 572, and the item PI2 that is "I will continue to purchase the paid course of the OEP" has the lowest average, at 5. 184. The average of the rest measurement items also exceeds 5. 1, which explains that users of OEP are still very likely to purchase online courses.

According to average value, the average value of each item is between 4. 274 and 5. 716. From the results, it can be concluded that responses to items generally show a positive attitude and orientation. According to standard deviation, the standard deviation of all items is between 1. 255-1. 609, which indicates that the score of the items done by respondents does not fluctuate greatly, and the overall distribution of the data is reasonable.

5.3 Reliability Validity and Data Test

5.3.1 Reliability and Validity Analysis of Questionnaire Data

(1) Reliability analysis of questionnaire data

Reliability is used to measure the credibility or stability within a scale. The α coefficient proposed by Cronbach in 1951 has been used to measure the consistency of each item. The higher α value means the better character of each item in the questionnaire, indicating that the reliability of the questionnaire is higher (Meng, 2013; Liu, 2016; Hou, 2018). Statistical analysis of the reliability of the nine variables that are PV, WM, PR, CFT, PEU, TSA, PU, PI, and PC was performed by IBM

SPSS software, and its results can be seen in Table 5-6.

Table 5-6   Summary of Cronbach's alpha of variables

Variable	Number of items	Cronbach's alpha
CFT	4	0.834
PC	4	0.844
PEU	4	0.859
PI	4	0.871
PR	4	0.855
PU	4	0.876
PV	4	0.836
TSA	4	0.891
WM	4	0.886
Internal consistency: 36		0.861

When the Cronbach's alpha coefficient is greater than 0.7, it indicates the internal consistency of the questionnaire is credible. From Table 5-6, it can be learned that the overall alpha value of the questionnaire is 0.861, which indicates that the questionnaire has a high reliability. The alpha value of the remaining 9 variables is all greater than 0.8, indicating that each variable has good reliability. It can be concluded that the questionnaire as a whole has good reliability.

(2) Validity analysis of questionnaire data

Under the condition that the reliability of the questionnaire has reached the standard, in order to ensure that questions in the questionnaire can honestly and effectively reflect the meaning of the research variables, its validity was analyzed. The "factor analysis" function in the IBM SPSS analysis software has been used to access Kaiser-Meyer-Olkin (KMO) and the Bartlett sphericity test has been performed. If KMO is greater than 0.8, the validity is very high (Fang, 2016).

Table 5-7   KMO and Bartlett sphericity test

The number of KMO sample applicableness		0. 917
Bartlett sphericity	approximate chi-square	12988. 833
	degree of freedom	630
	significance	0. 000

As shown from Table 5-7, the KMO value of the questionnaire in this study is 0. 917, indicating that the validity is very high. The approximate chi-square of the Bartlett sphericity test is 12988. 833, and the significance is 0. 000 < 0. 001, indicating that the questionnaire is very significant, so the data structure of the questionnaire has excellent validity (Meng, 2013; Liu, 2017).

5. 3. 2   Reliability and Validity Analysis of the Model

This study has combined the PLS Algorithm and Bootstrapping of SmartPLS to calculate the meansurement model's combined reliability, internal consistency coefficient, convergence validity and discriminant validity. The number of samples in Bootstrapping is set as 669.

Table 5-8   Factor load and cross factor load table

	CFT	PC	PEU	PI	PR	PU	PV	TSA	WM
CFT1	0. 815	−0. 109	0. 191	0. 244	−0. 179	0. 195	0. 199	0. 208	0. 286
CFT2	0. 813	−0. 081	0. 239	0. 270	−0. 215	0. 240	0. 234	0. 234	0. 241
CFT3	0. 834	−0. 145	0. 206	0. 259	−0. 209	0. 214	0. 222	0. 186	0. 304
CFT4	0. 805	−0. 052	0. 244	0. 263	−0. 189	0. 209	0. 191	0. 200	0. 257
PC1	−0. 110	0. 826	−0. 126	−0. 195	0. 148	−0. 154	−0. 342	−0. 141	−0. 101
PC2	−0. 108	0. 798	−0. 110	−0. 152	0. 118	−0. 136	−0. 267	−0. 085	−0. 097
PC3	−0. 094	0. 842	−0. 117	−0. 186	0. 138	−0. 143	−0. 334	−0. 146	−0. 082
PC4	−0. 081	0. 831	−0. 098	−0. 188	0. 184	−0. 123	−0. 311	−0. 082	−0. 122
PEU1	0. 203	−0. 110	0. 824	0. 278	−0. 236	0. 300	0. 309	0. 271	0. 239
PEU2	0. 216	−0. 081	0. 855	0. 300	−0. 259	0. 276	0. 314	0. 244	0. 191
PEU3	0. 236	−0. 136	0. 832	0. 272	−0. 248	0. 289	0. 330	0. 210	0. 204

Continuation

	CFT	PC	PEU	PI	PR	PU	PV	TSA	WM
PEU4	0.247	−0.129	0.840	0.333	−0.276	0.304	0.362	0.291	0.186
PI1	0.278	−0.202	0.290	0.856	−0.345	0.316	0.491	0.457	0.372
PI2	0.308	−0.202	0.319	0.890	−0.388	0.310	0.496	0.464	0.409
PI3	0.236	−0.164	0.296	0.804	−0.343	0.278	0.484	0.430	0.307
PI4	0.253	−0.178	0.297	0.848	−0.352	0.323	0.451	0.452	0.322
PR1	−0.203	0.164	−0.279	−0.360	0.836	−0.257	−0.431	−0.302	−0.218
PR2	−0.206	0.124	−0.233	−0.306	0.808	−0.221	−0.383	−0.248	−0.194
PR3	−0.196	0.168	−0.256	−0.382	0.871	−0.280	−0.433	−0.257	−0.206
PR4	−0.209	0.138	−0.246	−0.351	0.823	−0.273	−0.398	−0.261	−0.181
PU1	0.252	−0.134	0.250	0.300	−0.239	0.828	0.426	0.312	0.186
PU2	0.200	−0.127	0.303	0.303	−0.279	0.838	0.463	0.287	0.193
PU3	0.243	−0.164	0.300	0.328	−0.295	0.899	0.476	0.287	0.211
PU4	0.207	−0.151	0.334	0.301	−0.243	0.850	0.447	0.287	0.214
PV1	0.206	−0.318	0.357	0.467	−0.379	0.422	0.831	0.361	0.234
PV2	0.237	−0.286	0.324	0.457	−0.409	0.442	0.823	0.373	0.273
PV3	0.182	−0.329	0.291	0.462	−0.430	0.393	0.798	0.347	0.190
PV4	0.224	−0.319	0.316	0.466	−0.398	0.480	0.821	0.359	0.262
TSA1	0.215	−0.153	0.268	0.488	−0.277	0.311	0.425	0.885	0.267
TSA2	0.240	−0.146	0.263	0.480	−0.303	0.300	0.386	0.887	0.269
TSA3	0.248	−0.098	0.275	0.432	−0.261	0.299	0.353	0.818	0.253
TSA4	0.179	−0.084	0.252	0.438	−0.270	0.279	0.359	0.883	0.216
WM1	0.303	−0.076	0.225	0.353	−0.222	0.184	0.253	0.248	0.894
WM2	0.305	−0.107	0.252	0.406	−0.243	0.236	0.293	0.263	0.902
WM3	0.289	−0.138	0.194	0.334	−0.205	0.201	0.244	0.238	0.862
WM4	0.249	−0.102	0.166	0.338	−0.152	0.191	0.217	0.251	0.794

It can be known from Table 5-8, and Table 5-9 that: (1) The factor load of all factors is more significant than 0.5, and the level is relatively high; (2) The composite reliability (CR) of the nine latent variables is greater than or equal to 0.8; (3) Cronbach's alpha coefficient of all latent variables is higher than 0.7; the combined reliability CR value of the latent variable and the minimum Cronbach's alpha coefficient is not less than 0.7, indicating that the measurement model has good internal consistency reliability (Straub, Boudreau, & Gefen, 2004; Luo, 2014; Wang, 2017). Based on the above analysis, the measurement model of this study can be considered to have good reliability.

The validity of the measurement model is usually measured by content validity, convergence validity, and discriminant validity. All measurement items in this study were adapted from the previous research literature. The pre-investigation before the formal questionnaire survey was conducted to ensure the validity of the content of the scales. Therefore, it is rational to consider that the research scales are clear, accurate, and valid in content. And it has content validity.

The average variance extracted (AVE) is greater than 0.5, which indicates that the variables have ideal convergence validity. Table 5-9 shows that the AVE value of the model is greater than 0.6, further suggesting that the measurement model has outstanding convergence validity (Zhou, 2014; Shangguan, 2015; Liu, 2016).

Discriminant validity can be tested by comparing the square root of AVEs of the latent variable with the correlation coefficient of other latent variables (Fornell & Larcker, 1981; Zhang, 2012; Zeng, 2013; Yu, 2015). Table 5-10 shows the correlation coefficient of the latent variable and the square root of AVE. In the lower triangular region in the matrix, the correlation coefficient between the variables has been listed, and the square root of the variable AVE can be seen along the angular bisector. It can be seen that the AVE square root of each latent variable in the measurement model is greater than the correlation coefficient between the latent variable and other latent variables, indicating that the measurement model has good discriminant validity.

The factor load and cross factor load can be used to test the internality and discriminability of the measurement model. As can be seen from Table 5-10, there is a relatively high correlation coefficient between each measurement variable and its latent variable. The factor load (bold ones) of all the measurement items of the latent variable is much larger than the cross-factor load with other latent variables. It further indicates that the measurement model of this study has good internal consistency and differentiation (Jiang，2013；Chen，2015；Liang，2017).

Table 5-9　AVE, Communality, CR and Cronbach's alpha of the measurement model

Latent variable	Number of items	Convergence validity	communality	Reliability	
		AVE		Composite Reliability	Cronbach's alpha
CFT	4	0.667	0.667	0.889	0.834
PC	4	0.680	0.680	0.895	0.844
PEU	4	0.702	0.702	0.904	0.859
PI	4	0.722	0.722	0.912	0.871
PR	4	0.697	0.697	0.902	0.855
PU	4	0.729	0.729	0.915	0.876
PV	4	0.670	0.670	0.890	0.836
TSA	4	0.754	0.754	0.925	0.891
WM	4	0.747	0.747	0.922	0.886

Table 5-10　Correlation coefficient between latent variables and AVE square root

	CFT	PC	PEU	PI	PR	PU	PV	TSA	WM
CFT	0.817								
PC	−0.119	0.825							
PEU	0.270	−0.137	0.838						
PI	0.317	−0.220	0.354	0.850					
PR	−0.243	0.179	−0.304	−0.421	0.835				
PU	0.263	−0.169	0.349	0.361	−0.310	0.854			
PV	0.260	−0.383	0.393	0.566	−0.493	0.531	0.818		
TSA	0.254	−0.140	0.304	0.530	−0.320	0.343	0.440	0.868	
WM	0.332	−0.122	0.244	0.416	−0.240	0.236	0.293	0.290	0.864

Note：The lower triangular region in the matrix is the correlation coefficient between the variables，and the value on the angular bisector is the square root of the variable AVE.

5.3.3　Common Method Deviation Test

The questionnaire in this study were all conducted by a single online survey. The self-report study of respondents collected the survey date. The self-inflicted standard method biases may seriously plague research results and even mislead this study's conclusions (Doty & Glick, 1998; Du, Zhao, & Liu, 2003; Zhou & Long, 2004; Zhu & Li, 2019). Based on previous research, this study has reduced the impacts caused by common method biases from program control and statistical control (Podsakoff & Organ, 1986).

(1) Program control

In term of program control, the following four strategies were implemented to reduce the impacts of common method bias.

Firstly, during the questionnaire survey, respondents were informed that the study results were only used for academic research rather than for any other purposes. Secondly, the online questionnaire survey was all anonymous. The measurement items in the questionnaire did not involve any sensitive information about personal privacy. Thirdly, all variables in the questionnaire was measured by using multiple measurement items. Fourthly, based on the previous in-depth interviews and pre-investigation, the items in scales were optimized. The expression ambiguity was reduced by modifying some expressions and descriptions into more clear and accurate wording.

(2) Statistical control

Harman's one-factor test was used for statistical control of common method biases. Harman's one-factor test has been widely used in questionnaire surveys conducted by self-report scale. For example, respondents may tend to choose the middle option when answering the Likert scale to avoid extreme scores, while Harman's one-factor test can estimate the common method bias. Using the exploratory factor analysis (EFA) function in the IBM SPSS analysis software, the EFA was performed on all the measurement items in the questionnaire. In the unrotated factor analysis results, if the explained variance of the first factor is less than 40%, it can be considered that the impacts of the standard method biases are minor (Cui, 2010; Yang, 2017; Deng, Li, &

Chen，2018）. A total of 8 factors with eigenvalues greater than 1 were extracted from all the items，and the explained variance of the factor was 28.184%. There is not the situation where a particular factor explains the majority of the conflict，so it is reasonable to assume that the standard method biases impose significant impacts on the results of the research.

5.3.4 Multicollinearity Test

When constructing a research model，it is also necessary to check whether multi-collinearity in the structural model. Hair et al. （2016） considered that when the tolerance in the model is less than 0.20 or the variance inflation factor （VIF） is greater than 5；they indicate serious collinearity in this model. Through SmartPLS calculation，the VIF of each variable is less than 5，and the VIF satisfies the critical level of collinearity described in Table 5-11 and Table 5-12. Therefore，this model has no multicollinearity problem，and the results estimated in the model are relatively stable.

Table 5-11　Inner VIF Values

	Age	CFT	Edu	Income	PC	PEU	PR	PU	PV	TSA	WM	PV * WM
PI	1.733	1.191	1.408	1.733	1.191		1.389		1.758	1.333	1.222	1.012
PU						1.000						
PV		1.159			1.056	1.259	1.241	1.291		1.257		

Table 5-12　Outer VIF Values

Item	VIF	Item	VIF	Item	VIF
CFT1	1.864	PI1	2.197	PV1	1.905
CFT2	1.713	PI2	2.633	PV2	1.832
CFT3	1.917	PI3	1.771	PV3	1.686
CFT4	1.744	PI4	2.210	PV4	1.816
PC1	1.782	PR1	1.930	TSA1	2.586

Continuation

Item	VIF	Item	VIF	Item	VIF
PC2	1.804	PR2	1.830	TSA2	2.648
PC3	1.951	PR3	2.267	TSA3	1.916
PC4	1.911	PR4	1.889	TSA4	2.716
PEU1	1.898	PU1	2.076	WM1	2.956
PEU2	2.210	PU2	1.993	WM2	2.910
PEU3	1.941	PU3	2.857	WM3	2.426
PEU4	1.933	PU4	2.133	WM4	1.736
income	1.000	PV * WM	1.000	age	1.000
				education	1.000

5.4　Model Hypothesis Test and Analysis

5.4.1　Structural Model Validation

In this study, SmartPLS was used to construct the model. After the calculation using PLS Algorithm, the model was analyzed to obtain the calculation results of the PLS structural equation model. Based on Sarstedt, Henseler, and Ringle (2011) recommendations for the number of samples, the study used a self-service method to select 5,000 pieces with resamples to analyze the significance of the path coefficients. The PLS structural equation model for users' PI of courses on OEP is shown in Figure 5-1.

When the T value is larger than 1.96 in the PLS-SEM model, the model has reached a significant level when the α value is 0.05 (shown by*). When the T value is larger than 2.58, the model has reached a significant level when the α value is 0.01 (shown by**). When the T value is larger than 3.29, this indicates that the model has reached a significant level when the α value is 0.001 (shown by***) (Xie & Zhang,

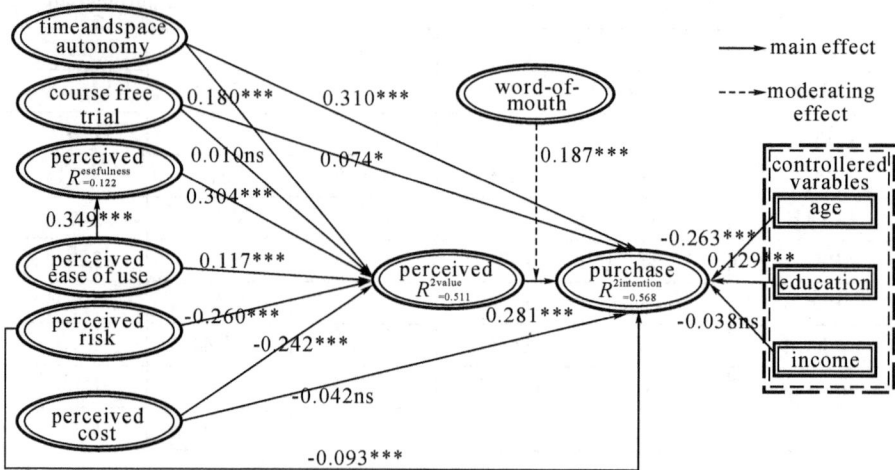

Note: **P<0.001; **P<0.01; *P<0.05; ns: not-significant

Figure 5-1   PLS structural equation model for OEP users' willingness
to purchase courses

2014; Zhu & Liao, 2017).

The results of the final calculation of the model show that the T values of CFT→PV and PC→PI are all less than 1. 96. The impacts of hypotheses H5 and H11 are not significant, so hypotheses H5 and H11 are not established. As for the control variables, the T value of the path of income to PI does not reach a significant level, indicating that H14c is not supported. As for the rest hypotheses that include H1, H2, H3, H4, H6, H7, H8, H9, H10, H12, H13, H14a, and H14b, hypotheses H1, H2, H4, H6, H7, H8, H9, H12, H13, H14a, and H14b have reached a significant level with an alpha value at 0. 001, hypothesis H3 has reached a significant level with an alpha value at 0. 01, and hypothesis H10 has reached a significant level with alpha value at 0. 05.

As for hypothesis H1, the path coefficient of users' PV to PI is 0. 281, the T value is 8. 073, and the P value is 0. 000, significant at the 0. 010 level. It indicates that the PV of the user has a significant and positive effect on the PI of the course, and that greater PV imposes greater impacts on PI of users on online educational platforms.

As for hypothesis H2, the path coefficient of the WM moderating PV to PI is 0. 187, the T value is 6. 961, and the P value is 0. 000, significant at the 0. 000 level. It illustrates that WM has substantial and positive moderation on the impacts of PV on the PI. The hypothesis H2 is supported indicates that greater PV delivers more potent PI on OEP under the circumstance of relatively high WM. Meanwhile, the PV and PI have significant and positive impacts.

As for the hypothesis H3, the path coefficient of PR to PI is -0.093, the T value is 3. 145, and the P-value is 0. 002, significant at 0. 010 level. It indicates that the PR has significant and negative impacts on PI, and that greater PR reduces users' PI.

As for the hypothesis H4, the path coefficient of PR to PV is -0.260, the T value is 8. 780, and the P value is 0. 000, which is significant at the 0. 000 level. It indicates that the PR has a negative effect on PV. That the hypothesis H4 is established means that the PR has a significant effect on PV.

As for the hypothesis H5, the path coefficient of users' PC to PI of is -0.042, the T value is 1. 523, and the P-value is 0. 128, which indicates that the significance has not been verified. It means that the hypothesis that PC has a negative impact on PI is invalid. The hypothesis H5 is not established means that users' PC does not significantly affect their PI.

As for the hypothesis H6, the path coefficient of users' PC to PV is -0.242, the T value is 8. 775, and the P value is 0. 000, significant at the 0. 000 level. It means that PC has a negative impact on PV, and it can be concluded that the higher PC reduces users' PV of courses.

As for the hypothesis H7, the path coefficient of users' PU to PV is 0. 304, the T value is 9. 864, and the P-value is 0. 000, significant at the 0. 001 level. It indicates that the PU has a substantial and positive impact on PV, and the greater users an percive on OEP, the greater value users will perceive.

As for the hypothesis H8, the path coefficient of users' PEU to PV is

0.17, the T value is 3.658, and the P value is 0.000, which is significant at the 0.001 level. It indicates that the PEU has a significant and positive impact on PV, and that when the PEU is high, users will have considered the courses with higher value.

As for the hypothesis H9, the path coefficient of users' PEU to PU is 0.349. When the path coefficient is greater than 0.2, the level of the impact is relatively high. T value is 10.135, and P-value is 0.000, which means significance at the 0.0001 level. It indicates that the PEU has a significant and positive impact on PU. The hypothesis H9 is supported illustrates that the higher PEU delivers higher PU to users.

As for the hypothesis H10, the path coefficient of the CFT to PI is 0.074, the T value is 2.522, and the P value is 0.012, significant at the 0.05 level. It indicates that the CFT has a significant and positive impact on PI, which means that if OEP provides CFT from which users gain good experiences; they will have more robust PI.

As for the hypothesis H11, the path coefficient of the CFT to PV is 0.010, the T value is 0.335, and the P-value is 0.738. The significance is not proved, which indicates that the hypothesis that CFT has a positive impact on PV does not support. Therefore, it can illustrate that the CFT services and experience provided by OEP do not significantly affect users' PV.

As for the hypothesis H12, the path coefficient of TSA to PI is 0.310, T value is 9.756, and the P value is 0.000, which is significant at the 0.001 level. It indicates that TSA has a significant and positive impact on PI, and it can be concluded that the stronger TSA perceived by users can bring stronger PI.

As for the hypothesis H13, the path coefficient of TSA to PV is 0.180, T value is 5.739, and the P value is 0.000, significant at the 0.000 level. It indicates that TSA has a substatial and positive impact on PV, and it can be concluded that the stronger TSA delivers more PV.

As for the hypothesis H14a, the path coefficient of users' age to PI is 0.263, the T value is 7.123, and the P value is 0.000, which is significant at the 0.000 level. It illustrates that the user's age has a negative impact on PI, which means that older users are more likely not to buy courses.

As for hypothesis H14b, the path coefficient of users' educational background to PI is 0.129, the T value is 4.299, and the P value is 0.000, which is significant at the 0.000 level. It illustrates that the user's educational level has significant and positive impacts on PI, which means that users with higher academic levels tend to have strong PI.

As for the hypothesis H14c, the path coefficient of income to PI is -0.038, the T value is 1.106, and the P-value is 0.269, which indicates that the significance is not proved. It states that the hypothesis that income has a positive impact on PI does not establish. The hypothesis H14c is not valid, which means that the user's income level does not have a significant and positive impact on the PI.

5.4.2　Model Goodness-of-fitness Test

The coefficient of determination (R^2) can measure the accuracy of explanatory relevance and predictive relevance of the model within the structual equation model framework. R^2 ranges from 0 to 1, and a higher value indicates a more vital explanatory relevance of each variable in the model to the dependent variable.

Chin (1998) believed that an R^2 greater than 0.333 indicates a level exceeding the average, indicating high explanatory relevance. It can be noted that R^2 of PV is 0.511, R^2 of PI is 0.568, and R^2 of PU is 0.122 from Figure 5-1. The overall explanatory relevance of this model in this study is 0.568, indicating that the model has a good prediction effect (Straub, Boudreau, & Gefen, 2004).

In PLS-SEM, the model's overall indicator can be used to test the Goodness-of-Fitness (GoF) represents the predictive utility of the entire model. The GoF is calculated as the square root of the product of the average commonality and the average R^2. A GoF at 0.36 indicates a good fitness (Wetzels, Odekerken, & Van-Oppen, 2009; Zhou, 2014).

It can be seen from Table 5-9 that the average commonality of the measurement model is 0. 708, and the average R^2 is 0. 401. After the calculation, the GoF is 0. 533, indicating a good fitness in the overall model (Hair et al. , 2016).

The standardized root means square residual (SRMR) can be used to evaluate GoF. SRMR is defined as the difference between the observed correlation matrix and the predicted correlation matrix of the model to reflect the average magnitude of the difference. When the SRMR value is less than 0. 08, the model has a good fitness (Hu & Bentler, 1998; Hair et al. , 2016; Cheng, 2017; Cai, Shi, & Chen, 2019).

The SRMR value is 0. 035, less than the critical value of 0. 08 through SmartPLS operation, which further demonstrates that the overall model of this study has a good fitness and can explain the factors influencing users' willingness to buy courses on OEP.

5. 4. 3　Model Prediction Relevance Analysis

This study used the Blindfolding function to analyze the predictive relevance of the model used the Cross-validation method of Stone-Geisser's to calculate the predictive relevance of the model and used Q^2 to evaluate the predictive relevance of the model (Tenenhaus, Vinzi, & Chatelin, 2005; Jiang, 2013). The formula for Q^2 is $Q^2(=1\text{-}SSE/SSO)$. If Q^2 is less than 0, it means that the model has no predictive relevance; if Q^2 is more than 0, it means that the model has good predictive relevance (Chin, 1998; Zhang, 2012).

Through the calculation of SmarPLS software, the Q^2 of three endogenous variables, PU, PV and PI is 0. 383, 0. 321 and 0. 083 respectively, which are all greater than 0, indicating that the model constructed in this research to study users' course PI on OEP has good predictive relevance.

5.4.4   Mediation Effect Analysis

The research model of this study introduced a mediation variable of PV, so the mediation effect of PV needs to be analyzed. When selecting a method to test, the literature review on related methods testing mediation effect has been conducted. It can be noted that the most commonly used 4 methods are bootstrapping, the product of results approach, distribution of the product strategy causal steps approach. After comparing these 4 methods and according to Zhao and Han (2007) and Hair et al. (2016), this study finally adopted Bootstrapping to test and analyze the mediation impacts of the mediator.

In the SmartPLS software, the results of the PLS-SEM algorithm and bootstrap functions contain direct impacts, total impacts, and specific indirect impacts. According to the setting recommended by Hair et al. (2016), the number of bootstrap samples was set at 5,000, and the confidence interval was set at 95%. The calculation results are shown in Table 5-13.

In the mediation effect analysis, (1) if the indirect effect is not significant, it indicates no mediation effect; (2) if the indirect effect is significant, but the direct effect is not significant, it indicates that the mediation effect is a complete mediation; (3) if the indirect effect and the direct effect are both significant, the mediation effect is a partial mediation (Hair et al., 2016; Zhang, 2017).

As can be seen from Table 5-13, the indirect effect of CFT on PI is 0.003 with the confidence interval range from -0.015 to 0.020, which contains 0, so the indirect effect is not significant. The direct effect of CFT to PI is 0.074 with the confidence interval range from 0.015 to 0.129, which does not contain 0, indicating the direct effect is significant. Therefore, PV does not act as a mediation role between CFT and PI.

The indirect effect of PC to PI is -0.068 with the confidence interval range from -0.094 to -0.046, which contains 0, so the indirect effect is significant. The indirect effect of PC to PI is -0.042 with the confidence interval range from -0.094 to 0.012, which contains 0, so the direct effect is not significant. Therefore, PV acts as a complete mediation on the relationship between PC and PI.

Table 5-13 Analysis result of mediation effect

Path	Effect	Initial sample(O)	95% confidence intervals	T value	Significant	Type of mediation
CFT→PV→PI	Direct	0.074	[0.015, 0.129]	2.522	Yes	No
	Total	0.077	[0.014, 0.134]	2.511	Yes	
	Indirect	0.003	[−0.015, 0.020]	0.333	No	
PC→PV→PI	Direct	−0.042	[−0.094, 0.012]	1.523	No	Complete
	Total	−0.110	[−0.163, −0.054]	3.923	Yes	
	Indirect	−0.068	[−0.094, −0.046]	5.672	Yes	
PR→PV→PI	Direct	−0.093	[−0.153, −0.038]	3.145	Yes	Partial
	Total	−0.166	[−0.227, −0.111]	5.565	Yes	
	Direct	−0.073	[−0.100, −0.052]	6.118	Yes	
TSA→PV→PI	Direct	0.310	[0.244, 0.370]	9.756	Yes	Partial
	Total	0.361	[0.300, 0.419]	11.842	Yes	
	Direct	0.051	[0.031, 0.077]	4.466	Yes	
PEU→PU→PV	Direct	0.117	[0.053, 0.178]	3.658	Yes	Partial
	Total	0.224	[0.158, 0.285]	5.201	Yes	
	Indirect	0.106	[0.079, 0.137]	7.182	Yes	

The indirect effect of PR to PI is -0.073 with the confidence interval range from -0.100 to -0.052, which does not contain 0, so the indirect effect is significant. The direct effect of PR to PI is -0.093 with the confidence interval rang from -0.153 to -0.038, which does not contain 0, so the direct effect is significant. Therefore, PV act as a partial mediation on the relationship between PR and PI.

The indirect effect of TSA to PI is 0.051, with the confidence interval range from 0.031 to 0.077 which contains 0, so the indirect effect is significant. The direct effect of TSA to PI is 0.310, with the confidence interval range from 0. 244 to 0. 370, which does not contain 0, so the direct effect is significant. Therefore, PV act as a partial mediation on the relationship between TSA and PI.

The indirect effect of PEU to PV is 0. 106 with the confidence interval range from 0. 079 to 0. 137, which does not contain 0, so the indirect effect is significant. The direct effect of PEU to PV is 0. 117, with the confidence interval range from 0. 053 to 0. 178, which does not contain 0, so the direct effect is significant. Therefore, PV act as a partial mediation on the relationship between PEU and PV.

In summary, perceived profit (TSA, PEU, PU) and perceived loss (PC, PR) affect the user's PI through the mediator PV, in line with previous research results about PV (Zeithaml, 1988; Butz, 1996; Parasuraman & Grewal, 2000; Zhao, 2013; Fang, Lu, & Liu, 2018).

5. 4. 5   Moderation Effect Test

This study also used the SmartPLS analysis software to test the moderation effect. A model in which WM moderates the impacts of PV on PI was established in SmartPLS into which questionnaire data were imported later. The PLS algorithm and bootstrapping functions were used for hierarchical regressions (Al-Gahtani, Hubona, & Wang, 2007; Zhou, 2014; Zhang, 2018), and the results of the moderation effect are shown in Table 5-14.

As shown in Table 5-14, the path coefficient β of moderation effect item (PV * WM) and PI is 0. 187, indicating that PV * WM has a positive. When WM is used as a reference point, the relationship between PV and PI is 0. 281. However, when WM increases, the relationship between PV and PI will change with the moderation impacts to 0. 468 (0. 281+0. 187), which shows that, the explanatory relevance of PV will be strengthened when WM is high.

The conclusions mentioned above must be established on the premise that the moderation effect is significant. The calculation results in Table 5-14 show that the path coefficient β of PV and PI is 0. 281 with T-value at

8.703，and the path coefficient β of WM and PI is 0.186 with T-value at 6.044. The path coefficient β of the moderation effect item (WM * PV) and PI is 0.187 with T-value at 6.961. All T-values are greater than 1.96，certifying the significance. Therefore，WM imposes a significant positive moderating effect on PV and PI.

Table 5-14 Test result of moderation effect

Hypothesis path	Without Moderator			With Moderator			Hypothesis test result
	Path coefficient β	T-value	Signifi-cance	Path coefficient β	T-value	Signifi-cance	
PV→PI	0.288	7.899	* * *	0.281	8.703	* * *	Hypothesis is supported.
WM→PI				0.186	6.044	* * *	
PV * WM→PI				0.187	6.961	* * *	
R²	0.509			0.568			
f²				0.066			

Note：* * * p<0.001；* * p<0.01；* p<0.05；ns：not significant

After adding the moderator of WM，R^2 increased from 0.509 to 0.568，indicating that the PI is affected by the moderator of WM (Lin，2018). Effect size (f^2) can be used to explain the impacts of exogenous variables on endogenous variables. $0.02 < f^2 < 0.15$ is a weak impact，$0.15 < f^2 < 0.35$ is a moderate impact，and $0.35 < f^2$ is a strong impact (Jiang，2013；Hair et al.，2016). It can be seen from the table that the f^2 of the moderation effect is 0.066，indicating that WM has a weak moderation effect on the relationship between PV and PI.

5.4.6 Analysis of Impacts of Control Variables

By running the SmartPLS software to obtain the standardized path coefficient β and T-value to confirm whether the three control variables，education，age，and income have a significant impact on the model (Li，2015；Li，2018).

From Table 5-15，it is a confirmed hypothesis that the user's age (β= 0.129，T = 4.299，p<0.001) has a negative impact on PI，and it is significant. It is a confirmed hypothesis that the user's education background ($\beta=0.073$, $T=7.123$, $p<0.001$) positively affects PI and it is significant. The hypothesis that the user's income level has a positive impact on PI is not supported.

Table 5-15   Control variable impact analysis

Path	T-value	Signifi-cance	Hypothesis test result
education→PI	4.299	* * *	Support
age→PI	7.123	* * *	Support
income→PI	1.106	ns	Not support

5.4.7   Analysis of Moderated Mediation Effect

To further explore whether WM can moderate the mediation effect of PV to PI, model 14 in the Process tool of SPSS was used to test moderated mediation effect. The number of Bootstrap samples is 5000 (Rodríguez, Roldán, & Ariza-Montes, 2014; Wen & Ye, 2014; Fang, Zhao, & Gu, 2014; Chen, 2015; Hayes, 2019), and calculation result are shown in Table 5-16.

From Table 5-16, it can be noted that that path of TSA-PV-PI with WM as the moderator has the index of moderated mediation and the 95% confidence interval of mediator index is from 0.032 to 0.067, without 0. It indicates a significant difference in the mediation effect of PI when the WM is at different levels. When WM is in the low score group, the mediation effect is 0.041, and the 95% confidence interval is from 0.015 to 0.072, which does not contain 0, indicating that the mediation effect is significant. When WM is in the high score group, the mediation effect is 0.156, and the 95% confidence interval is from 0.112 to 0.205, which does not contain 0, indicating that the mediation effect is significant. The mediation 0.156 in the high score group is higher than the mediation 0.041 in the low score group, thus indicating that the mediation is positively moderated.

Table 5-16   Moderated mediation effect test

Mediation Path	Moderator	Group (score)	Effect	Boot SE	Bias Corrected (95%)		Index of moderated mediation		
					LLCI	ULCI	Index	LLCI	ULCI
TSA-PV-PI	WM	Low	0.041	0.015	0.015	0.072	0.049	0.032	0.067
		High	0.156	0.023	0.112	0.205			
CFT-PV-PI	WM	Low	0.012	0.007	0.001	0.027	0.014	0.001	0.027
		High	0.044	0.020	0.005	0.084			
PC-PV-PI	WM	Low	−0.036	0.013	−0.063	−0.013	−0.043	−0.059	−0.028
		High	−0.137	0.020	−0.178	−0.100			
PR-PV-PI	WM	Low	−0.044	0.016	−0.077	−0.016	−0.053	−0.071	−0.036
		High	−0.169	0.021	−0.212	−0.129			

Note: ULCI is the upper limit of the confidence interval, and LLCI is the lower confidence interval.

That path of CFT-PV-PI with WM as the moderator has the index of moderated mediation, and the 95% confidence interval of the mediator index is from 0.001 to 0.027, without 0. It indicates a significant difference in the mediation effect of PV when the WM is at different levels. When WM is in low score group, the mediation effect is 0.012, and the 95% confidence interval is from 0.001 to 0.027 which does not contain 0, indicating that the mediation effect is significant. When WM is in the high score group, the mediation effect is 0.044, and the 95% confidence interval is 0.005 to 0.084, which does not contain 0, indicating that the mediation effect is significant. The mediation 0.044 in the high score group is higher than the mediation 0.012 in the low score group, thus indicating that the mediation is positively moderated.

The path of PC-PV-PI with WM as the moderator has the index of moderated mediation and the 95% confidence interval of the mediator index is from −0.059 to −0.028, without 0. It indicates a significant difference in the mediating impacts of PV when the course reputation is at different levels. When WM is in low score group, the mediation effect is −0.036, and the 95% confidence interval is from −0.063 to −0.013 which does not contain 0, indicating that the mediation effect is

significant. When WM is in the high score group, the mediation effect is
−0.137, and the 95% confidence interval is from −0.178 to −0.100
which done not contain 0, indicating a significant mediating effect. The
mediation −0.137 in the high score group is lower than the mediation
−0.036 in the low score group, thus indicating that the mediation is
negatively moderated.

The path of PR-PV-PI with WM as the moderator has the index of
moderated mediation and the 95% confidence interval of the mediator
index is from −0.071 to −0.036, without 0. It indicates that there is a
significant difference in the mediation effect of PV when the WM is at
different levels. When WM is in the low score group, the mediation effect
is −0.044, and the 95% confidence interval is from −0.077 to −0.016
which does not contain 0, indicating that the mediation effect is
significant. When WM is in the high score group, the mediation effect is
−0.169, and the 95% confidence interval is from −0.212 to −0.129,
which does not contain 0, indicating a significant mediation effect.
However, the mediation −0.044 in a low score, the group is higher than
the mediation −0.169 of high score group, thus indicating that the
mediation is negatively moderated.

5.5　Multi-group Analysis

This study used Multi-Group Analysis (MGA) in PLS-SEM to test
whether users who once bought online courses and those never bought
online courses are affected by the same factors when they make decisions
on buying online courses (Wolfgang, Andreas, & Lars, 2010; Sarstedt,
Henseler, & Ringle, 2011). The results obtained by running the MGA
function of the SmartPLS software are shown in Table 5-17.

Table 5-17 shows that the CFT ($\beta=0.205$, $p<0.001$) significantly
affects the PI of users who do not have experience in buying online
courses, but CFT does not significantly affect the PI of users who have

experience in buying online courses ($\beta=0.007$, $p>0.8$). It can illustrate that CFT can impose significant impacts on PI who have never bought courses on OEP before.

Table 5-17   PLS-MGA results

	path coefficient		T value		significant	
	bought	not purchased	bought	not purchased	bought	not purchased
AGE→PI	−0.325	−0.173	7.275	3.075	* * *	* *
CFT→PI	0.007	0.205	0.174	4.809	ns	* * *
CFT→PV	0.018	0.003	0.424	0.069	ns	ns
EDUCATION→PI	0.065	0.189	1.670	3.967	ns	* * *
INCOME→PI	−0.021	−0.034	0.486	0.683	ns	ns
PC→PI	−0.036	−0.023	1.032	0.474	ns	ns
PC→PV	−0.314	−0.204	8.611	4.584	* * *	* * *
PEU→PU	0.183	0.544	3.768	12.035	* * *	* * *
PEU→PV	0.018	0.270	0.450	5.563	ns	* * *
PR→PI	−0.052	−0.184	1.469	3.472	ns	* * *
PR→PV	−0.172	−0.328	4.180	8.194	* * *	* * *
PU→PV	0.267	0.295	7.057	5.340	* * *	* * *
PV→PI	0.262	0.274	6.340	4.405	* * *	* * *
TSA→PI	0.389	0.197	10.624	3.901	* * *	* * *
TSA→PV	0.248	0.035	6.197	0.748	* * *	ns
WM→PI	0.187	0.179	4.805	3.721	* * *	* * *
moderation→PI	0.210	0.155	6.879	3.418	* * *	* * *

Note: *** $p<0.001$; ** $p<0.01$; * $p<0.05$; ns: not significant

The CFT has no significant impacts on the PV of users who have experienced in purchasing courses on OEP.

PI users who once bought online courses and have never bought online courses are not significantly affected by PC.

The PC owned by users who have experience in purchasing online courses ($\beta=-0.314$, $p<0.001$) has a significant impact on PV. The PC owned by users who has never bought any online courses ($\beta = -0.204$, $p < 0.001$) also significantly affects PV.

Among users who have never bought courses on OEP, PEU ($\beta = 0.544$, $p < 0.000$) significantly affects PU and PEU ($\beta = 0.270$, $p < 0.000$) significantly affect PV. For users who have bought courses on OEP, PEU ($\beta = 0.183$, $p < 0.000$) significantly affects PU, and PEU ($\beta = 0.018$, $p > 0.6$) does not significantly affects PV. Therefore, users who have no experience in purchasing online courses are more likely to think highly of the usability of online courses than those who have bought online courses once.

Among users who have bought courses on OEP once, their PR ($\beta = -0.052$, $p > 0.1$) does not significantly affect their PI, and their PR ($\beta = -0.172$, $p < 0.000$) significantly affects their PV. Among the users who have never bought online courses before, the PR ($\beta = -0.184$, $p < 0.000$) significantly affects their PI, and their PR ($\beta = -0.328$, $p < 0.000$) significantly affects their PV.

The PU ($\beta = 0.267$, $p < 0.000$) of users who have bought courses on OEP once significantly affects PV, and the PU ($\beta = 0.295$, $p < 0.000$) of users without experience buying online courses also considerably affects their PV.

On the path of PV→PI, the PV of the two groups of users who are with and without experience in buying online courses has a significant impact on the PI.

The TSA ($\beta = 0.389$, $p < 0.000$) of users who have bought courses on OEP significantly affect their PI, and the TSA ($\beta = 0.197$, $p < 0.000$) of users who have never bought courses on OEP before also significantly affects their PI. The TSA T — value of users with online courses purchasing experience is significantly more extensive than that of users without online courses purchasing experience, indicating that greater impacts of TSA impose users with the purchasing expertise.

The TSA ($\beta = 0.248$, $p < 0.000$) of users who have bought courses on OEP significantly affects their PV, but the PV of users without online practices purchasing experience is not significantly affected by TSA (β = 0. 035, p>0. 4).

The WM (β = 0. 187, p<0. 000) of users who once purchased online courses significantly affects their PI, and the WM (β = 0. 179, p<0. 000) of users who have never bought online courses also significantly affects the PV. However, when users have experience purchesing online courses, WM positively and significantly affects the PI, and for users without related knowledge, WM also ultimcrtely and significantly affects the PI. The two groups of users have significant impacts in the same direction.

Among the three control variables of age, education, and income, age showed significant impacts on PI whether users previous experience buying courses. However, the control variable of education has different results in groups with different purchasing experience. As for the group without experience in buying online course, their education background (β = 0. 189, p<0. 001) significantly affects their PI, but as for the group with experience in buying online courses, their PI is not significantly affected by education background (β = 0. 065, p>0. 09). The control variables of the income of the two groups do not significantly affect their PI.

The moderator MW exerts the same impacts on groups of users with different buying experiences. The WM (β = 0. 210, p<0. 001) exerts a significant positive moderation effect on PV and PI in the group of users who once bought online course, but did not exert the course reputation of users who purchase experience (β = − 0. 155, p<0. 001). It has a significant positive moderating effect on PV and PI.

5.6 Chapter summary

This chapter presented statistics and analysis on the data that were collected to explore the factors influencing the users' PI in buying courses on OEP and the path between various factor variables. This chapter contains five parts: data analysis methods and tool selection, descriptive statistical analysis, reliability and validity analysis, model hypothesis testing analysis, and multi-group analysis.

In order to test the theoretical model proposed in this study, IBM SPSS V24. 0 and SmartPLS 3. 2. 8 were selected for data analysis. A descriptive statistical analysis of 669 questionnaires from the Internet was conducted to describe the basics of the sample, after which reliability and validity analysis proved that the sample data of this study has good reliability and validity, and there was no standard method bias or multicollinearity in this data. The model hypothesis test showed that the model has a good fitness, and 13 out of the 16 hypotheses proposed in this study passed the hypothesis test.

Our results show that PV, TSA, CFT, and PR are the key factors directly affecting PI. At the same time, TSA, PU, PEU, PC, PR also affect PI indirectly through affect PV, but the hypothesis CFT indirectly affects PI through PV was not confirmed. Age and education in the control variables also directly affect PI, but income does not significantly affect PI (hypothesis failing the test). The study also found that WM has a significant and positive moderation effect on PV and PI. Therefore, it is rational to believe that WM is also one of the factors that are critical to PI in online courses.

In addition, this study also carried out a deeper analysis of multiple groups. In the user group with purchasing experience, TSA is the critical factor of PV and it passed the hypothesis test, but this hypothesis was not supported in user group without purchasing experience. On the contrary, in the user group without purchasing experience, CFT, PR, and education have significant impacts on PI and passed the hypothesis test, and PU also has significant impacts on PV. These 4 hypotheses are not valid in the user group with the purchasing experience.

第6章 结论与展望

6.1 研究结论与管理启示

6.1.1 课程购买意愿直接影响因素探讨

通过运行 SmartPLS 3.2.8 计算在线教育平台用户课程购买意愿 PLS-SEM 得出运算结果,从中发现直接影响课程购买意愿的因素有感知价值(β=0.281)、时空自主性(β=0.310)、感知风险(β=−0.093)、课程免费试听(β=0.074)。这 4 个潜在变量对因变量购买意愿均有不同程度的影响作用,也都通过了显著性的检验。

6.1.1.1 感知价值

分析结果显示,感知价值是影响购买意愿非常关键的因素之一。消费者在进行在线教育课程这类虚拟产品选购时,会充分收集相关信息,最终进行比较后得出个人的感知价值来进行决策,感知价值会影响用户的购买行为,这也与之前学者们的研究成果相符(Zeithaml,1988;王小丽,2017;储林,2018;洪菲等,2019)[59,163,165,166]。当用户进行感知价值的判断时,感知价值通过感知利得与感知利失的比较评估后,得出自我的感知价值,最终驱动用户决定是否购买在线教育平台的课程。

管理启示:感知价值显著影响购买意愿,因此在市场营销策略的制定上需要突出展示在线教育平台课程的感知利得,让用户能够感知到更多的价值、收获与利益。从而让消费者在自主选择或者通过口碑分享选购这些商品的时候,能够充分了解该课程能够给用户带来的收益,明确该课程的价值。这也要求在线教育平台的运营方和课程的制作方需要注重提炼本课程的卖点,同时在课程制作的阶段就需要对本课程的目标客户进行定位,把本

218

课程的特点贯穿到课程内容中,这样也会让课程更加具有针对性,减少不必要的营销推广成本,同时提炼了课程的针对性并形成独特卖点。感知利得与感知利失两者的比较最后形成感知价值,这也为后期在线教育平台提供了分类管理的参考。

在多群组比较分析中,不管是否拥有在线教育平台课程购买经验,用户的感知价值都显著地影响了在线教育平台潜在消费者的在线课程购买意愿。

6.1.1.2　时空自主性

通过实证分析得出时空自主性对用户购买意愿有着显著的影响作用,这也说明在线教育课程的时空自主性成为提升用户购买意愿的关键因素之一(舒宁,2016;杨佳绮,2016;苏幂遮,2019)[135,149,243]。在多群组的比较分析中发现,有课程购买经验和不曾拥有课程购买经验的用户都通过了时空自主性的显著影响检验。

时空自主性是指在线教育平台课程的学习方式不受时间和空间的束缚,允许用户自主地决定学习的内容、进度、时间和地点。在线课程不需要用户耗费时间前往教室参加培训,录播的课程允许用户自主决定学习时间和地点,而直播的课程虽然不能自主选择学习时间却有更强的互动性,允许用户与教师进行实时互动并获得反馈。

时空自主性也给授课方式带来了巨大的变化。在线学习打破了时间空间的限制之后,允许更多的用户通过手机、电脑等联网的终端设备同时进行学习和在线互动。在线课程拓宽了教学的方式和载体,在线的方式可以结合许多新的教学软件、多媒体技术来增强教学的效果和趣味性。

管理启示:

(1)时空自主性扩大了在线教育平台的目标客户覆盖人群。在线课程的学习更加方便快捷,因此在线教育平台的营销可以针对线下课程学习的用户,这类用户也成为在线教育平台营销的潜在对象。

(2)在线教育平台和课程的制作方应更加注重时空自主性的特点,充分利用新技术来提高用户的学习效率和便捷性。结合目前流行的 5G、移动互联网、虚拟现实、物联网等技术,充分发掘时空自主性对用户学习在线教育平台课程所带来的方便快捷。

(3)允许用户利用碎片化时间学习。时空自主性有利于实时的跟踪和反馈,提升用户的学习效率。

6.1.1.3 课程免费试听

在线教育平台用户课程购买意愿模型中,课程免费试听对用户的课程购买意愿产生显著影响作用,由此说明课程免费试听会直接影响在线教育平台用户的课程购买意愿(李雅筝,2016;许亚楠等,2018;李正峰等,2019)[10,11,177]。可见,课程免费试听也是直接影响课程购买意愿的关键因素之一。

在用户多群组比较分析中,不拥有在线课程购买经验用户的课程免费试听($\beta=0.205$,$p<0.001$)显著影响课程购买意愿,也说明其更加注重在线课程的免费试听。而拥有购买经验用户的课程免费试听并未显著影响课程购买意愿。通过两者的比较,发现课程免费试听对不同购买经验的用户拥有不同的影响。

由于在线课程作为虚拟的电子商务产品,一般以视频、文字、图片等形式存在,用户对在线课程难以有直观的评价和感受,只能通过课程的相关介绍来了解。但课程免费试听为用户提供了解课程内容、授课老师、授课方式、授课质量的机会。课程免费试听的感受相比文字、图片了解的形式更加直观,也能帮助用户做出更理智的购买决策。

管理启示:在线教育平台应提供更多的课程免费试听服务,提升课程免费试听的服务质量。课程免费试听体现出在线教育平台和课程的制作方对课程的一种自信,能够帮助用户直观了解课程详细内容。课程免费试听可以让用户直观地了解授课的内容、形式、质量等,帮助用户做出购买的决策。从数据分析得出课程免费试听会增强用户购买意愿,因此在线教育平台应该提供课程免费试听的服务,注重试听服务的质量,帮助用户直观地感受课程的具体内容和形式,提升在线课程的销售转化率。

在多群组比较分析当中,不同购买经验的两组用户,其课程免费试听对课程购买意愿产生不同的影响作用。其中,不曾拥有课程购买经验的用户更加注重课程免费试听。由于之前未曾拥有同类的课程购买经验,所以难以有课程购买后的使用体会,因此这些用户更希望使用课程免费试听来体验在线课程。在营销推广中,针对没有购买经验的用户要加大课程免费试听的服务推介,以增强他们的课程购买意愿。

6.1.1.4 感知风险

通过分析可知感知风险也是影响因变量的关键因素之一(王英迪,2016;王小丽,2017;向云峰,2018;崔剑峰,2019)[55,88,166,169]。在多群组比较分析中发现,缺乏购买经验的消费者其感知风险对因变量在线课程购买意愿产生负向的显著影响。而有购买历史的消费者却未产生显著影响。在线课程作为虚拟产品,用户会担心课程的质量无法达到预期、课程内容无法帮助达到学习目的,也会担心自己无法坚持完成所有的课程。由于用户通过课程介绍和网站资料来了解课程的相关内容,并无直观的体验,所以用户会产生担心和忧虑并影响课程的购买意愿。

管理启示:

(1)提供课程的 7 天无理由退货。允许用户在限定的条件下申请退款,以此来降低用户对课程质量和课程内容达不到自己预期的担忧。从而减少用户的顾虑,以提升用户购买意愿。

(2)增加在线客服的功能,提升联系客服的便捷性。优化客服联系的功能和及时性,以保证用户在犹豫不决或拥有顾虑时能够及时联系客服,解除忧虑,获得解答,降低用户对售后服务无法保证的顾虑。

(3)提供免费重学的服务。允许用户在未完成本期课程的前提下,参与下一期课程,降低用户对自己无法按时完成课程的忧虑。

在多群组比较分析当中,缺乏购买经验的消费者其感知风险对因变量在线课程购买意愿产生负向的显著影响,由于该组用户不曾拥有类似产品的购买经验,其感知风险会较大可能性的存在。然而拥有类似购买经验的用户,由于已经拥有类似课程的购买经验和相关学习体验,对课程的质量、内容和学习安排的顾虑,不再是影响课程购买的关键因素。在市场营销中应更加注重降低没有购买经验用户的感知风险,以提高该类用户的课程购买意愿。

6.1.2 课程购买意愿间接影响因素探讨

在线教育平台用户课程购买意愿的 PLS 结构方程模型显示,感知有用性($\beta=0.304$)、感知易用性($\beta=0.117$)、时空自主性($\beta=0.180$)都显著正向影响中介变量感知价值,之后再经过用户的感知价值来影响在线教育平台消费者的在线课程购买意愿;在线教育平台用户的感知风险($\beta=-0.260$)与用户的感知成本($\beta=-0.242$)负向且显著影响在线教育平台用户课程购买意愿模型的中介变量感知价值。

6.1.2.1 时空自主性

在未进行分组分析的情况下,时空自主性显著正向影响用户感知价值,然后通过感知价值间接影响购买意愿(杨永清等,2012;玄海燕等,2018;腾讯研究院,2019)[4,179,182]。因此时空自主性也是影响用户购买意愿的重要因素之一。

在进行分组比较分析的情况下,拥有购买经验的用户时空自主性显著影响用户感知价值变量,再间接地影响在线教育平台用户的在线课程购买意愿。然而没有购买经验的用户,其时空自主性并不显著影响用户感知价值。没有购买经验的用户对课程内容、质量等方面的考虑更多,而未将课程学习的时间和空间摆在重要考虑的位置。

管理启示:

(1)优化时空自主性的课程学习功能,以提升用户的购买意愿。时间和空间的自主性往往需要配合在线教育平台提供的无线终端学习软件,这样才会允许用户决定学习的内容与配套的功能。

(2)对拥有购买经验的用户重点宣传时空自主性所带来的方便快捷。拥有购买经验的用户群组中,其时空自主性显著影响购买意愿和感知价值。因此要加强对拥有购买经验用户的针对性宣传,优化自主学习功能的便利性,以降低用户的流失率,提高拥有购买经验用户的复购率。

6.1.2.2 感知成本

用户感知成本对在线教育平台消费者的感知价值有显著的负向影响作用,再通过感知价值间接地影响在线教育平台用户的在线课程购买意愿,在线教育平台消费者的感知成本成为作用在线课程购买意愿的一个因素。(程兴火,2006;陈湘青,2016;王晰巍等,2017;宋金倩,2018;董庆兴等,2019)[81,171,172,244,245]。在多群组比较分析中,不管用户是否拥有课程的购买经验,用户感知成本对感知价值都有显著的负向影响。

较高的在线课程价格会显著影响用户课程的感知价值,课程所花费的时间、精力同样会影响用户的感知价值。因此降低用户的感知成本不仅限于课程定价的优化,还包括课程的学习方式、学习计划的改善,以适应用户个性化的学习需求。

管理启示:

(1)以用户接受的价格范围来制定课程价格。课程的定价不该是在线教育平台单方面的定价策略,而是建立在用户调查的基础上,定价在用户能够接受的范围来扩大销量,也可保证在线教育平台获得最大化的收入。

(2)根据用户自身的知识储备,提供个性化和针对性的课程方案。根据用户已经掌握知识的层次和个人的时间安排,可以对课程内容进行适当的切割和分块。这样不仅可以降低课程的单价,同时可以允许用户来选择适合自己的课程模块。用户对于自己掌握的内容可以选择跳过或者暂时不学,而直接学习自己所需要的内容。

6.1.2.3　感知有用性

从在线教育平台用户课程购买意愿模型的分析中得出感知有用性显著影响用户感知价值,而后间接影响购买意愿。因此感知有用性也是影响购买意愿的重要因素之一(欧阳映泉,2014;杨秀云等,2017;方爱华等,2018;李梦吟、王成慧,2019)[56,69,174,246]。在多群组比较分析当中,拥有购买经验的消费者和不曾拥有购买经验的使用者,他们的感知有用性都会显著地影响在线教育平台消费者的感知价值。

在线教育平台的课程更加需要精工细作,更加需要提升课程的内容质量,让用户感知到在线课程有利于提高学习效率,也更加轻松。

管理启示:

(1)注重课程内容对于学习者提升学习效率和学习效果的卖点宣传。在线教育平台应对课程内容持续优化,以提升用户的学习效率和学习效果。提供高质量且全面的课程介绍,深入描述课程的定位、目标、学情分析与教学方法,更加有利于提高用户的感知有用性。

(2)在线教育平台课程软件的开发过程中要注重软件的有用性和便利性,在课程内容的编排上也要注意课程内容的有效性和便利性。

6.1.2.4　感知易用性

在未进行分组比较的情况下,感知易用性显著影响用户感知价值,这也符合之前学者们的相关研究成果(刘遗志、汤定娜,2015;刘晓庆,2016;白玉,2017;刘昊达,2018)[31,173,247,248]。感知易用性先通过显著影响在线教育平台消费者的感知价值,再间接地影响到在线教育平台消费者的课程购买意愿。因此感知易用性也是影响购买意愿的因素之一。

在进行分组比较分析中,不拥有购买经验的用户感知易用性显著影响感知价值。而拥有购买经验的用户感知易用性并没有显著影响感知价值。这也说明没有购买经验的用户更加担心在线教育平台所提供的课程学习方式和软件是否易用。没有购买经验的用户对于在线教育课程的学习和客服联系等功能模块处于一个陌生的状态,因此他们会更加关注课程的学习方式和软件的使用方法。而拥有购买经验的用户对于课程学习的方式和软件操作已有一定的了解,因此感知易用性并未显著影响有购买经验用户的感知价值。

管理启示:

(1)提升在线教育平台课程学习软件的易用性。在线教育平台在软件开发和课程学习方式上,应注重用户所反馈的意见,开发人性化并且符合用户操作习惯的软件和课程学习方式,以提升用户的购买意愿。

(2)持续优化在线课程的教学方式和学习体验。新的多媒体技术、5G技术、移动互联网的普及为全息投影教学、高清视频教学、VR 教学带来更多的可能性。在线教育平台要注重新技术带来的便捷性,提升在线课程学习的易用性。

(3)针对没有购买经验的用户加大感知易用性的宣传。在多群组比较分析中,没有购买经验的用户感知易用性显著影响其感知价值,间接影响其购买意愿,这也说明没有购买经验的用户更加注重在线教育课程是否易学和软件是否易用。

6.1.2.5　感知风险

用户感知风险显著负向影响感知价值,这与前人的研究结果相同(万苑微,2011;杨秀云等,2017;方爱华等,2018;郭朋,2019)[69,174,249,250]。在多群组比较分析当中,不同购买经验的用户,其感知风险都显著影响感知价值。

当在线教育平台用户选择课程时,会担心课程的质量无法达到预期,课程学习的效果不能达到自己的预期,也会担心后期的售后服务质量。因此有必要降低潜在消费者的感知风险来提高在线教育平台消费者的购买意愿,这也是非常行之有效的措施。

管理启示:

(1)配合课程的免费试听,提供用户免费试听课程的机会。通过试听让用户对课程的质量、学习形式和学习方式获得一定认知后,再考虑做出相应的决策,有利于降低用户的感知风险。

(2)优化在线客服的联系功能。为减少用户对售后服务和课程功能使用的一些顾虑,可以通过提供更加具有便捷性的客服功能来降低用户的感知风险,从而提升用户的感知价值。

6.1.3　关于课程口碑的探讨

课程口碑作为感知价值和课程购买意愿之间关系的调节变量,通过了显著性的检验并有显著正向调节作用。这与之前学者所得的研究结论相同（钟凯、张传庆,2013;陈超等,2017;王建军等,2019)[47,68,251]。在进行分组比较时发现课程口碑也显著调节用户的感知价值和购买意愿之间的关系。可见课程口碑也是影响用户课程购买意愿的关键因素之一。加大对课程口碑的建设,也是提升用户感知价值和购买意愿非常行之有效的措施。

课程口碑都是之前已购买用户所反馈的点评,对于还未进行购买的用户具有参考意义。用户往往会在购买在线课程前参考课程的相关评论,也会分辨评论的真实性,分清哪些评论对自己选购商品起到指导性作用。课程口碑往往给用户一种比较客观的反馈,相比较课程介绍是由在线教育平台来发布的,课程口碑更具有真实性特点,尤其是在这种虚拟电子商务产品的选购上,课程口碑会更加具有参考性。

管理启示:

(1)在线教育平台需要注重课程口碑的积累。在线教育平台中不拥有任何口碑的课程,难以获得用户的信赖,因此其要积累有质量的课程口碑,以供用户参考并做出理智的购买决策。真实的课程口碑也有助于提升用户的感知价值和购买意愿。

(2)收集课程口碑的反馈以对在线课程进行改善。在用户进行课程口碑的点评或课程学习的反馈时,在线教育平台可以对这些口碑内容进行归类,有针对性地去研究用户发出该点评的原因,以达到收集用户意见来促进课程优化的目的。

(3)及时反馈用户口碑,建立良好的双向互动机制。在用户留下课程反馈时,在线教育平台的工作人员也可以及时与用户进行沟通,避免客户发送反馈后了无音讯。同时也可以给用户一种课程建设的参与感,更好地维护与客户之间的关系。

(4)发掘潜在的口碑营销对象。发掘愿意分享给亲朋好友的用户,通过用户发布课程反馈来了解用户对于课程的感受。在此过程中可以发掘愿意分享该课程给亲朋好友的用户,有利于开展低成本的口碑营销。

6.1.4　关于用户年龄、教育的探讨

6.1.4.1　用户年龄

在控制变量的分析中,用户年龄显著影响用户的课程购买意愿(高瑜,

2013;钱英杰,2013;陈芳草,2018)[184,252,253]。在多群组分析当中用户年龄同样显著影响用户的课程购买意愿,由此说明用户年龄也是影响用户课程购买意愿的重要因素之一。

用户年龄显著负向影响课程购买意愿,说明随着用户年龄的增长,其对在线课程的购买意愿下降了。年龄相对较小的用户,其所处的学习氛围更浓,好奇心也相对更强。在线教育平台的课程作为新颖的学习方式,也更容易被这些正处于学习氛围当中的年轻一代所接受。

管理启示:根据用户年龄阶段进行分组的课程营销。针对性的推广有利于提高用户的课程购买意愿,减少无效推广,减少对用户的广告骚扰,提升用户体验。在进行多群组比较分析中同样发现用户年龄都显著负向影响课程购买意愿,进一步证明用户年龄是影响在线教育平台消费者购买意愿的一个重要因素。根据潜在消费者的年龄变量进行分层次的推广,有助于提高用户的课程购买意愿。

6.1.4.2　用户教育

在线教育平台课程用户购买意愿模型当中用户教育显著影响课程购买意愿,这也符合学者们的研究结论(冯建英等,2008;范琳琳,2015;腾讯研究院,2019)[4,183,254],说明用户教育也是影响课程购买意愿的重要因素之一。

在进行多群组比较分析当中,发现没有购买在线课程经验的用户教育显著影响课程购买意愿,而拥有购买经验的用户教育并未显著影响课程购买意愿。这说明没有购买经验的用户群中,高学历用户会通过资料收集和自我判断做出相应的决策。而拥有购买经验的用户,对在线课程已经获得一定的认知,因此用户教育并不显著影响其课程购买意愿。

管理启示:加大对学历层次较高用户的营销推广力度。在线教育平台可以借助数据分析来了解用户是否有相关课程的购买记录,并利用自身和第三方数据库来分析用户的学历层次并判断用户是否属于没有购买经验的高学历用户,再启动相应的推荐机制。这样的过程可以减少不必要的营销支出,也可获得更好的推广效果。

6.2　研究建议

(1)保证课程质量,提供口碑参考。保证课程质量以提升课程的感知价值,对于提升课程购买意愿有着非常关键的作用。在线教育平台用户通过点击量、购买人数、口碑来筛选课程,这些脱离课程内容专业性的数据指标难以真正判断课程质量。单纯从互联网指标来筛选课程容易受到营销手段的刺激,导致用户购买的课程并不适合自身,花费了时间、金钱却无法获得良好的学习效果。把握课程的质量,通过优秀的课程积累用户口碑,收获更多忠实用户,这也是在线教育平台形成自身独特优势的契机,有助于实现在线教育平台的可持续发展。

(2)根据购买经验分组,通过 AI 推荐在线课程。不同购买经验的用户在课程免费试听、感知成本、感知易用性、时空自主性、用户教育上拥有不同的显著性,这也要求细化用户画像和标签,分组分层地进行课程推荐。加强课程内容多元化与个性化需求的匹配,通过人工智能(AI)技术来分析用户需求并针对性地推荐课程,以此提高课程购买意愿。

(3)优化时空自主性功能,利用 5G、VR、AR 提升用户体验。在线教育课程允许用户在任何时候和任何地点学习,对于碎片化的时间可以进行有效的利用,不再受上课地点的限制。利用 5G、VR、AR 等新技术对在线教育平台进行功能升级,为用户提供“随时随地学习,自主掌握进度”的学习环境。

(4)借助云服务、大数据技术,降低课程价格。提供优惠的在线课程价格有利于提高用户的课程购买意愿。云服务和大数据技术的应用,允许更多用户进行在线课程的学习,为在线教育平台用户提供更加优质的服务并大幅度下降边际成本。

(5)提供更多课程免费试听,降低用户感知风险。提前试听有助于用户了解课程内容、质量、适用性等,帮助客户做出购买决策。尤其是对于没有课程购买经验的用户,可以提供免费试听资格来提升其购买意愿。如 CCtalk 等 B2B2C 在线教育平台都提供免费试听的机会,以此来提升客户购买率。

6.3　研究创新

(1)数据来源的创新。本书调研的样本数据全部来自真实商业环境的用户反馈。主要数据来自数据城堡(DataCastle)、腾讯课堂、淘宝教育等真实在线教育平台的用户,而不是采用学生问卷的方式来获得样本数据,因此本研究较大程度还原了真实商业场景中的消费行为。相比较采用学生问卷的方式,本研究更加具有说服力和商业的参考价值,能够给在线教育平台企业和从业者一些参考。

(2)研究模型的整合创新。本研究的在线教育平台用户课程购买意愿模型将技术接受模型、感知价值和感知风险理论进行了整合创新。根据中国在线教育平台的情境,引入了课程免费试听和时空自主性两个情境变量,加入了口碑调节变量和控制变量,扩大了模型的解释范围,完善了感知价值理论。

(3)研究方法上的创新。本研究采用了 PLS-SEM 研究方法对在线教育平台用户课程购买意愿影响因素构建模型并且进行相关检验,然后对拥有在线教育平台课程购买经验和不曾拥有购买经验的用户进行分组讨论。采用 PLS-MGA 进行多群组比较分析,进一步讨论具有不同购买经验的用户购买意愿影响模型中各潜在变量之间的相互关系与强度,以探讨不同用户分组的购买意愿所包含的因素与对应因素的影响强度。

6.4　研究局限与展望

本研究在查阅文献并借鉴之前学者的研究成果基础上,开展了中国在线教育平台用户课程购买意愿的影响因素研究,并取得了一定的成果。鉴于人财物等客观原因,本研究的内容还十分有限,也存在一些不足之处,但这些不足之处同样是未来开展进一步研究的建议。

第 1 点:增加经济回报方面的研究内容。

后期的研究中可以增加经济回报方面的潜在变量,并调查用户在学习前后所产生的收入差异,以研究经济回报和学习前后的收入差异是否对用户的购买决定产生相关影响。鉴于在线课程类型的多样性,这方面的调查同时可以了解经济回报是否会对用户选择课程类型产生影响,以丰富相关领域研究内容。

第 2 点:数据采集方式和样本数量的优化。

本次调研的数据全部来自在线问卷的回收,这些问卷数据都是用户在一个时点回复的内容。因此,问卷数量和代表性会存在一定的片面性。在数字化和大数据的发展趋势下,可以考虑跟踪用户的行为轨迹和对用户画像的记录,从而获取更多的数据样本和更全面的数据来分析用户课程购买意愿。

第 3 点:更多潜在变量、研究方法的探索。

后续的研究可以采用定性研究方法与本研究所用的定量研究方法。之后的研究中,可以通过焦点访谈的方式进行深度沟通来发现更多潜在变量。两种研究方法可以进行有效的互补。通过对用户的深度访谈可以获得更多创新的潜在变量来完善研究。

第 4 点:开展更深入的纵向研究。

本研究主要聚焦在线教育平台用户课程的购买意愿,后续可以聚焦用户的购买行为研究。之后通过跟踪用户从浏览、注册、使用到购买、复购或流失的整个行为流程,持续对用户行为进行研究,以更加准确了解用户整个生命周期的信息行为。

Chapter 6   Conclusions and Prospects

6.1   Research Conclusions and Management Implications

By running SmartPLS 3.2.8, the PLS-SEM estimates the impacts of PI of OEP usage identifies the factors that directly affect PI: TSA, CFT, PR and, PV. These four potential variables have different impacts on the dependent variable, PI, and all have passed the significance test. The path coefficients of each potential variable to dependent variable are PV ($\beta=0.281$), TSA ($\beta=0.310$), CFT ($\beta=0.074$), PR ($\beta=-0.093$).

6.1.1   Factors Directly Affecting PI

(1) PV

The results show that PV is one of the critical factors affecting PI. When consumers purchase virtual products such as online courses, they fully collect relevant information and compare different options and then obtain their PV to make decisions, which is consistent with previous research (Zeithaml, 1988; Wang, 2015; Chu, 2018; Hong, Zheng, & Zhou, 2019). When users make a judgment of PV, they compare and evaluate perceived benefits and losses, based on which they obtain the self-perceived value, and it ultimately drives users' intention to purchase the course on OEP.

Enlightenment for management: PV significantly affects PI. Therefore, in the formulation of marketing strategies, it is necessary to highlight the perceived benefits of courses on the OEP so that users can perceive more value, gains, and benefits. In this way, consumers can fully understand the benefits that the course can bring to them and clarify the value of the course when they choose their products or share them through WM. It also requires the OEP operators and the courses producers to focus on refining the selling points of the course. At the same time, we should meet the needs of the course's target costomers, and the characteristics of the course need to be integrated into the content of the course. It also makes the course more targeted and reduces unnecessary promotion costs in marketing, and the targets of the course are refined, thus creating unique selling points. The comparison between perceived benefits and losses finally forms PV, which also provides a reference for classification management for the OEP.

According to the multi-group comparative analysis, whether users once bought OEP courses or not, their PV significantly affects the user's PI. Therefore, it is imperative to impact the PI of users through PV.

(2) TSA

Through empirical analysis, TSA has a significant impact on users' PI, which shows that the TSA of online courses has become a key factor in enhancing users' PI (Shu, 2016; Yang, 2016; Su, 2019). In the multi-group comparative analysis, it was found that users with and without experience in buying course on OEP passed the significant test of TSA.

TSA means that the learning method on OEP is not restrained by time and space, allowing users to decide the content, progress, time and place of learning autonomously. The online course does not require users to go to the classroom to participate in the training. The recorded course has allowed the user to decide the time and place to study. Although the live course does not allow users to choose when to study, it is more interactive, engaging users and teachers in real-time interaction and feedback.

TSA has brought about tremendous changes in the way of teaching. Since online learning breaks the limitations of time and space, online learning has allowed more users to learn and interact online simultaneously through networked terminal devices such as mobile phones and computers. The online course broadens the teaching method and carrier. The online method can combine many new teaching software and multimedia technology to enhance the results and entertainment of teaching.

Enlightenment for management inspiration: ① TSA has expanded the target customer coverage of the OEP. Online learning is more convenient and faster, so the marketing of OEP can be targeted at users of offline learning by providing a different learning experience. These users are also potential target consumers for OEP marketing.

② The OEP and course producers should pay more attention to the characteristics of TSA, make full use of new technologies to improve user learning efficiency and convenience. Combining the popular 5G, virtual reality (VR), Internet of Things, and mobile Internet technologies, the convenience brought by TSA can be fully explored for users on the OEP.

③ To learn with fragmented time should be allowed. TSA facilitates real-time tracking and feedback. New technologies, features, and wearable devices allow users to participate in the teaching process without time and space constraints, Breaking the time limit also allows users to take advantage of the fragmented time for phased learning.

(3) CFT

In the model of users' intention of purchasing courses on OEP, the CFT has a significant impact on users' willingness to buy courses, which indicates that CFT directly affects users' intention of purchasing courses on OEP (Li, 2016; Xu, Zhang, & Dong, 2018; Li, Zhang, & Hu, 2019). It can be seen that CFT is also one of the critical factors that directly affect the willingness to purchase the course.

In the multi-group comparison analysis, users who have never bought online courses before, the CFT ($\beta=0.205$, $p<0.001$) significantly affect their PI, which indicates that they pay more attention to the CFT of the online course. For users who once bought online courses before, CFT does not significantly affect their willingness to buy an online course. By comparing the two groups, it is found that CFT imposes different impacts on users with different purchasing experiences.

Because online courses are virtual e-commerce products, they generally exist in video, text, and pictures. It is difficult for users to have an intuitive evaluation and to feel about the online course. It can only be understood through the relevant introduction of the course. However, the CFT provides users with the opportunity to understand the content, the instructor, the method of teaching, and the quality of the lecture in the course. The experience provided by the free trial of the course is more intuitive than the text and image; thus, it is more helpful for users to make rational purchasing decisions.

Enlightenment for management: The OEP should provide more free trial services for users and improve the quality of CFT. The CFT reflects the confidence of the OEP and the course producer, which can help the user to understand the details of the course straightway. The CFT allows the user to intuitively understand the lecture's content, form, quality, etc. Thus helping the user make the purchase decision. From the data analysis, CFT enhances the user's willingness to purchase. Therefore, the OEP should provide CFT service, pay attention to the quality of CFT, and help the user to feel the specific content and form of the intuitively course, thereby raising the sales conversion rate of the online course.

In the multi-group comparative analysis, CFT imposes different impacts on PI of users in two groups with different purchasing experiences. Among them, users who never bought online courses before pay more attention to CFT. Due to the lack of similar purchase experience before, it is difficult for them to assume the subsequent experiences of buying an online course, so these users prefer to use CFT to taste of the online course. In marketing promotion, more tremendous efforts should be made to promote CFT recommendations to users who never bought online courses before to enhance their willingness to start buying courses.

(4) PR

This study has found that PR significantly affects PI, which indicates that PR is also one of the critical factors affecting the willingness to purchase online courses (Wang, 2016; Wang, 2017; Xiang, 2018; Cui, 2019). In the multi-group comparative analysis, it was found that PR of users without purchasing experience has a significant negative impact on the PI. PR of users with purchasing experience does not have a significant impact on PI. Users worry that the quality of the course may not meet their expectations since the online course is a virtual product the course, and they also worry that they cannot achieve the purpose of learning through learning the online course, or they cannot complete learning all the course. Since the user understands the content of the course only through the course introduction on the website, there is no intuitive way to inform themselves of information about the course, so the user has fears and worries that hinders their intention to buy courses.

Enlightenment for management: ① A 7-day return of goods without reasons can be offered. Users are allowed to request refunds under limited conditions, which reduces users' fears that the quality and content of the course cannot meet their expectations. This practice can reduce the concerns of users to enhance their willingness to buy online courses.

② The function of online customer service can be added to improve the convenience of contacting customer service. Optimization of online customer service ensures that users can contact customer service when they are hesitant or have concerns, and the service can relieve their worries answer their inquiries, and reduce users' concerns about the after-sales service.

③ The free re-learning service can be provided, which allows users to participate in the next course if they are not able to complete the current course, thereby reducing the user's fear of not being able to complete the course in time.

In the multi-group comparative analysis, for users without buying experience, their PR exerts a significant negative impact on their PI. Since the group of users have never bought similar products before, their PR is more likely to be high. However, users with experience in buying online courses because they already have related buying and learning experiences. Their concerns about the course's quality, content and learning arrangements of the course are no longer the key factors hindering them from buying online courses. In marketing, more attention should be paid to the reduction of PR of users who never bought online courses before to increase the PI of this group of users.

6.1.2 Discussion on Factors Indirectly Affecting PI

The PLS structural equation model of users' intention in buying courses on OEP shows that PU ($\beta=0.304$), PEU ($\beta=0.349$), and TSA ($\beta=0.180$) all significantly and positively affect the mediator variable, PV. Then, through PV, these factors mentioned above further affect the PI of users. PC ($\beta=-0.242$) and PR ($\beta=-0.260$) negatively affect the PV's mediator variable.

(1) TSA

Before conducting the group analysis, TSA significantly and positively affects users' PV, and then indirectly affects PI through PV (Yang, Zhang, & Man, 2012; Xuan, Dai, & Lin, 2018; TRI, 2019). Therefore, TSA is also one of the essential factors that affect users' PI.

In the case of group comparison analysis, A significantly affects their PV and indirectly affects their PI for users with experience in buying online courses. However, for users who never bought online courses before, TSA does not significantly affect their PV. Users without related experience have more considerations about the content and quality of the course, and they do not prioritize the time and space of learning the course when making their decisions.

Enlightenment for management: ① Optimize learning function of TSA to enhance the user's PV, which indirectly affects their PI. Realizing TSA often relies on the wireless terminal learning software provided by the OEP so that the user can be allowed to decide the content of learning and the supporting functions.

② For the users who have the purchasing experience, the marketing should focus on the convenience brought by TSA. In the group of users with purchasing experience, TSA significantly affects the user's PI and PV. Therefore, it is necessary to strengthen the targeted publicity and advertisement for users with purchasing experience and optimize the convenience of self-learning functions to reduce the user turnover rate and improve the repurchase rate of users who have purchasing experience.

(2) PC

According to H6, PC has a significant negative impact on PV and then indirectly affects PI through PV. PC is also one of the important factors affecting users' PI (Cheng, 2006; Chen, 2016; Wang, Li, & Wang, 2017; Song, 2018; Dong, Zhou, & Mao, 2019). In the multi-group comparative analysis, regardless of the users' previous course purchase experience, PC has a significant and negative impact on PV.

The higher price of online courses can significantly affect users' PV of the course, and the time and effort spent on the course also affect users' PV. Therefore, reducing the PC of the user is not limited to pricing optimization of the course, and it also includes the improvement of the learning mode of the course and the learning plan to adapt to the users' individual learning needs.

Enlightenment for management: ① course price based on the price range accepted by the user. The course pricing should not be a unilateral pricing strategy by the OEP. On the contrary, it should be based on the user survey, and the pricing should be within the price range that can be accepted by users to boost sales, thus maximizing income for the OEP.

② Provide personalized and targeted curriculum programs in line with users' knowledge reserve. According to the level of knowledge that the user has mastered and their individual time schedule, the course content can be appropriately divided into several course modules. It reduces the unit price of the course and allows the user to choose the course module that suits them. Users can choose to skip or temporarily not learn the content they have mastered and directly learn what they need based on the

236

course module.

(3) PU

From the analysis of the intention model in purchasing courses on OEP, it is concluded that PU significantly affects the user's PV and indirectly affects their PI. Therefore, PU is one of the important factors affecting PI (Ouyang, 2014; Yang, Jiang, & Ma, 2017; Fang, Lu, & Liu, 2018; Li & Wang, 2019). In a multi-group comparative analysis, the PU of users with and without purchasing experience significantly affects their PV.

On the OEP, the course needs to be more elaborated and exquisite, and the quality of the course content should be improved. In this way, users can perceive that the online course is conducive to improve learning efficiency and learning results and help them to acquire more knowledge. In addition, the learning process should be produced with better interestingness, enjoyment and relaxation because it is more conducive to enhancing the users' PV, thus affecting their PI.

Enlightenment for management inspiration: ① Pay attention to the content of the course and target the selling point of how the course can improve the learning efficiency and learning effect. The OEP should continuously optimize the content of the course to improve the learning efficiency and learning effect of users. The OEP should also provide a high-quality and comprehensive curriculum introduction, in-depth description of the course's positioning, goals, academic analysis and teaching methods, which is more conducive to improving users' PU.

② In developing the course software, the OEP should pay attention to the usefulness and convenience of the software and to the effectiveness and convenience of the course content when arranging the course content.

(4) PEU

Before the multi-group comparison, PEU significantly affects users' PV, which is also consistent with previous research results (Liu & Tang, 2015; Liu, 2016; Bai, 2017; Liu, 2018). PEU indirectly affects PI by significantly affecting PV. Therefore, PEU is one of the factors that impact PI.

In the multi-group comparison analysis, the PEU of users who do not have purchasing experience significantly affects their PV. PEU of users with purchasing experience does not significantly affect their PV. It also illustrates that users without purchasing experience is more worried about whether the methods and software provided by the OEP are easy to use. This group of users who have no purchasing experience are unacquainted with function modules of the online course, such as the learning module and customer service contacts module, so they tend to pay more attention to how the course is learned and the way how the software is used. Users with purchasing experience have a certain understanding of course learning and software operation, so PEU does not significantly affect their PV.

Enlightenment for management: ① Improve the ease of using the learning software where the online course is provided. When developing the learning software and learning methods, the OEP should pay attention to the feedback from the users, develop the learning software and learning methods that are user-friendly and conform to the user's habits of operating software, thus enhancing the user's PI.

② Continuously optimize the teaching methods and learning experience of online courses. The popularity of new multimedia technologies, 5G technologies, and mobile Internet brings more possibilities for holographic projection teaching, high-definition video teaching, and VR teaching. OEPs should focus on the convenience of new technologies and improve the ease of use of online courses.

③ Targeted dissemination and publicity with a focus on PEU have no experience in purchasing online courses. In the multi-group comparative analysis, the PEU of users without purchasing experience significantly affects their PV, indirectly affecting their PI. It indicates that users who have no purchasing experience pay more attention to whether online education courses are easy to learn and whether the software is easy to use.

(5) PR

Users' PR is significantly and negatively affected by their PV; a finding confirms previous empirical research (Wan, 2011; Yang, Jiang, & Ma, 2017; Fang, Lu, & Liu, 2018; Guo, 2019). In the multi-group comparative analysis, the PR of users with different purchasing experiences significantly affect both their PV, which further explains that PR is one of the important factors influencing the user's intention to purchase online courses.

When users are selecting courses on OEP, they worry that the quality of the courses cannot meet their expectations, the effect of the course cannot meet their expectations, and they also worry about the quality of after-sales service. Therefore, it is necessary to reduce users' PR to improve their PV and indirectly improve user' PI, and this is a very effective and necessary measure.

Enlightenment for management: ① Provide users with FCT opportunities to inform them of the course better. Through the FCT, users understand the course's quality, learning, and learning style, and then consider making corresponding decisions. This practice is beneficial to reduce users' PV.

② Optimize the contact function and contact information of online customer service. In order to reduce some users' concerns about the after-sales service and how to use some course functions, the user's PR can be reduced by providing more convenient customer service contact, thereby enhancing the user's PV.

6.1.3   Discussion on WM

As a moderator variable of PV to PI, WM has passed the significant test and significantly and positively moderates the impacts from PV to PI. It is the same as the previous research results (Zhong & Zhang, 2013; Chen, Wu, & Zhang, 2017; Wang, Wang, & Yang, 2019). In the multi-group comparison, WM significantly moderates the impacts of PV on PI, so it can be concluded that WM is one of the key factors affecting the intention of users to purchase online courses. Intensifying efforts in building WM of the course is an effective measure to improve users' PV and PI.

Since WM is the feedback from users who have previously purchased the course, it has reference significance for users who have not yet purchased it. Users often refer to the relevant comments of the course before purchasing it and distinguish the authenticity of the comments and distinguish which comments can guide them. WM often provides users with relatively objective feedback. Compared with the course introduction that the OEP publishes, WM is more authentic, especially when purchasing virtual e-commerce products when WM is more informative and of the greater reference value.

Enlightenment for management: ① The OEP needs to pay attention to the accumulation of WM. If the OEP does not have any WM, it will be challenging to obtain users' trust. Therefore, the accumulation of quality course feedback and comments provide users with references for making rational purchasing decisions. Authentic WM helps to enhance the user's PV and PI.

② Collect feedback about the course to improve online courses. The OEP can classify the WM when users comment or give feedback on the course, and specifically study the reasons why the user makes the comment to achieve the purpose of collecting user opinions to promote course optimization.

③ Timely feedback to users' WM, establish a suitable two-way interaction mechanism. When the user leaves the course feedback and WM, the staff of the OEP can communicate with the user in time to prevent one-way communication. At the same time, this practice can offer users a sense of participation in curriculum building and better maintain the relationship between the OEP with customers.

④ Discover potential WM marketing objects. Discover the WM marketing objects which are willing to share for the second time, which means that they are willing to share their learning experience with their friends and relatives and understand the user's feelings about the course through the user's comments. In this process, it can be discovered that users who are willing to do second-time-sharing, which is beneficial to the OEP, are likely to carry out low-cost WM marketing.

6.1.4   Discussion on Users' Age and Education Background

(1) Users' age

In the analysis of control variables, users' age significantly affects the PI (Gao, 2013; Chen, 2018). In the multi-group analysis, the user's age also significantly affects the user's PI, which indicates that the user's age is one of the crucial factors that affect the user's intention to purchase online courses.

The users' age significantly and negatively affects their intention to purchase online courses, which indicates that as the users' age increases, the intention to purchase online course will decrease. Relatively young users have a more vital learning atmosphere, more substantial curiosity, and longer time to extract economic rents from the investment in human capital. The OEP curriculum is a novel way of learning and is readily accepted by the younger generation immersed in the learning atmosphere.

Enlightenment for management: Course marketing grouped according to the age of the user. Targeted promotion improves users' willingness to purchase courses and user experience while reducing users' invalid promotion and advertisement distraction. In the multi-group comparative analysis, this research also found that the user's age has a significant and negative impact on users' PI, further indicating that the user's age is one of the critical factors affecting their willingness to purchase the course. The OEP can promote the course hierarchically according to users' age, which helps to increase the user's willingness to purchase the course.

(2) Users' education background

In the model of users' intention in purchasing courses on OEP course, users' education background significantly affects their intention to purchase the course, which is also in line with previous research results

(Feng, Mu, & Zhang, 2008; Fan, 2015; TRI, 2019) and explains that user education background is one of the important factors affecting their intention topurchase online courses.

In the multi-group comparative analysis, it was found that the education background of users without experience in purchasing online courses significantly affects their PI. The educational background of users with purchasing experience does not significantly affect their PI. It shows that in the user group without purchasing experience, highly educated users make corresponding decisions through data collection and self-judgment. Users with purchasing experience have gained a certain understanding of online courses, so their education level does not significantly affect their intention to purchase courses.

Enlightenment for management: increase efforts in the marketing promotion for users with higher education levels. The OEP can use data analysis to understand whether the user has a purchase record or not, and OEP can also use its own and third-party database to analyze the user's education level to determine whether the user without purchasing experience is highly-educated, and then launch a corresponding recommendation mechanism. Such a process can reduce unnecessarlly marketing expenses and achieve better promotion results.

6.2　Research Recommendations

1. To ensure the quality of the course, provide WM for reference. PV significantly affects PI and WM significantly and positively affects the impacts of PV on the PI. Ensuring the quality of the course and enhancing the PV of the course is critical to enhancing PI. Users on the OEP filter select the course by the number of clicks, purchases, and WM. With these professional data indicators derived from the course content, it is not easy to truly judge the quality of the course. Selecting a course based on Internet data indicators is easily stimulated by marketing methods,

resulting in the situation that courses are not suitable for some users who spend time and money, ending in poor learning results. Grasping the quality of the course, accumulating reputation through excellent courses and accessing more loyal users are opportunities for the OEP to form its own unique advantages and realize the sustainable development of the OEP.

2. According to the user group classified based on their purchase experience, recommend online courses through AI. Users with different purchasing experience have different salience in terms of CFT, PC, PEU, TSA and education, which requires refining user portraits and labels, and recommending courses in different groups and layers. OEPs can enhance the alignment of content diversification and individualized needs and analyze users' needs and recommend courses in a targeted manner through AI technology to enhance users' PI.

3. Optimize TSA function and use 5G, VR, and AR to enhance the user experience. TSA significantly affects users' PI. PU and PEU significantly affect PV and indirectly affect users' PI. Therefore, improving TSA, PU and PEU helps to increase intention in purchasing courses. The online education program allows users to learn at any time and any where, while taking advantage of fragmented time, and their learning is no longer limited by the location of the class, making the learning process easier and more convenient. Utilize new technologies such as 5G, VR, and AR to upgrade the OEP to provide users with a learning environment of "learning at any time and self-control progress".

4. With cloud services, big data technology to reduce the price of the course. PC significantly and negatively affects PV and indirectly affects PI. Providing online courses at preferential prices is conducive to improving the user's intention to purchase the course. The application of cloud services and big data technology can increase users to learn online courses, provide better service for OEP users and signticantly reduce the marginal cost.

5. Provide more CFT to reduce users' PR. Free trials in advance of

the course help users understand the course's content, quality, applicability, etc. and helps customers make their purchasing decisions. In particular, for users who never bought online courses before, CFT can be provided to increase their PI. OEPs such as Taobao OEP, Tencent OEP, and CCtalk all offer opportunities for a free trial to enhance purchase rates.

6.3 Research Innovation

(1) Innovation in data sources. The sample data in this research is all from user feedback in a natural business environment. The primary data comes from user surveys of real OEPs such as DataCastle, Tencent OEP, and Taobao OEP, rather than using student questionnaires to obtain the sample data, therefore this study restores consumer behavior in real business scenarios to the most corsiderable extent. Compared with the way of student questionnaire, this study is more persuasive, enjoys most exellent commercial reference value, and gives guidance to OEP companies and practitioners.

(2) Integration and innovation of the research model. The model of users' intention in purchasing courses on OEP of this study integrates and innovates the TAM, PV, and PR theory. According to the situation of China's OEP, two situational variables, FCT and TSA, were introduced. The moderator variable, WM, and control variables were also added to expand the scope of the model and improve the theory of PV.

(3) Innovation in research methods. In this study, the PLS-SEM research method was used to construct a model for researching factors influencing users' intention in purchasing courses on the OEP and conduct related tests. Then group discussions were carried out based on whether users have experience in purchasing courses on OEP before. PLS multi-group analysis (PLS-MGA) was used for multi-group comparison analysis further discuss the relationship between different variabes in the model in

two different groups with different purchase experiences to explore the factors involved in the PI and the impacts strength of the corresponding factors in two groups.

6.4   Limitations and Outlook

Based on the literature review and the research results of previous researchers, this study researched factors influencing users' intention in purchasing courses on OEP in China, achieving significant results. However, due to objective restrains such as the shortage of workforce, the lack of material resources, time and energy, the scope of this study is still minimal with some shortcomings, but these shortcomings can also be interpreted as suggestions for further research in the future.

Point 1: Future research on economic returns of students.

Future research can consider the potential variables of economic returns and investigate the income differences gained by users of online courses before and after learning to study whether the economic returns and income differences before and after learning have a relevant impact on their purchasing decisions. In light of the diversity of online course types, this survey can also understand whether the economic returns affect the user's choice of course type to enrich the research content in related fields.

Point 2: Optimization of data collection methods and sample size.

The data of this survey came from online questionnaires issuing and collection, which means that all questionnaires were replied to and collected at a one time point. Therefore, the number and representativeness of the questionnaire are somewhat one-sided. Under the trend of digitization and big data, researchers can consider working with OEP companies to track the behavior of users on the platform and record user portraits to obtain more promient and more comprehensive data samples to analyze users' intention in purchasing courses.

Point 3: Exploration of more latent variables and research methods.

Subsequent studies can combine qualitative research with quantitative research. In empirical research, deep communication can be conducted through focus interviews to discover more latent variables. The combination of the two research methods is conducive to making up for the lack of quantitative research. Through in-depth interviews with users, more innovative and latent variables can be obtained to improve the research.

Point 4: In-depth longitudinal study.

This study focuses on users' intention to purchase an online course, and the follow-up study can focus on researching the user's purchase behavior. Then, by tracking the entire behavior process from browsing, registering, using, purchasing, repurchasing to customer loss, users' behavior is continuously studied to understand the information of users' life cycle behavior accurately.

附录　调查问卷正文

在线教育平台课程购买影响因素研究问卷

尊敬的先生/女士,您好!

本问卷主要探讨在在线教育平台上购买课程意愿的影响因素。问卷中的选项没有对错之分,请您如实填写。本次调查使用不记名方式,严格遵循保密原则,仅用于学术研究。您的意见对本次研究结果影响重大,再次为您的支持表示感谢。

1. 您拥有使用在线教育平台的经验吗?[单选题] *

○有　○没有

2. 性别[单选题] *

○男　○女

3. 年龄[单选题] *

○18岁以下　○19~25岁　○26~35岁　○36~45岁　○46岁以上

4. 学历[单选题] *

○高中(中专)及以下　○大学专科　○大学本科　○硕士研究生○博士研究生

5. 职业[单选题] *

○在校学生　○企业职员　○事业单位工作人员　○公务员　○社会团体工作人员　○企业主、个体从业者　○其他

6. 年收入[单选题] *

○3万元以下　○4万~10万元　○11万~20万元　○21万~30万元　○31万元以上

7. 您使用过哪些在线教育平台（有在线教育平台使用经验则请继续往下填）〔多选题〕＊

□网易云课堂（有道精品课）　　□沪江网校（含 CCtalk）　　□淘宝教育（淘宝大学）

□腾讯课堂　　□百度传课　　□YOUKU 学堂（优酷教育频道）

□YY 教育　　□多贝网　　□淘客网
□新浪公开课　　□其他＿＿＿＿＿＿

8. 您是否购买过 B2B2C 在线教育平台的在线付费课程？〔单选题〕＊
○暂时不打算购买　○正在打算选购　○已购买正在学习　○曾经购买已学完

9. 您学习的在线付费课程包含的内容有哪些？〔多选题〕＊
□证书获取　□职业技能　□专升本、考研课程　□公务员考试培训
□英语培训　□兴趣爱好　□其他＿＿＿＿＿＿

10. 感知价值（1＝非常不认同,7＝非常认同）〔矩阵量表题〕＊

	1	2	3	4	5	6	7
相比我付出的金钱,购买在线课程是值得的	○	○	○	○	○	○	○
相比我付出的时间,购买在线课程是值得的	○	○	○	○	○	○	○
相比我付出的精力,购买在线课程是值得的	○	○	○	○	○	○	○
我认为购买在线课程是具有价值、意义的	○	○	○	○	○	○	○

11. 课程口碑（1＝非常不认同,7＝非常认同）〔矩阵量表题〕＊

	1	2	3	4	5	6	7
购买在线课程前,我会参考课程的相关评论	○	○	○	○	○	○	○
在线课程评论区的点评信息比较真实	○	○	○	○	○	○	○
在线课程评论区的点评信息比较可靠	○	○	○	○	○	○	○
在线课程评论区的点评信息比较客观	○	○	○	○	○	○	○

12. 感知风险（1＝非常不认同,7＝非常认同）〔矩阵量表题〕＊

	1	2	3	4	5	6	7
我在购买在线课程时,会担心课程质量无法达到预期	○	○	○	○	○	○	○
我在购买在线课程时,会担心课程达不到学习的目的	○	○	○	○	○	○	○
我在购买在线课程时,会担心自己不能坚持完成课程学习	○	○	○	○	○	○	○
我在购买在线课程时,会担心售后服务无法保证	○	○	○	○	○	○	○

13. 感知成本(1=非常不认同,7=非常认同)[矩阵量表题] *

	1	2	3	4	5	6	7
我认为在线课程的定价相对较高	○	○	○	○	○	○	○
购买在线课程会让我花费更多金钱	○	○	○	○	○	○	○
在线课程没有缩短我掌握知识的时间或节省精力	○	○	○	○	○	○	○
选择适合我的在线课程很消耗我的时间、精力	○	○	○	○	○	○	○

14. 感知有用性(1=非常不认同,7=非常认同)[矩阵量表题] *

	1	2	3	4	5	6	7
我认为在线课程能提高我的学习效率	○	○	○	○	○	○	○
我认为在线课程能提高我的学习效果	○	○	○	○	○	○	○
我认为在线课程能帮我获得更多的知识	○	○	○	○	○	○	○
我认为在线课程能使我学习变得更轻松	○	○	○	○	○	○	○

15. 感知易用性(1=非常不认同,7=非常认同)[矩阵量表题] *

	1	2	3	4	5	6	7
我能轻松地通过在线教育平台找到所需的课程	○	○	○	○	○	○	○
我能轻松地使用在线教育平台进行课程学习	○	○	○	○	○	○	○
我能轻松地联系到在线课程的供应商	○	○	○	○	○	○	○
我能轻松地使用在线教育平台的新功能、新版本	○	○	○	○	○	○	○

16. 课程免费试听(1＝非常不认同,7＝非常认同)〔矩阵量表题〕＊

	1	2	3	4	5	6	7
支持免费试听的在线课程能帮助我进行更理智的购买决策	○	○	○	○	○	○	○
试听的在线课程若达到我的预期,我的购买意愿会增强	○	○	○	○	○	○	○
试听的在线课程老师授课形式能吸引我,我的购买意愿会增强	○	○	○	○	○	○	○
在线课程是否支持试听会影响我的购买意愿	○	○	○	○	○	○	○

17. 时空自主性(1＝非常不认同,7＝非常认同)〔矩阵量表题〕＊

	1	2	3	4	5	6	7
在线课程学习时,我可以自主决定学习内容	○	○	○	○	○	○	○
在线课程学习时,我可以自主决定学习进度	○	○	○	○	○	○	○
在线课程学习时,我可以自主决定学习时间	○	○	○	○	○	○	○
在线课程学习时,我可以自主决定学习地点	○	○	○	○	○	○	○

18. 购买意愿(1＝非常不认同,7＝非常认同)〔矩阵量表题〕＊

	1	2	3	4	5	6	7
未来,我会尝试购买在线教育平台的付费课程	○	○	○	○	○	○	○
未来,我会继续购买在线教育平台的付费课程	○	○	○	○	○	○	○
如果在线课程是我需要的,我很愿意购买	○	○	○	○	○	○	○
我愿意将优质的在线课程推荐给朋友	○	○	○	○	○	○	○

Appendix: Questionnaire content

Research Questionnaire for Influencing Factors of Online Education Platform Course Purchase

Dear Sir / Madam,

Thank you very much for taking the time to participate in this survey. This questionnaire is purely for academic research, aiming at investigating the factors that influence your intention to purchase courses on online education platforms (OEPs). There is no right or wrong answers. You are kindly requested to fill it out according to your real situation. This survey is anonymous, and strictly follows the principle of confidentiality, only used for academic research purposes. Your opinion will have a significant impact on the results of this research. Thank you again for your support.

Congratulations: Happy new year and all the best.

1. Do you have experience using OEPs? [You can choose only one option] *

○Yes ○No

2. Gender [You can choose only one option] *

○Male ○Female

3. Age [You can choose only one option] *

○Below 18 ○19~25 ○26~35 ○36~45 ○Above 46

4. Education background [You can choose only one option] *

○High school (technical secondary school) and below ○Diploma's degree ◯Bachelor's degree ◯Master's degree ◯Ph. D

5. Occupation [You can choose only one option] *

◯Student ◯Private sector ◯Public institution ◯Civil servant
◯Social group ◯Company owner and individual business ◯Others

6. Annual income (unit: thousand) [Multiple choice] *

◯Below 30 ◯40～100 ◯110～200 ◯210～300 ◯Above 310

7. Which OEPs have you used (If you have experience using online education platform, please continue) [You can choose more than one options] *

☐NetEase Cloud Class (ke. Youdao)	☐Hujiang Online School (including CCtalk)	☐Taobao Education (Taobao College)
☐Tencent Classroom	☐Baidu Chuanke	☐YOUKU Academy (Youku education channel)
☐YY Education	☐Duobei	☐Gxtaoke
☐Sina Open Class	☐Others _____	

8. Have you purchased a paid course from an online education platform? [You can choose only one option] *

◯Not planning to buy ◯Planning to buy ◯Have purchased and learning ◯Have purchased and learned

9. What are the content of your courses? [You can choose more than one options] *

☐ Certificate ☐Professional skills ☐Training on upgrade from junior college student to university student or undergraduate to postgraduate ☐ Civil servant exam training ☐English training ☐Hobbies ☐ Others _____

10. Perceived value (1 = Highly disagree ～ 7 = Highly agree) [Matrix scale] *

	1	2	3	4	5	6	7
Compared to the money I paid, it is worth buying online courses.	○	○	○	○	○	○	○
Compared to the time I paid, it is worth buying online courses.	○	○	○	○	○	○	○
Compared to the effort I put in, it is worth buying online courses	○	○	○	○	○	○	○
I think buying online courses is valuable and meaningful.	○	○	○	○	○	○	○

11. Word-of-Mouth (1 = Highly disagree ～ 7 = Highly agree) [Matrix scale] *

	1	2	3	4	5	6	7
Before I buy an online course, I will refer to the relevant reviews of the course.	○	○	○	○	○	○	○
The review in the online course review area is more authentic.	○	○	○	○	○	○	○
The review in the online course review area is more reliable.	○	○	○	○	○	○	○
The review in the online course review area is more objective.	○	○	○	○	○	○	○

12. Perceived Risk (1＝Highly disagree ～ 7＝Highly agree) [Matrix scale] *

	1	2	3	4	5	6	7
When I buy an online course, I am concerned that the quality of the course is not as expected.	○	○	○	○	○	○	○
When I buy an online course, I am worried that the course will not achieve the purpose of learning.	○	○	○	○	○	○	○
When I buy an online course, I worry about not being able to complete the course.	○	○	○	○	○	○	○
When I purchase an online course, I worry that after-sales service is not guaranteed.	○	○	○	○	○	○	○

13. Perceived Cost (1＝Highly disagree ～ 7＝Highly agree) [Matrix scale] *

	1	2	3	4	5	6	7
I think online courses are relatively expensive.	○	○	○	○	○	○	○
Buying online courses will cost me more money.	○	○	○	○	○	○	○
Online courses have not shortened my time and effort to acquire knowledge.	○	○	○	○	○	○	○
Choosing the right online course is a waste of my time and energy.	○	○	○	○	○	○	○

14. Perceived Usefulness (1＝Highly disagree ～ 7＝Highly agree) [Matrix scale] *

	1	2	3	4	5	6	7
I think online courses can improve my learning efficiency.	○	○	○	○	○	○	○
I think online courses can improve my learning result.	○	○	○	○	○	○	○
I think online courses can help me gain more knowledge.	○	○	○	○	○	○	○
I think online courses will make my learning easier.	○	○	○	○	○	○	○

15. Perceived Ease of Use (1＝Highly disagree ～ 7＝Highly agree) [Matrix scale] *

	1	2	3	4	5	6	7
I can easily find the courses I need through the online education platform.	○	○	○	○	○	○	○
I can easily use the online education platform to learn my course.	○	○	○	○	○	○	○
I can easily contact the supplier of the online course.	○	○	○	○	○	○	○
I can easily use the new features and new versions of the online education platform.	○	○	○	○	○	○	○

16. Course Free Trial (1＝Highly disagree ～ 7＝Highly agree) [Matrix scale] *

	1	2	3	4	5	6	7
Online courses that support free trials help me make more informed buying decisions.	○	○	○	○	○	○	○
If the online course that I listened to meets my expectations, my willingness to buy will increase.	○	○	○	○	○	○	○
If the way of lecturing can attract me, my willingness to buy will increase.	○	○	○	○	○	○	○
Whether the online course supports trial affects my purchase intention.	○	○	○	○	○	○	○

17. Time and space autonomy (1 = Highly disagree ~ 7 = Highly agree) [Matrix scale] *

	1	2	3	4	5	6	7
I can decide what I want to learn while studying online.	○	○	○	○	○	○	○
I can decide on my own learning progress while learning online.	○	○	○	○	○	○	○
I can decide when I want to study while learning online.	○	○	○	○	○	○	○
I can decide where I want to study while learning online.	○	○	○	○	○	○	○

18. Purchase Intention (1 = Highly disagree ~ 7 = Highly agree) [Matrix scale] *

	1	2	3	4	5	6	7
In the future, I will try to purchase paid courses on the online education platform (OEP).	○	○	○	○	○	○	○
In the future, I will continue to purchase paid courses from OEPs.	○	○	○	○	○	○	○
If online courses are what I need, I would love to buy.	○	○	○	○	○	○	○
I would recommend quality online courses to friends.	○	○	○	○	○	○	○

参考文献

[1] 中国互联网络信息中心(CNNIC).第 47 次《中国互联网络发展状况统计报告》[EB/OL]. http://www.cac.gov.cn/2021-02/03/c_1613923423079314.htm,2021-2-28.

[2] 中国人民银行. 2020 年支付体系运行总体情况[EB/OL]. http://www.gov.cn/xinwen/2021-03/24/content _ 5595427.htm,2021-04-27.

[3] 工业和信息化部,国家发展和改革委员会.扩大和升级信息消费三年行动计划(2018—2020 年)[EB/OL]. http://www.miit.gov.cn/n1146295/n1652858/n1652930/n3757022/c6309188/content.html,2018-8-11.

[4] 腾讯研究院.2019 中国在线职业教育市场发展报告[EB/OL]. http://www.100ec.cn/detail-6504749.html,2019-3-13.

[5] 艾瑞咨询.2017 年中国 B2B2C 在线教育平台行业研究报告[EB/OL]. http://report.iresearch.cn/report/201712/3117.shtml,2018-8-7.

[6] 网经社-网络经济服务平台.2018 年度中国在线教育市场发展报告[EB/OL]. http://www.100ec.cn/zt/2018zxjybg/,2019-5-27.

[7] 极光大数据.2017 年 8 月在线教育市场 app 研究报告[EB/OL]. http://www.199it.com/archives/637393.html,2019-04-28.

[8] 前瞻产业研究院.2019 年中国在线教育行业市场前瞻分析报告[EB/OL]. https://bg.qianzhan.com/report/detail/1812171643422217.html,2018-12-17.

[9] 冯建英,穆维松,傅泽田.消费者的购买意愿研究综述[J].现代管理科学,2006(11):7-9.

[10] 李雅筝.在线教育平台用户持续使用意向及课程付费意愿影响因

素研究[D].合肥:中国科学技术大学博士论文,2016.

[11] 许亚楠,张孟琪,董治华,等.大学生在线网络课程付费意愿的因素[J].管理观察,2018(32):117-118.

[12] 陈昊,焦微玲,李文立.消费者知识付费意愿实证研究——基于试用视角[J].现代情报,2019,39(2):136-144.

[13] 问卷星.关于我们——问卷星[EB/OL]. https://www.wjx.cn/html/aboutus.aspx,2018-8-28.

[14] Eagly A H, Chaiken S. Harcourt Brace Jovanovich College Publishers[M]. New York: Harcourt Brace Jovanovich College Publishers,1993.

[15] Fishbein M A, Ajzen I. Belief, attitude, intention and behavior: An introduction to theory and research[M]. London: Addison-Wesley,1975.

[16] Bagozzi R P, Burnkrant R E. Attitude organization and the attitude - behavior relationship[J]. Journal of personality and social psychology, 1979, 37(6): 913-929.

[17] Burke J J, Hatfield J L, Klein R R. Accumulation of heat shock proteins in field-grown cotton[J]. Plant physiology, 1985, 78 (2): 394-398.

[18] Dodds W B, Monroe K B, Grewal D. Effects of price, brand, and store information on buyers' product evaluations [J]. Journal of marketing research, 1991, 28(3): 307-319.

[19] Ajzen I, Driver B L. Application of the theory of planned behavior to leisure choice[J]. Journal of leisure research, 1992, 24(3): 207-224.

[20] Spears N, Singh S N. Measuring attitude toward the brand and purchase intentions[J]. Journal of current issues & research in advertising, 2004, 26(2): 53-66.

[21] 韩睿,田志龙.促销类型对消费者感知及行为意向影响的研究[J].管理科学,2005(2):85-91.

[22] 张金鑫.在线负面评论对网络购买意愿的影响研究——消费者品牌认同的调节作用[D].南京:南京师范大学硕士论文,2017.

[23] 庞玉玮. 知识付费类课程用户付费意愿影响因素研究[D]. 广州：暨南大学硕士论文, 2018.

[24] 刘遗志, 胡争艳, 汤定娜. 研究型购物者为何回归离线渠道购买？——基于感知风险和感知成本视角[J]. 北京工商大学学报（社会科学版）, 2019, 34(1)：52-62.

[25] Monroe K B. Buyers' subjective perceptions of price[J]. Journal of marketing research, 1973, 10(1)：70-80.

[26] Teas R K, Agarwal S. The effects of extrinsic product cues on consumers' perceptions of quality, sacrifice, and value[J]. Journal of the Academy of marketing Science, 2000, 28(2)：278-290.

[27] Tam J L M. Customer satisfaction, service quality and perceived value：an integrative model[J]. Journal of marketing management, 2004, 20(7-8)：897-917.

[28] Wu C, Hsing S. Less is more：How scarcity influences consumers' value perceptions and purchase intents through mediating variables[J]. Journal of American Academy of Business, 2006, 9(2)：125-132.

[29] 宋亦平, 王晓艳, 许云莲. 网上商店形象对网上购物者商店忠诚度的影响[J]. 管理评论, 2006(11)：31-38＋62-64.

[30] 钟凯. 网络消费者感知价值对购买意愿影响的研究[D]. 沈阳：辽宁大学博士论文, 2013.

[31] 刘遗志, 汤定娜. 多渠道环境下消费者感知价值与离线向在线渠道迁徙行为研究[J]. 山西财经大学学报, 2015, 37(8)：11-20.

[32] 王赟芝. 自媒体用户信息内容消费意愿影响因素研究[D]. 合肥：安徽大学硕士论文, 2017.

[33] 林婷婷, 曲洪建. 网红营销要素对服装消费者购买意愿的影响[J]. 丝绸, 2019, 56(3)：54-62.

[34] 黄英, 朱顺德. 二十一世纪的口碑营销及其在中国的发展潜力[J]. 管理现代化, 2003(6)：33-36.

[35] Park D H, Lee J, Han I. The effect of on-line consumer reviews on consumer purchasing intention：The moderating role of

involvement[J]. International journal of electronic commerce, 2007, 11(4): 125-148.

[36] Lee M, Youn S. Electronic word of mouth（eWOM）How eWOM platforms influence consumer product judgement[J]. International Journal of Advertising, 2009, 28(3): 473-499.

[37] Cui G, Lui H K, Guo X. The effect of online consumer reviews on new product sales[J]. International Journal of Electronic Commerce, 2012, 17(1): 39-58.

[38] Hennig-Thurau T, Walsh G, Walsh G. Electronic word-of-mouth: Motives for and consequences of reading customer articulations on the Internet [J]. International journal of electronic commerce, 2003, 8(2): 51-74.

[39] 毕继东. 网络口碑对消费者购买意愿影响实证研究[J]. 情报杂志, 2009, 28(11): 46-51.

[40] 李佳. 社交网络下网络口碑、价值共创对消费者购买意愿的影响[D]. 北京: 北京邮电大学硕士论文, 2015.

[41] 黄文彦, 劳陈峰. 网络口碑质量对顾客感知价值和购买意愿的影响研究[J]. 消费经济, 2013, 29(5): 48-53.

[42] 卢长宝, 黄桂艳, 李娜. 秒杀对电商网站人气聚集的影响机制: 基于时间压力的实证研究[J]. 东南学术, 2017(05): 154-164+248.

[43] 张景. 网络口碑对消费者购买决策行为的影响研究[D]. 包头: 内蒙古科技大学硕士论文, 2015.

[44] 毕继东. 负面网络口碑对消费者行为意愿的影响研究[D]. 济南: 山东大学博士论文, 2010.

[45] 郭菲. 负面网络口碑对消费者购买意愿的影响研究[D]. 济南: 山东大学硕士论文, 2015.

[46] 叶阳, 王涵. 有声阅读平台用户内容付费意愿影响因素研究[J]. 图书馆学研究, 2018(1): 82-88.

[47] 王建军, 王玲玉, 王蒙蒙. 网络口碑、感知价值与消费者购买意愿: 中介与调节作用检验[J]. 管理工程学报, 2019, 33(4): 80-87.

[48] 王君萍, 汪玥, 杨晶. 网络口碑来源特征与信息特征对保健食品购买意愿的影响[J]. 企业经济, 2019, 38(4): 75-82.

［49］ Sharma A. Trends in Internet-based business-to-business marketing[J]. Industrial marketing management，2002，31(2)：77-84.

［50］ Belanger F，Hiller J S，Smith W J. Trustworthiness in electronic commerce：the role of privacy，security，and site attributes[J]. The journal of strategic Information Systems，2002，11(3-4)：245-270.

［51］ Pavlou P A. Consumer acceptance of electronic commerce：Integrating trust and risk with the technology acceptance model[J]. International journal of electronic commerce，2003，7(3)：101-134.

［52］周劲松.我国消费者对 B2C 网站信任度的实证研究[J].现代管理科学，2005(11)：61-62.

［53］孙娇娇，孙永波.消费者决策风格和感知价值对生鲜移动网购意愿的影响研究[J].商业经济研究，2017(16)：77-79.

［54］孙小丽.消费者网购体验、体验价值与购买意愿[J].商业经济研究，2018(12)：60-63.

［55］崔剑峰.感知风险对消费者网络冲动购买的影响[J].社会科学战线，2019(04)：254-258.

［56］李梦吟，王成慧.社会化媒体是否能促进网络购买？——基于技术接受模型的实证研究[J].中国流通经济，2019，33(05)：90-99.

［57］范秀成，罗海成.基于顾客感知价值的服务企业竞争力探析[J].南开管理评论，2003(06)：41-45.

［58］ Peter J P，Tarpey Sr L X. A comparative analysis of three consumer decision strategies[J]. Journal of consumer research，1975，2(1)：29-37.

［59］ Zeithaml V A. Consumer perceptions of price，quality，and value：a means-end model and synthesis of evidence[J]. Journal of marketing，1988，52(3)：2-22.

［60］ Butz Jr H E，Goodstein L D. Measuring customer value：gaining the strategic advantage[J]. Organizational dynamics，1996，24(3)：63-77.

［61］ Gardial S F，Clemons D S，Woodruff R B，et al. Comparing consumers' recall of prepurchase and postpurchase product evaluation experiences［J］. Journal of consumer research，1994，20(4)：548-560.

［62］ Woodruff R B. Customer value：the next source for competitive advantage［J］. Journal of the academy of marketing science，1997，25(2)：139-153.

［63］ Grewal D，Monroe K B，Krishnan R. The effects of price-comparison advertising on buyers' perceptions of acquisition value，transaction value，and behavioral intentions［J］. Journal of marketing，1998，62(2)：46-59.

［64］ A Parasuraman，D Grewal. The impact of technology on the quality-value-loyalty chain：a research agenda［J］. Journal of the academy of marketing science，2000，28(1)：168-174.

［65］ 江林，袁宏福.基于个性的顾客感知价值研究［J］.市场营销导刊，2009(02)：22-28.

［66］ 郝俊峰.企业创新行为对顾客感知价值及购买行为的影响研究［D］.天津：天津大学博士论文，2011.

［67］ 赵岩.科特勒顾客价值理论及其发展研究［J］.商业时代，2013(09)：47-49.

［68］ 陈超，吴佩，张明杨.消费者感知价值对转基因食品购买意愿的影响研究——以转基因大豆油口碑为调节变量［J］.江苏农业科学，2017，45(07)：325-330.

［69］ 方爱华，陆朦朦，刘坤锋.虚拟社区用户知识付费意愿实证研究［J］.图书情报工作，2018，62(06)：105-115.

［70］ 陈凯，顾荣，胡静.基于感知收益—感知风险框架的新能源汽车购买意愿研究［J］.南京工业大学学报(社会科学版)，2019，18(02)：61-70＋112.

［71］ Keeney R L. The value of Internet commerce to the customer［J］. Management science，1999，45(4)：533-542.

［72］ Bourdeau L，Chebat J C，Couturier C. Internet consumer value of university students：E-mail-vs.-Web users［J］. Journal of

Retailing and Consumer Services，2002，9（2）：61-69.

[73] 钟小娜.网络购物模式下的顾客感知价值研究[J].经济论坛，2005(15)：131-133.

[74] 许统邦，梁嘉成，夏剑龙.B2C 模式下的顾客感知价值研究[J].商场现代化，2006(21)：106-107.

[75] 孙强，司有和.网上购物顾客感知价值构成研究[J].科技管理研究，2007(07)：185-187.

[76] 张明立.顾客价值——21 世纪企业竞争优势的来源[M].北京：电子工业出版社，2007.

[77] 高翔.消费者感知质量对线上购买意愿的影响机理研究[J].商业经济研究，2019(06)：73-76.

[78] Bauer R A. Dynamic Marketing for a Changing World[M]. Chicago：American Marketing Association,1960.

[79] Stone R N, Grønhaug K. Perceived risk：Further considerations for the marketing discipline[J]. European Journal of marketing, 1993, 27(3)：39-50.

[80] Jacoby J, Kaplan L B. The components of perceived risk[J]. Advances in Consumer Research，1972(3)：382-383.

[81] 王晰巍，李师萌，王楠阿雪，等.新媒体环境下用户信息交互意愿影响因素与实证——以汽车新媒体为例[J].图书情报工作，2017,61(15)：15-24.

[82] 赵士雯，陈立文，杜泽泽.基于结构方程模型的智慧社区购买意愿影响因素研究[J].资源开发与市场，2018,34(04)：575-581.

[83] Klemperer P. Markets with consumer switching costs[J]. The quarterly journal of economics，1987，102(2)：375-394.

[84] Dick A S, Basu K. Customer loyalty：toward an integrated conceptual framework[J]. Journal of the academy of marketing science，1994，22(2)：99-113.

[85] Venkatesh V, Morris M G, Davis G B, et al. User acceptance of information technology：Toward a unified view[J]. MIS quarterly，2003：425-478.

[86] Jones M A, Mothersbaugh D L, Beatty S E. Why customers

stay: measuring the underlying dimensions of services switching costs and managing their differential strategic outcomes[J]. Journal of business research, 2002, 55(6): 441-450.

[87] Lam S Y, Shankar V, Erramilli M K. Customer value, satisfaction, loyalty, and switching costs: an illustration from a business-to-business service context[J]. Journal of the academy of marketing science, 2004, 32(3): 293-311.

[88] 王英迪. 微信支付用户使用意愿影响因素研究[D]. 太原:山西财经大学硕士论文,2016.

[89] 万静. 感知价值与顾客多渠道购物意愿的关系探讨[J]. 商业经济研究,2018(06):50-53.

[90] 卢恒,张向先,张莉曼. 语音问答社区用户知识付费意愿影响因素研究——基于现状偏差的视角[J]. 情报科学,2019,37(06):119-125+162.

[91] Arndt J. Role of product-related conversations in the diffusion of a new product[J]. Journal of marketing Research, 1967, 4(3): 291-295.

[92] Brown J J, Reingen P H. Social ties and word-of-mouth referral behavior[J]. Journal of Consumer research, 1987, 14(3): 350-362.

[93] File K M, Judd B B, Prince R A. Interactive marketing: the influence of participation on positive word - of - mouth and referrals[J]. Journal of services marketing, 1992, 6(4): 5-14.

[94] Gelb B, Johnson M. Word-of-mouth communication: Causes and consequences[J]. Journal of health care marketing, 1995, 15: 54-54.

[95] Chatterjee P. Online Reviews: Do Consumers Use Them? [J]. Advances in Consumer Research, 2001, 28(1), 129-133.

[96] Bhatnagar A, Ghose S. Online information search termination patterns across product categories and consumer demographics [J]. Journal of Retailing, 2004, 80(3): 221-228.

[97] Sun T, Youn S, Wu G, et al. Online word-of-mouth (or

mouse）：An exploration of its antecedents and consequences [J]. Journal of Computer-Mediated Communication，2006，11 (4)：1104-1127.

[98] Porter M E. Competitive Advantage：Creating and Sustaining Superior Performance[M]. New York：Free Press,1985.

[99] Annika R，Christian G. The value concept and relationship marketing[J]. European journal of marketing，1996，30(2)：19-30.

[100] [美]菲利普·科特勒(Philip Kotler). 市场营销[M]. 1988. 俞利军译. 北京：华夏出版社,2003.

[101] Wood C M，Scheer L K. Incorporating perceived risk into models of consumer deal assessment and purchase intent[J]. Advances in Consumer Research，1996，23 (1)：399-404.

[102] Shim S，Eastlick M A，Lotz S L. An online prepurchase intentions model：the role of intention to search：best overall paper award—The Sixth Triennial AMS/ACRA Retailing Conference，2000 ☆ [J]. Journal of retailing，2001，77(3)：397-416.

[103] McKnight D H，Choudhury V，Kacmar C. The impact of initial consumer trust on intentions to transact with a web site：a trust building model[J]. The journal of strategic information systems，2002，11(3-4)：297-323.

[104] 孟陆,焦腾啸,刘凤军. 网络语言广告与调节定向对消费者购买意愿的影响[J]. 中国流通经济,2019,33(06):98-108.

[105] Davis F D. A technology acceptance model for empirically testing new end-user information systems：Theory and results [D]. Boston：Massachusetts Institute of Technology Doctorial Thesis，1986.

[106] Venkatesh V，Davis F D. A model of the antecedents of perceived ease of use：Development and test [J]. Decision sciences，1996，27(3)：451-481.

[107] 李同强. 在线外卖平台用户重复购买意向的实证研究[D]. 长春：

吉林大学硕士论文,2016.

[108] 黄彬.网络社区知识服务的购买意愿研究[D].上海:华东师范大学硕士论文,2017.

[109] 马健.移动互联网直播平台用户使用及付费意愿研究[D].北京:北京邮电大学硕士论文,2018.

[110] Williams V, Peters K. Faculty incentives for the preparation of web-based instruction [M]. Englewood Cliffs: Educational Technology Publications,1997.

[111] Miltiadou M. Motivational constructs as predictors of success in the online classroom. [J]. Dissertation Abstracts International, 2001, 61(9-A):3527.

[112] Piccoli G, Ahmad R, Ives B. Web-Based virtual learning environments: a research framekwork and a preliminary assessment of effectiveness in basic IT skills training[J]. Mis Quarterly, 2001, 25(4): 401-426.

[113] Harasim L M, Hiltz S R, Teles L. Learning networks: A field guide to teaching and learning online[M]. Boston: MIT press, 1995.

[114] 何克抗.从 Blending Learning 看教育技术理论的新发展[J].国家教育行政学院学报,2005(09):37-48+79.

[115] 上海市教科院智力开发研究所. 美国教育部教育技术白皮书[EB/OL]. https://www. docin. com/p-82683329. html,2019-04-29.

[116] 毛向辉.2003 年美国 10 项最佳教学技术应用项目[J].计算机教与学.IT 搜索,2003(12):28-33.

[117] Moallem M. An interactive online course: A collaborative design model [J]. Educational Technology Research and Development, 2003, 51(4): 85-103.

[118] Carson S E. MIT OCW Program Evaluation Findings Report [EB/OL]. http://ocw. mit. edu/NR/rdonlyres/3DFAB417-0966-4CC-8025-94F1991302F6/0/Program_Eval_March_2004. pdf,2019-07-18.

[119] Wikipedia. Massive open online course[EB/OL]. https://en. wikipedia. org/wiki/Massive_open_online_course，2018-7-29.

[120] 董晓迪. 国内在线教育的商业模式探析[D]. 北京:北京印刷学院硕士论文,2015.

[121] Allen I E, Seaman J. Online Report Card - Tracking Online Education in the United States ［EB/OL］. https:// onlinelearningsurvey. com/reports/onlinereportcard. pdf，2019-2-5.

[122] 余胜泉,林君芬. 2002 年教育信息化应用回顾与展望[J]. 中国电化教育,2003(02):5-12.

[123] 丁兴富. 论加快远程教育学科专业建设[J]. 中国远程教育,2004(19):17-22＋78.

[124] 方柏林,刘常庆. 美国马歇尔大学网络教育的组织管理及思考[J]. 开放教育研究,2006(05):39-42.

[125] 彭立宏,周丽涛. 对在线教育质量问题的若干思考[J]. 高等教育研究学报,2006(03):64-66.

[126] 高峻. 基于引领式在线学习模式的网络课程设计与研究[D]. 上海:上海师范大学硕士论文,2008.

[127] 姜卉,张振虹,黄荣怀. 在线协作学习中教师交互言语特征分析——以《e-Learning 导论》在线课程为案例[J]. 中国电化教育,2008(04):35-38.

[128] 胡晶,韩晓东,武喜春. 在线课程教学设计探索[J]. 中国远程教育,2010(06):39-41.

[129] 张玲燕. 网购消费的信息认知、感知价值和说服抵制——以意见领袖为例[J]. 商业经济研究,2018(12):70-72.

[130] 陈巍. 成人高等教育机构开展网络教育的实证研究[J]. 开放教育研究,2010,16(05):27-34.

[131] 齐振国. 关于网络教育的几个认识误区[J]. 教育探索,2012(11):83-85.

[132] 韩勇. Web 2.0 下以人为本的网络教育新模式探究[J]. 现代计算机(专业版),2012(30):53-55.

[133] 王立慧,徐文清. 搭建成人学历教育"立交桥"的思路设计——兼

论成人教育、网络教育、自考教育的融合发展[J].现代教育管理,2012(03):7-10.

[134] 中商产业研究院. 2019 年中国在线教育市场前景研究报告 [EB/OL]. http://www. askci. com/news/chanye/20190301/ 1500101142564. shtml,2019-3-1.

[135] 苏幕遮. 2019 中国 K12 在线教育行业研究报告[EB/OL]. https://www. iimedia. cn/c400/64177. html,2019-6-28.

[136] 李晓明.MOOC 理念打开了一扇创新的大窗户[J].中国教育网络,2013(4):24.

[137] 袁莉,Stephen Powell,马红亮,等. MOOC 对高等教育的影响:破坏性创新理论视角[J].现代远程教育研究,2014(02):3-9.

[138] 李明华.MOOCs 革命:独立课程市场形成和高等教育世界市场新格局[J].开放教育研究,2013,19(03):11-29.

[139] 顾小清,胡艺龄,蔡慧英.MOOCs 的本土化诉求及其应对[J].远程教育杂志,2013,31(05):3-11.

[140] 汪琼.MOOCs 与现行高校教学融合模式举例[J].中国教育信息化,2013(11):14-15.

[141] 焦建利,贾义敏.国际开放教育资源典型案例研究之反思与展望[J].现代教育技术,2011,21(12):13-17.

[142] 黄荣怀.2017 互联网教育服务产业研究报告[EB/OL]. http:// sli. bnu. edu. cn/a/xinwenkuaibao/yanjiudongtai/20171228/ 480. html, 2019-8-7.

[143] 极光大数据.知识付费的风口,谁飞得更高?[EB/OL].http:// www. shujuju. cn/lecture/detail/2719? attachmentId = 2872, 2019-8-17.

[144] 庞东梅.B2B2C 在线教育平台受青睐[EB/OL]. http://kns. cnki. net/kns/detail/detail. aspx? FileName=JRSB201802100062&DbName=CCND2018,2018-2-10.

[145] Docebo. E-Learning Market Trends and Forecast 2017 - 2021 [EB/OL]. https://www. waitang. com/report/6029. html, 2019-2.8.

[146] Allen I E, Seaman J. Distance Education Enrollment Report

2017[EB/OL].

https://onlinelearningsurvey.   com/reports/
digtiallearningcompassenrollment2017.pdf，2017-5-1.

[147] Bestcolleges. Online-Education-Trends-Report-2018[EB/OL].
https://www.bestcolleges.com，2019-9-7.

[148] 李大力.MOOC 提供商的经营策略[J].现代经济信息，2014
(02):25.

[149] 舒宁.美国 MOOC 对我国高校在线教育的启示[D].金华:浙江
师范大学硕士论文，2016.

[150] U.S Department of Education. The Future Ready District
Professional Learning Through Online Communities of Practice
and Social Networks to Drive Continuous Improvement[EB/
OL]. https://tech.ed.gov/wp-content/uploads/2014/11/
Section7-FutureReadyDistrictBrief-Final.pdf，2019-8-7.

[151] Dhawal S. A Review of MOOC Stats and Trends in 2017[EB/
OL]. https://www.class-central.com/report/moocs-stats-
and-trends-2017，2018-1-22.

[152] The Open University. About The Open University[EB/OL].
http://www.open.ac.uk/about/main，2019-2-9.

[153] Kpmg，Google. Online Education in India 2021[EB/OL].
https://home.kpmg/in/en/home/insights/2017/05/internet-
online-education-india.html，2019-3-2.

[154] 中国互联网络信息中心.第 43 次《中国互联网络发展状况统计
报告》[EB/OL]. http://www.cac.gov.cn/2019-02/28/c_
1124175677.htm，2019-2-28.

[155] 倪明.在线教育普遍严重亏损[EB/OL]. http://finance.ce.cn/
stock/gsgdbd/201807/27/t20180727 _ 29867154.shtml，2018-
7-27.

[156] 中国科技部火炬中心，长城战略咨询. 2017 中国独角兽企业发
展报告 [EB/OL]. http://www.shujuju.cn/lecture/detail/
2448，2019-2-1.

[157] CCtalk. CCtalk 简介 [EB/OL]. https://www.cctalk.com/

about/introduction,2018-2-2.

[158] CCtalk. 2017 年度网师用户画像行为报告[EB/OL]. http://tech. ifeng. com/a/20180202/44869533_0. shtml,2018-2-2.

[159] 腾讯课堂. 腾讯课堂服务协议[EB/OL]. https://ke. qq. com/proService. html,2018-8-18.

[160] 网易云课堂. 网易云课堂介绍[EB/OL]. http://study. 163. com/about/aboutus. htm♯/about? aboutType＝1,2018-8-17.

[161] Kim H W, Xu Y, Gupta S. Which is more important in Internet shopping, perceived price or trust? [J]. Electronic commerce research and applications, 2012, 11(3)：241-252.

[162] 王茂彬. 消费者对知识付费产品购买意愿影响因素的实证研究[D]. 济南：山东大学硕士论文,2018.

[163] 洪菲,郑辉,周颖帆,等. 在线评论对大学生消费者购买意愿的影响研究[J]. 商业经济研究,2019(08)：52-56.

[164] 何海英. 综合型 B2C 网店形象对消费者购买意愿影响研究[D]. 沈阳：辽宁大学博士论文,2015.

[165] 储林. 老字号线上品牌体验对顾客购买意愿影响的实证研究[D]. 合肥：安徽财经大学硕士论文,2018.

[166] 王小丽. 感知价值对模仿品牌购买意愿的影响研究[D]. 郑州：郑州大学硕士论文,2017.

[167] 季文静. 网络消费者购买意愿影响因素研究[D]. 济南：山东大学硕士论文,2013.

[168] 王睿. 智能移动终端应用商店的用户购买意愿影响因素研究[D]. 北京：北京邮电大学硕士论文,2013.

[169] 向云峰. 网店促销策略对消费者感知风险的影响研究[D]. 北京：中国地质大学(北京)硕士论文,2018.

[170] Rabinovich E, Knemeyer A M, Mayer C M. Why do Internet commerce firms incorporate logistics service providers in their distribution channels?：The role of transaction costs and network strength [J]. Journal of Operations Management, 2007, 25(3)：661-681.

[171] 宋金倩. 线上知识付费用户持续使用意愿影响因素的研究[D].

济南：山东大学硕士论文,2018.

[172] 董庆兴,周欣,毛凤华,等.在线健康社区用户持续使用意愿研究——基于感知价值理论[J].现代情报,2019,39(03):3-14＋156.

[173] 刘晓庆.网络教育付费意愿影响因素研究[D].福州：福建农林大学硕士论文,2016.

[174] 杨秀云,蒋园园,马思睿.网络文化产品消费意愿的影响因素研究[J].西安交通大学学报(社会科学版),2017,37(05):94-103.

[175] 蒋晓茜.A 在线培训平台的创业成长问题及策略研究[D].成都：电子科技大学硕士论文,2018.

[176] 高晨璐.在线教育平台用户学习效果提升策略研究[D].天津：天津大学硕士论文,2018.

[177] 李正峰,张丽君,胡月琴.试用信息对广告说服效果的影响——基于渐进式新产品的研究[J].中国流通经济,2019,33(04):100-110.

[178] Lee T M. The impact of perceptions of interactivity on customer trust and transaction intentions in mobile commerce [J]. Journal of Electronic Commerce Research, 2005, 6(3): 165-180.

[179] 杨永清,张金隆,满青珊,等.移动互联网用户采纳研究——基于感知利益、成本和风险视角[J].情报杂志,2012,31(01):200-207.

[180] 傅颖.企业微博营销对消费者购买意愿的影响研究[D].杭州：浙江工商大学硕士论文,2013.

[181] 杨根福.MOOC 用户持续使用行为影响因素研究[J].开放教育研究,2016,22(01):100-111.

[182] 玄海燕,戴天骄,蔺全录,等.APP 营销对群体购买行为影响研究[J].商业经济研究,2018(03):103-106.

[183] 范琳琳.企业慈善捐赠行为对消费者购买意愿影响的实证研究[D].杭州：浙江工商大学硕士论文,2015.

[184] 陈芳草.越南消费者网购意愿的影响因素研究[D].上海：华东师范大学硕士论文,2018.

［185］ Schumacker R E，Lomax R G. A Beginner's Guide to Structural Equation Modeling［M］. New Jersey：Lawrence Erlbaum Associates，1996.

［186］孙晓军,周宗奎.探索性因子分析及其在应用中存在的主要问题［J］.心理科学,2005(06):162-164＋170.

［187］李梦莹.基于 PLS-SEM 的虚拟社区交互对用户购买意愿影响研究［D］.北京:首都经济贸易大学硕士论文,2018.

［188］刘金兰,何涛,宁禄乔,等.结构方程模型的偏最小二乘算法及其几何意义［J］.哈尔滨商业大学学报(自然科学版),2005(06):776-780.

［189］张军.结构方程模型构建方法比较［J］.统计与决策,2007(18):137-139.

［190］赵耀华,韩之俊.基于结构方程的高校顾客满意度模型［J］.系统工程,2007(11):85-90.

［191］ Urbach N，Ahlemann F. Structural equation modeling in information systems research using partial least squares［J］. Journal of Information technology theory and application，2010，11(2)：5-40.

［192］ Ringle C M，Sarstedt M，Straub D. A Critical Look at the Use of PLS-SEM in MIS Quarterly［J］. MIS Quarterly，2012，36(1)：3-21.

［193］王绍峰,黄荣怀.在线主动学习意愿的产生机理与提升策略［J］.开放教育研究,2020,26(05):99-110.

［194］百度指数.在线教育百度指数 20190504 的人群画像报告［EB/OL］. http://index. baidu. com/v2/main/index. html ♯/crowd/％E5％9C％A8％E7％BA％BF％E6％95％99％E8％82％B2? words＝％E5％9C％A8％E7％BA％BF％E6％95％99％E8％82％B2,2019-5-4.

［195］侯军利.创新价值链视角下非核心企业创新行为模式演化研究［D］.沈阳:辽宁大学博士论文,2018.

［196］刘春艳.产学研协同创新团队内部知识转移影响机理研究［D］.长春:吉林大学博士论文,2016.

[197] 方艺文.企业家内外控人格特质对创新行为的影响机理研究 [D].长春:吉林大学硕士论文,2016.

[198] 孟佳佳.双元营销能力对企业绩效的影响研究[D].大连:大连理 工大学博士论文,2013.

[199] 刘晓琴.差序式领导对员工职场非伦理行为的影响机制研究 [D].广州:华南理工大学博士论文,2017.

[200] Straub D, Boudreau M C, Gefen D. Validation guidelines for IS positivist research[J]. Communications of the Association for Information systems,2004(13):380-427.

[201] 罗红霞.公司治理、投资效率与财务绩效度量及其关系[D].长 春:吉林大学博士论文,2014.

[202] 王磊.企业信息化领导力形成机理及对竞争优势的影响研究 [D].长春:吉林大学博士论文,2015.

[203] 上官彩霞.城乡建设用地增减挂钩实施中宅基地置换的模式选 择及其对农民福利的影响研究[D].南京:南京农业大学博士论 文,2015.

[204] 周驷华.信息技术对供应链风险管理的影响[D].上海:上海交通 大学博士论文,2014.

[205] Fornell C, Larcker D F. Evaluating structural equation models with unobservable variables and measurement error [J]. Journal of marketing research,1981,18(1):39-50.

[206] 张辉.制造企业服务导向战略研究:战略的制定与执行视角[D]. 上海:复旦大学博士论文,2012.

[207] 曾薇.金融监管对商业银行产品创新绩效的影响研究[D].长沙: 湖南大学博士论文,2013.

[208] 郁玉兵.关系资本对供应链质量整合与绿色管理的影响研究 [D].杭州:浙江大学博士论文,2015.

[209] 姜岩.消费者购物网站依恋机理研究[D].大连:大连理工大学博 士论文,2013.

[210] 梁乙凯.电子政务云服务采纳、吸收及其价值影响机制研究[D]. 济南:山东大学博士论文,2017.

[211] 陈志明.企业知识基础、开放式创新与创新绩效关系研究[D].广

州：华南理工大学博士论文,2015.

[212] Doty D H, Glick W H. Common methods bias：does common methods variance really bias results? [J]. Organizational research methods, 1998, 1(4)：374-406.

[213] 杜建政,赵国祥,刘金平.测评中的共同方法偏差[J].心理科学, 2005(02):420-422.

[214] 周浩,龙立荣.共同方法偏差的统计检验与控制方法[J].心理科学进展,2004(06):942-950.

[215] 朱海腾,李川云.共同方法变异是"致命瘟疫"吗？——论争、新知与应对[J].心理科学进展,2019,27(04):587-599.

[216] Podsakoff P M, Organ D W. Self-reports in organizational research：Problems and prospects[J]. Journal of management, 1986, 12(4)：531-544.

[217] 邓稳根,黎小瑜,陈勃,等.国内心理学文献中共同方法偏差检验的现状[J].江西师范大学学报(自然科学版),2018,42(05): 447-453.

[218] 崔瑜.基于知识的企业家异质性人力资本形成机制研究[D].上海：复旦大学博士论文,2010.

[219] 杨明远.顾客参与价值共创和智力资本对企业绩效的影响研究[D].西安：西安电子科技大学硕士论文,2017.

[220] Hair Jr J F, Hult G T M, Ringle C. A primer on partial least squares structural equation modeling (PLS-SEM)[M]. Los Angeles：Sage Publications,2016.

[221] Sarstedt M, Henseler J, Ringle C M. Multigroup analysis in partial least squares (PLS) path modeling：Alternative methods and empirical results[J]. Advances in International Marketing, 2011(22):195-218.

[222] 谢佳琳,张晋朝.用户在线生成内容意愿影响因素研究[J].信息资源管理学报,2014,4(01):69-77.

[223] Chin W W. The partial least squares approach to structural equation modeling[J]. Modern methods for business research, 1998, 295(2)：295-336.

[224] Tenenhaus M，Vinzi V E，Chatelin Y M. PLS path modeling [J]. Computational statistics & data analysis，2005，48(1)：159-205.

[225] Wetzels M，Odekerken-Schröder G，Van O C. Using PLS path modeling for assessing hierarchical construct models：Guidelines and empirical illustration[J]. MIS quarterly，2009，33 (1)：177-195.

[226] Hu L，Bentler P M. Fit indices in covariance structure modeling：Sensitivity to underparameterized model misspecification[J]. Psychological methods，1998，3(4)：424.

[227] 成升.暴雨灾害中公众持续使用微博获取灾害信息意愿的影响因素研究[D].武汉：武汉大学硕士论文，2017.

[228] 蔡杨，石文典，陈晓惠.员工内外部动机对隐性知识共享意愿和创新行为的影响[J].心理研究，2019，12(01)：56-66.

[229] Davadas S D，Lay Y F. Factors affecting students' attitude toward mathematics：A structural equation modeling approach [J]. Eurasia Journal of Mathematics，Science and Technology Education，2017，14(1)：517-529.

[230] Zhao X，Lynch Jr J G，Chen Q. Reconsidering Baron and Kenny：Myths and truths about mediation analysis[J]. Journal of consumer research，2010，37(2)：197-206.

[231] Hair Jr J F，Hult G T M，Ringle C，Sarstedt M. A primer on partial least squares structural equation modeling (PLS-SEM) [M]. 2nd Ed. Los Angeles：Sage Publications，2017.

[232] 张亚运.信息技术能力对船舶产业链价值共创的影响研究[D].镇江：江苏科技大学硕士论文，2017.

[233] 杨爽，郭昭宇.品牌幸福感对顾客忠诚行为的影响研究[J].消费经济，2018，34(06)：68-74.

[234] Al-Gahtani S S，Hubona G S，Wang J. Information technology (IT) in Saudi Arabia：Culture and the acceptance and use of IT [J]. Information & management，2007，44(8)：681-691.

[235] 张梦雪.中小企业微信公众号采纳行为的影响机理研究[D].扬

州：扬州大学硕士论文,2018.

［236］林峥峥.探究手机银行系统的延伸使用［D］.合肥：中国科学技术大学博士论文,2018.

［237］李洪琳.大型企业 IaaS 云服务对企业绩效影响的过程机理研究［D］.北京：北京邮电大学硕士论文,2015.

［238］Hayes A F. Process：A Versatile Computational Tool For Observed Variable Mediation，Moderation，and Conditional Process Modeling［EB/OL］. http://www. afhayes. com/public/process2012. pdf，2019-11-10.

［239］Leal-Rodríguez A L，Roldán J L，Ariza-Montes J A，et al. From potential absorptive capacity to innovation outcomes in project teams：The conditional mediating role of the realized absorptive capacity in a relational learning context［J］. International Journal of Project Management，2014，32（6）：894-907.

［240］方杰,张敏强,顾红磊,等.基于不对称区间估计的有调节的中介模型检验［J］.心理科学进展,2014,22(10):1660-1668.

［241］陈志明.企业知识基础、开放式创新与创新绩效关系研究［D］.广州：华南理工大学博士论文,2015.

［242］Henseler J，Ringle C M，Sinkovics R R. The Use of Partial Least Squares Path Modeling in International Marketing［J］. Advances in International Marketing，2009（20）：277-320.

［243］杨佳绮.在线教育的盈利模式研究［D］.昆明：云南财经大学硕士论文,2016.

［244］程兴火.基于游客感知价值的森林生态旅游景区竞争优势研究［D］.杭州：浙江大学博士论文,2006.

［245］陈湘青.O2O 电子商务顾客满意度分析［J］.商业经济研究,2016(14):46-48.

［246］欧阳映泉.付费在线学习采纳意愿影响因素研究［D］.成都：西南财经大学硕士论文,2014.

［247］白玉.学术虚拟社区持续意愿的影响因素研究［J］.图书馆学研究,2017(05):2-6.

［248］刘昊达.第三方移动支付用户使用意愿影响因素研究［D］.北京：北京邮电大学硕士论文,2018.

［249］万苑微.感知利益、感知风险和购买成本对网络消费者购买意向影响的研究［D］.广州：华南理工大学硕士论文,2011.

［250］郭朋.新零售模式下顾客感知价值研究［D］.石家庄：河北科技大学硕士论文,2019.

［251］钟凯,张传庆.消费者感知价值对网络购买意愿影响研究——以在线口碑为调节变量［J］.沈阳师范大学学报(社会科学版),2013,37(03)：53-56.

［252］高瑜.植入模式、受众感知匹配性与广告植入效果的关系研究［D］.杭州：浙江工商大学硕士论文,2013.

［253］钱英杰.物流终端服务质量、顾客满意及顾客重复购买意愿的关系研究［D］.杭州：浙江工商大学硕士论文,2013.

［254］冯建英,穆维松,张领先,等.基于消费者购买意愿的农机市场需求分析［J］.商业研究,2008(02)：191-194.

［255］Sirdeshmukh D,Singh J,Sabol B. Consumer trust,value,and loyalty in relational exchanges［J］. Journal of marketing, 2002,66(1)：15-37.

［256］Kankanhalli A,Tan B C Y,Wei K K. Contributing knowledge to electronic knowledge repositories：an empirical investigation ［J］. MIS Quarterly, 2005, 29 (1), 113-143.

［257］Davis F D. Perceived usefulness, perceived ease of use, and user acceptance of information technology［J］. MIS Quarterly, 1989, 13 (3), 319-399.